ESTATE PLANNING

AFTER THE

2001 Tax Act

Also available from
Bloomberg Press

Wall Street Secrets for Tax-Efficient Investing:
From Tax Pain to Investment Gain
by Robert N. Gordon with Jan Rosen

Deena Katz on Practice Management:
for Financial Advisers, Planners, and Wealth Managers
by Deena B. Katz

Deena Katz's Tools and Templates for Your Practice:
for Financial Advisers, Planners, and Wealth Managers
by Deena B. Katz

Getting Started as a Financial Planner
by Jeffrey H. Rattiner

Best Practices for Financial Advisors
by Mary Rowland

Protecting Your Practice
by Katherine Vessenes, in cooperation with the
International Association for Financial Planning

A complete list of our titles is available at
www.bloomberg.com/books

BLOOMBERG ® WEALTH MANAGER magazine is the premiere professional information resource for independent financial planners and investment advisers who are serving clients of high net worth. See wealth.bloomberg.com or call 1-800-681-7727.

ESTATE PLANNING
AFTER THE
2001 Tax Act

*Guiding Your Clients
through the Changes*

MARTIN M. SHENKMAN, CPA, M.B.A., J.D.

Bloomberg Press
Princeton

Books are available for bulk purchases at special discounts. Special editions or book excerpts can also be created to specifications. For information, please write: Special Markets Department, Bloomberg Press.

BLOOMBERG, BLOOMBERG NEWS, BLOOMBERG FINANCIAL MARKETS, OPEN BLOOMBERG, BLOOMBERG PERSONAL, THE BLOOMBERG FORUM, COMPANY CONNECTION, COMPANY CONNEX, BLOOMBERG PRESS, BLOOMBERG PROFESSIONAL LIBRARY, BLOOMBERG PERSONAL BOOKSHELF, and BLOOMBERG SMALL BUSINESS are trademarks and service marks of Bloomberg L.P. All rights reserved.

This publication contains the author's opinions and is designed to provide accurate and authoritative information. It is sold with the understanding that the author, publisher, and Bloomberg L.P. are not engaged in rendering legal, accounting, investment-planning, or other professional advice. The reader should seek the services of a qualified professional for such advice; the author, publisher, and Bloomberg L.P. cannot be held responsible for any loss incurred as a result of specific investments or planning decisions made by the reader.

First edition published 2002
1 3 5 7 9 10 8 6 4 2

Library of Congress Cataloging-in-Publication Data

Shenkman, Martin M.
   Estate planning after the 2001 tax act : guiding your clients through the changes / Martin M. Shenkman.-- 1st ed.
      p. cm. -- (Bloomberg professional library)
   Includes index.
   ISBN 1-57660-121-8 (alk. paper)
   1. Inheritance and transfer tax--Law and legislation--United States. 2. Tax planning--United States. 3. Estate planning--United States. I. Title. II. Series.

KF6572 .S5882 2002
343.7305'32--dc21   2002020067

Acquired and edited by Kathleen A. Peterson

To my parents Jack and Miriam Shenkman, whose encouragement and support throughout the years have provided a foundation; and to my three sons: Yoni, Dovi, and Daniel, whose joy and well-being are my greatest pleasure.

Estate planning is not only about the transmission of wealth; it should be about the transmission of values. As such, this book is dedicated in honor of my parents and sons, and also to the memory of all those lost in the September 11 tragedy and to the honor of the many who have helped in the rescue and healing process thereafter. To acknowledge the victims of this tragedy, 10 percent of this book's royalties will be donated to The September 11th Fund.

CONTENTS

<hr>

PART I

General Considerations for Estate Planning

PART II

Specific Techniques and Planning Strategies

INTRODUCTION

The Economic Growth and Tax Relief Reconciliation Act of 2001 (the "2001 Tax Act") is one of the most comprehensive and complex estate tax laws passed in decades, perhaps ever. There have been few, if any, tax bills that have made planning so uncertain as the 2001 Tax Act. The estate tax is being modified extensively through 2009, repealed in 2010, and re-enacted in 2011 unless a future Congress acts to maintain the repeal. This confusing estate planning environment, exacerbated by the myriad of income tax, personal, business, asset protection, and other issues affecting it, makes it essential for every estate, tax, financial, and investment adviser to understand planning in this new environment in order to serve his or her clients. Every high-net-worth taxpayer needing to address estate planning must have some understanding of the new planning environment in order to work with his or her advisers and to ensure that planning is properly done.

The stakes are significant. Obviously, failing to properly plan can trigger substantial estate taxes. Worse yet, assets may not be distributed as the testator wishes, insurance might be cancelled inappropriately, investment decisions could be made in a less than optimal manner, and so on. Thus, planning remains essential. Yet understanding the impact of the 2001 Tax Act is difficult. It affects different taxpayers differently. It affects planning for different assets in different ways. Not only is new planning affected, but taxpayers and their advisers must review existing planning and determine what steps, if any, can be taken to restructure prior to planning to address the new rules.

This book has been written to help a wide range of professional advisers (attorneys, estate planners, accountants, investment advisers, insurance consultants, tax advisers, and others) as well as sophisticated clients, understand how to plan in the new post-2001 Tax Act environment.

To facilitate meeting this planning objective, this book provides several different methods to access information and recommendations. The new laws are analyzed by section. The impact of the new rules on various assets are analyzed on an asset by asset basis. The impact of the new rules on different types of taxpayers is analyzed on a taxpayer by taxpayer basis. Finally, prior law planning techniques are explained and analyzed in light of the new rules. This analysis addresses both what to do with existing trusts and planning techniques and how the future use of those trusts and planning techniques should be handled in light of the 2001 Tax Act.

HOW TO USE THIS BOOK

Most books written about a tax bill tend to be organized in the same manner as the tax legislation, making it easy for the author but not accessible or practical for the reader. The organization of *Estate Planning after the 2001 Tax Act* enables the user to find the necessary information to plan under the new rules. Note in particular the following features:

- The discussions of the changes made by the 2001 Tax Act to the estate tax system and the discussions of the new post-estate tax repeal system (the modified carryover basis system) are presented in separate chapters. The analysis of the 2001 estate tax changes appears in Chapter 1, whereas the analysis of the new modified step-up in basis rules appears in Chapter 7 because the provisions are largely mutually exclusive.

- Chapter 4 is organized by types of taxpayer. Planning objectives, especially in light of the complex phase-ins and uncertain future of the 2001 Tax Act, will vary considerably depending on each person's circumstances. Someone who is elderly or infirm probably cannot afford to wait for the estate tax benefits to be phased in. For a person who is young and healthy, the circumstances may differ and may offer more options.

- Chapter 5 is organized by asset type. It provides answers to questions about planning for particular assets such as a personal residence, family business, or insurance.

- Chapter 6 discusses many common estate planning techniques and types of trusts to highlight what the 2001 Tax Act does to the effectiveness of these techniques and trusts. The chapter provides an overview of each technique or trust, then explains the impact of the 2001 Tax Act on that technique or trust. Each discussion can help in evaluating the options available if the taxpayer has used any of these techniques or trusts in the past (e.g., the person already has an insurance trust and wants to know what, if anything, to do with it in light of the 2001 Tax Act). Finally, each discussion helps clarify how and when to use each technique or trust in the future.

- A separate chapter (Chapter 3) is devoted to nontax aspects of estate planning. Although this is only a general discussion, it has been included in this book because most estate planners, financial advisers, and other professionals have so focused clients on saving taxes that many people have ignored the really important personal issues of estate planning. Even if the estate tax will no longer affect a taxpayer's estate, planning is still necessary to deal successfully with those central personal issues.

Whereas the preceding structure follows a logical sequence and makes the planning process easier, there will be some redundancy when reading through the entire book. However, it was felt that a bit of redundancy was a price worth incurring for a more accessible and logically organized presentation.

A note on style: The use of the pronoun *he* in reference to taxpayers and professionals is purely for simplicity and ease of reading. All information herein is equally applicable to both genders.

TAX REFERENCES AND NOTES

Most technical references and citations have been relegated to notes to make the text more readable for laypersons and professionals alike.

In some instances, a Tax Code provision number has been included in the text because the particular provision or tax benefit is known by the name of the Code Section that contains it (e.g., Code Section 529 college savings plans). Notes have been included for confirmation and ready reference purposes to assist professional tax, legal, and financial advisers in researching provisions discussed in this book.

SOURCES FOR BACKGROUND INFORMATION ON PLANNING TECHNIQUES

If you want additional information on the planning techniques and the pre-2001 Tax Act rules discussed in this book, many books are available through the Law Made Easy Press, LLC website: www. laweasy.com. Consult the book order section of the website to order. Among other books written by Martin M. Shenkman are the following:

- On trusts: *The Complete Book of Trusts.* This book provides an analysis of qualified personal residence trusts, grantor retained annuity trusts, charitable remainder annuity trusts, and other techniques. It does not contain an extensive analysis of dynasty trusts. The planning concepts and techniques presented can help you apply the updates discussed in Chapter 1 of this book.

- On organizing and record keeping: *The Beneficiary Workbook.* This book includes detailed chapters, sample forms (with a diskette) to help taxpayers organize all their personal, business, tax, legal, and financial records, including the records they should begin keeping yesterday in light of the potential repeal of step-up in basis rules. Although the book is not updated for the 2001 Tax Act, the record-keeping concepts haven't changed.

- On limited liability companies (LLCs) and family limited partnerships (FLPs): *Starting Your Own Limited Liability Company.* This book explains the details and steps necessary to form, operate, and plan with LLCs, an important tool in the post-2001 Tax Act environment, and the most common structure for closely held business and investment endeavors. Since FLPs and LLCs are treated in an identical manner for federal income tax purposes, the book is useful to those working with FLPs.

- On revocable living trusts: *The Complete Living Trust Program.* These trusts have been and will remain popular estate planning tools. Although the book has not been updated for the 2001 Tax Act, almost all of its analysis, if supplemented with the estate tax changes highlighted in this book, will continue to meet planning needs.

- On probate (postdeath planning): *The Complete Probate Guide.* This book provides a detailed analysis of the steps to handle the estate of someone who has died. The advice on tax planning, except for the dollar amount of the estate tax exclusion (discussed in Chapter 1) is still generally current.

UPDATES AND FORMS

Tax laws and planning strategies change at a rapid pace. Treasury Department and IRS guidance will be issued on many of the new tax provisions, states must react to address the many federal tax law changes in the 2001 Tax Act, and new planning strategies will need to be developed. Some of these postpublication developments will be highlighted on the website: www.laweasy.com.

Forms to apply the tax planning strategies are critical to ensuring that planning is up-to-date. Forms such as the sample Will, Durable Power of Attorney, Revocable Living Trust, and other documents on the Law Made Easy Press, LLC website: www.laweasy .com, are updated regularly so as to reflect many of the changes made by the 2001 Tax Act. Consult the website periodically for updates. Just be sure to check the date of the form and consult with an accountant, attorney, or estate planner as needed before proceeding.

Author's note: I want to acknowledge and thank Ron Bachrach, J.D., MSM, AEP, CLU, ChFC, for his editorial comments. Any errors that might be contained herein are my own.

In the preparation of this book, effort has been made to offer current, correct, and clearly expressed information. Nonetheless, inadvertent errors can occur, and tax rules and regulations often change. Further, the information in the text is intended to afford general guidelines on matters of interest to taxpayers. The application and impact of tax laws can vary widely from case to case, however, based on the specific or unique facts involved. Accordingly, the information in this book is not intended to serve as legal, accounting, or tax advice. Readers are encouraged to consult with professional advisers for advice concerning specific matters before making any decision, and the author and publisher disclaim any responsibility for positions taken by taxpayers in their individual cases or for any misunderstanding on the part of readers. Furthermore, the provisions of the 2001 Tax Act, on which the information in this book is based, are complex, controversial, and according to almost all tax experts, likely to be changed before they all become effective. Therefore, it is essential that you consult with your tax adviser concerning developments occurring after publication of this book.

MARTIN M. SHENKMAN

OVERVIEW

Congress enacted the Economic Growth and Tax Relief Reconciliation Act of 2001 (Tax Relief Act) as a substantial and major tax cut. It was intended, or at least advertised, as affecting a broad range of taxpayers and many types of taxes. In fact, the 2001 Tax Act—especially if all the phased tax reductions ultimately occur—constitutes one of the largest tax reduction acts in many decades.

GOALS OF THE ESTATE TAX REPEAL

In 1998, only 2 percent of decedents paid estate tax. They generated almost $30 billion in estate tax. Of the 2 percent subject to the estate tax, only 5 percent had estates greater than $5 million and these taxpayers paid almost one half of the estate tax. Family-held businesses and farms were not significantly at risk considering only 7 percent of the assets listed on estate tax returns were in those categories.

Under prior law, states were encouraged to enact state-level "estate" taxes because the federal estate tax gave a credit to each taxpayer for state estate taxes up to a specified maximum. Thus it would not cost an estate anything extra to pay a state death tax to the extent of this benefit. So states enacted estate taxes to "soak up" the credit available. These were called "sop" taxes. The state level "sop" tax (the state death tax credit) generated about $10 billion in revenue for the states that must be made up for if state budgets are to be unaffected. It remains to be seen how this can be done. Are states in the present environment in a position to create or increase inheritance or state estate taxes, or will they have to increase sales and other taxes?

The 2001 Tax Act was defined for a ten-year goal. To achieve the significant income tax cuts, repeal the estate tax, and enhance retirement and education savings, Congress had to back-end many of the cuts. Furthermore, the Act includes a sunset provision through which the legislators have basically shifted this problem to a future Congress. Thus, unless a future Congress acts, the entire estate tax repeal will end and the tax will revert to pre-2001 Tax Act law (i.e., a $1 million exclusion) in 2011. Similarly, the repeal of the income tax marriage penalty will not become effective for years.

BACK-END AND DEFERRED CHANGES

Congress has used some of its favorite techniques to achieve advertised tax reduction budget guesstimates at the cost of tremendous complexity and ultimate difficulty for taxpayers in taking advantage of those tax reductions. These include drawn-out *phase-in* of various tax benefits; thus, the advertised tax breaks that many taxpayers anticipate are to only occur over a lengthy time period, in some cases as long as ten years (most notably, for the estate tax repeal). This back-end loading also creates a tremendous risk in planning activities and investments. What happens if budget shortfalls caused by the slowdown of the economy result in a future Congress repealing or freezing tax reductions that have not yet taken effect? The war on terrorism, expanded security measures, a bailout of the airline industry, and other developments following the September 11 tragedy may all create further budget problems, adding to the pressure on a future Congress to either enact new taxes or to scale back promised estate tax breaks to raise revenues.

 Not all tax changes are back-ended. Some estate tax changes take effect now and are even retroactive. For example, the new IRC § 2632(c) provision provides for an automatic allocation of the generation skipping transfer (GST) exemption for certain transfers unless the taxpayer affirmatively files a gift tax return stating that the allocation is not wanted.

COMPLEXITY OF THE TAX BILL

The massive tax cuts contained in the 2001 Tax Act are extraordinarily complicated. The complexity of the bill itself and the tremendous amount of back-end–loaded tax changes mean that planning has become complicated for many taxpayers. The need for projections and alternative "what-if" planning scenarios has increased.

Not all the advertised tax changes are complicated. For example, the child care credit has increased. The maximum contribution limits for IRA and other retirement plan accounts also increase. These changes are favorable and easy to understand modifications of prior law. The reduction in income tax rates appears straightforward, and occurs on a set schedule. The complexity arises when taxpayers endeavor to plan and maximize the tax benefits of the rate reduction by accelerating deductions into an earlier year and deferring income to later, lower tax years. The analysis becomes further complicated because the reductions are not substantial enough to make the planning worthwhile in all instances.

The potential repeal of the automatic step-up in basis on death is one of the most complex provisions included in the 2001 Tax Act. The decedent's tax basis (investment plus capital improvements, less depreciation) is to become the heir's tax basis. It promises to require enormous amounts of record keeping by those affected, as explained in Chapter 7. It is also unworkable, which is why it was rescinded the previous two times Congress tried to enact it. Identifying what Aunt Edna paid to buy her vacation home in the 1950s and how much she spent on building improvements over the years will be as difficult as digesting her pot roast.

LIKELIHOOD OF ACTUAL ESTATE TAX REPEAL

Almost no one is convinced the repeal is real. However, many taxpayers on the lower end of the estate planning screen (say, aggregate family estates under $1 million, a figure to increase as the exemption increases) may now be reluctant to incur the costs and complexity of engaging in the type of planning they had heretofore addressed. Why bother with a complex will with a bypass trust if it appears that no tax will be due? On the other hand, older and high-net-worth taxpayers (say, $5 million and above) can only ignore the estate tax at their peril. The changes are complex. Much of the public's first impressions (that the estate tax has been repealed) are not consistent with the reality of the law (repeal may never happen). Thus, the major challenges in making decisions are to address planning and to navigate through the complex changes, phase-ins, phaseouts, and back-ins) of the legislation.

Charities are being hurt. The increase in the exclusion (such that taxpayers with estates of or under $1 million, later increasing to $3.5 million, won't pay tax) means many taxpayers won't need to use charitable planning to minimize estate taxes. For estates subject to tax, the lower tax rates mean that contributions will cost more to make. The wealthy will benefit. Planning involving charitable giving remains important, but the increased complexity combined with the fact that more taxpayers won't realize an estate tax savings will make many reluctant to tolerate the cost and complexity of such planning. And as noted, the changes also represent a major trap for unwary taxpayers who mistakenly assume that the tax is repealed, or that smaller estates can ignore planning.

The focus of a proper and comprehensive estate plan never should be solely on estate taxes. No matter what the impact of the 2001 Tax Act may be, a host of ongoing nontransfer tax issues must still be addressed as well. The 2001 Tax Act has created some substantial benefits for many taxpayers. The lower end of the estate tax spectrum may well be removed from the estate tax rolls. Beyond that, much confusion and uncertainty remain. The balance of this book analyzes these issues and identifies planning traps and opportunities. As with all tax legislation, those who plan will fare best.

PART I

General Considerations for Estate Planning

1

THE SCOPE OF ESTATE TAX CHANGES

Congress has indicated that it has helped the country by repealing the purportedly evil "death tax." As the following discussion makes clear however, despite significant reductions, the death tax has certainly not yet been eliminated. Substantial and complex tax traps remain for many taxpayers, especially those in high-net-worth positions.

The cost of the estate tax reduction and potential repeal has been estimated at $138 billion over the ten years following passage of the tax act. Consider that approximately three to four thousand families per year pay one-half of the tax. Doing the simple math would indicate that about 30,000 to 40,000 families will receive nearly $70 billion in tax breaks over the ten year period. This will provide substantial enhancement for the wealthiest component of the country. Further, the reduction and eventual repeal of the estate tax, if it is in fact effected, would have a detrimental impact on the ability of charities to raise charitable funds because the estate tax provided a substantial incentive for well-to-do families to make significant charitable gifts—a charitable lead trust is but one example. Finally, the phaseout of the state death tax credit will force states to raise taxes in other ways, perhaps through regressive sales and other taxes.

The tremendous back-ending of the estate tax reductions and eventual repeal pose the same risk associated with other back-ended tax benefits; if budget requirements change or the administration changes, the future anticipated reductions may be frozen, repealed, or changed.

ESTATE AND GENERATION-SKIPPING TRANSFER TAX REPEAL IN 2010

The estate tax is scheduled for repeal beginning in tax year 2010.[1] The generation-skipping transfer (GST) tax (a tax on transfers to persons at least two generations below the taxpayer) is scheduled for repeal beginning in tax year 2010.[2] There are five important exceptions to this apparent tax benefit:

1. The gift tax is modified, but not repealed, as explained later in this chapter.
2. The estate tax repeal has a sunset so that it is reintroduced in 2011 unless Congress acts.
3. Carryover basis rules, in a complex modified format, will apply, thus in theory substituting a capital gains tax for the estate tax.
4. The tax on a noncitizen spouse under Code Section 2056A continues in a modified format, as explained later.
5. The continued application of other recapture provisions postrepeal is not certain, although future regulations may clarify this.

LOWER ESTATE TAX RATES AND HIGHER ESTATE EXCLUSION

Two key aspects of planning for the gift and estate tax are the maximum tax rate and the exclusion amount (how much can be transferred free of tax). The 2001 Tax Act has made substantial changes to both of these items. The phase in of the benefits over a long time period creates additional planning complexity as explained below.

Exhibit 1.1 illustrates the reduction in the maximum estate tax rate and the maximum transfers that can be made free of estate taxes. The phaseout of the estate tax is set to follow a slow timetable.

Exhibit 1.1   Phaseout Schedule of Rates and Exclusions

Year	Top Transfer Tax Rate (%)[1]	Exemption Amount[2]
2002	50	$1 million
2003	49	1 million
2004	48	1.5 million
2005	47	1.5 million
2006	46	2 million
2007	45	2 million
2008	45	2 million
2009	45	3.5 million
2010	repealed[3]	N/A
2011	55	1 million

[1] IRC § 2001(c), amended by Act § 511. Note: does not reflect interplay of state estate taxes if applicable, which could raise the effective rate. The top tax rate applies for GST purposes as well.

[2] IRC § 2010(c), as amended by Act § 521(a).

[3] Following repeal of the estate and GST tax, the top gift tax rate is 35%, the top income tax rate for individuals.

Impact of Lower Estate Tax Rates

Notwithstanding the significant reduction in tax rates from 55 percent down to 45 percent in the year 2009, the tax bite remains at such a substantial level that anyone subject to the estate tax would probably continue to take the same measures that they took prior to the change.[3] It lessens the sting but does not eliminate the pain.

After 2009, the estate and GST taxes are repealed and the gift tax will remain with a lower rate at 35 percent, pegged to the top individual income tax rate.

NOTE

Setting the top gift tax rate at the same level as the top income tax rate following repeal of the estate and GST tax is consistent with the newly defined objective of the gift tax: preventing the use of inter vivos gifts to effect assignment of income to lower bracket taxpayers.

Effect of Higher Exclusion

A major impact of the changes in tax rates and exclusions is that beginning with the year 2002, the prior law $675,000 that can be transferred tax-free is increased to $1,000,000 (and more in subsequent years). These increases provide smaller estates (estates worth less than the exclusion available in the year of death) a method of avoiding estate tax. For wealthier clients, there is an increased opportunity to use gift planning to transfer assets and avoid the estate tax if that type of planning makes sense in light of the new rules depending on particular circumstances.

As with prior law, the exclusion amount is scheduled to increase, although in much larger increments. Thus, taxpayers would need to draft wills and trust documents in a flexible manner that would take advantage of the maximum exclusion amount at the time of their death. A bypass trust, as under current law, remains appropriate for taxpayers with significant estates.

Taxpayers should be cautious to avoid the problem that snared many taxpayers under prior law. Someone with an estate of perhaps $1,000,000, or with a combined estate for a family of $1,000,000, might think it is not necessary to plan since the estate is below the new increased exclusion amount. However, should a surviving spouse inherit $1,000,000, and the tax is not ultimately repealed or the surviving spouse dies prior to a further increase in the exclusion, and the assets increase in value, a tax could be due. For example, if husband and wife each had $500,000 in their names in 2003, they might opt simply for a will without any tax planning. However, if before year end the value of assets increased 10 percent, a tax of approximately $50,000 will be due if the husband dies and then the wife. A simple bypass trust would have avoided this tax. Thus, the same type of bypass or applicable exclusion trust planning as under prior law would continue to make sense for many clients. The difficulty and complexity of this approach would be to address how much of one's estate should be transferred to this type of trust.

 When evaluating the need for planning for smaller estates, keep in mind that most people underestimate their net worth, often forgetting to include valuable assets (such as insurance, which is not visible) or undervaluing a house or business. Further, it is necessary to consider the impact of inflation on a small estate if the estate tax is reintroduced in 2011. A $1,000,000 exclusion in 2011, in present dollar terms, may not be much more than the $675,000 exclusion that existed when the 2001 Tax Act was passed.

Under prior law, with a maximum that could be given away of $675,000, many people were comfortable transferring the full amount into the trust. However, as the amount that can be so transferred free of estate tax increases from the former $675,000 to $1,000,000 and eventually to $3,500,000 by the year 2009, taxpayers might prefer to give some component of their assets outright to the surviving spouse.

 Taxpayers should consider taking advantage of each increase in the exclusion to make additional lifetime gift transfers to dynasty trusts that can grow assets outside their estate if the estate tax is not ultimately eliminated, and may allow them access to those assets if needed.

Qualified Family-Owned Business Interests Deduction Affected by Increased Exclusion

The increase in the exclusion amount also obviates the need for the special deduction for qualified family-owned business interests[4] (QFOBI), which is tied to the amount of exclusion. Thus, this tax benefit is repealed in 2004.

Estate planning has far too often focused solely on tax minimization. The most significant threat to family business has always been the lack of succession planning, not estate taxes. Every business owner should be on guard not to lapse into inaction by the possible repeal of the estate tax. Succession, buyout of disabled or deceased partners, and other related planning remains essential.

Coordination of GST Exemption with Exclusion Delayed

The GST exemption amount increases to equal the estate tax exclusion amount from 2004 to 2009 after which the estate tax is scheduled for repeal. It appears that from 2001 to 2003 the GST exemption is to remain at the $1 million level indexed for inflation ($1,100,000 in 2002), as under prior law. The differences between the exclusion and GST exemption will continue to make planning complex.

This difference between the maximum amount that can be transferred without estate tax and the maximum amount that can be transferred without GST tax means that for 2002 and 2003 taxpayers can give more away for GST purposes than for estate tax purposes. To take maximum advantage of the difference between the estate tax and GST exclusion in those years, it might be preferable to bequeath the differential to grandchildren or other "skip" persons (defined later in this chapter), because the amount at stake is probably too small to warrant the complexity and expense of setting up a trust for this amount.

Investment of Bypass Trust and GST-Exempt Assets Post-2001 Tax Act

Tax-oriented investment planning has become common. Most investors, however, interpret this to mean income tax-oriented investing.

Proper tax and investment planning requires the consideration of gift, estate, and GST taxes in addition to income taxes.

The typical investment strategy for a surviving spouse has been, and for many will remain, investing bypass trust assets for growth. This is because the growth in those assets will be excluded from the surviving spouse's taxable estate. Thus, in a common estate plan of funding the bypass trust to the maximum and bequeathing the remaining estate to the surviving spouse outright or in a marital trust, investment planning often had the following pattern. The bypass trust contained primarily equities. If the estate were of modest size, the bypass trust would contain a significant portion of the family equity investments; in a larger estate, the growth-oriented equities might be concentrated in the bypass trust. The bond portion of the portfolio would be concentrated in the surviving spouse's name or in a marital trust (for example, a QTIP—the acronym for qualified terminable interest property trust) established for the surviving spouse. This is because the assets in the surviving spouse's name, or in a QTIP trust for the surviving spouse, will be taxed in the surviving spouse's estate. The objective of this typical plan is to concentrate growth in those areas not subject to estate tax.

The preceding plan can be complicated by the introduction of GST tax planning. In such cases, the objective is first to maximize growth that passes free of estate and GST tax to succeeding generations and also to maximize the growth that will not be taxed in the surviving spouse's estate. These objectives can be accomplished by first determining an asset allocation model appropriate for the taxpayer's assets, and then allocating those investment components in a manner that maximizes tax benefit. The assets likely to yield the highest growth over the long term should be held in GST tax-exempt, or dynasty, trusts that will likely pass on to future generations. The group of assets next most likely to appreciate would be held in a bypass trust format. The more conservative, income-oriented, assets would be held in the least estate tax–favored format (e.g., outright by the surviving spouse or in a non-GST tax-exempt QTIP trust).

The following examples can be changed somewhat to incorporate GST planning for future generations. As explained in this chapter and

---
EXAMPLE

Husband dies in 2002 with a $1,500,000 estate. Wife has a $750,000 estate. $1,000,000 is funded into a bypass trust under husband's will for the benefit of wife. The remaining $500,000 of husband's assets are contributed to a QTIP or marital trust for wife. The bypass trust, pursuant to the terms of husband's will, ends on the later of wife's death and the children attaining age 25. At that time, all assets are distributed to the children outright and unrestricted. Assume for simplicity that from an investment perspective a 50% equity allocation 50% bond allocation is determined to be appropriate for the family unit following husband's death. The combined investment estate (assuming all assets are investment assets) is $2,250,000 [$1,500,000+$750,000]. $1,125,000 should be invested in equities and $1,125,000 in bonds. Thus, the entire $1,000,000 bypass trust will be invested in equities. The QTIP trust might include only bonds to facilitate paying income to the wife (a QTIP must pay all income at least annually to the surviving spouse). The remaining $750,000 in wife's name would include $125,000 of equities and the remainder in bonds.

Chapter 6, dynasty trust planning is an important planning goal in light of the 2001 Tax Act. Dynasty trust planning will grow assets outside taxable estates in the event that the estate tax is reinstated in 2011. It will grow assets outside the reach of the $1 million gift tax lifetime exclusion, even if the estate tax is repealed.

EXAMPLE

Husband dies in 2002 with a $1,500,000 million estate. Wife has a $1,750,000 estate. $1,000,000 is funded into a bypass trust under husband's will for the benefit of wife. The husband's executor allocates $1,000,000 (almost all) of husband's GST tax exemption to the bypass trust so that it will never be subject to gift, estate, or GST tax. The remaining $500,000 of husband's assets are contributed to a QTIP or marital trust for wife. No GST tax exemption is allocated to this QTIP trust because the maximum GST tax exemption is only approximately $1,100,000 (2002 figure) and the husband's executor determines that the additional complexity of having two QTIP trusts (one GST tax exempt and one not) for the modest remaining exclusion is not worthwhile.

The bypass trust, pursuant to the terms of husband's will, does not end (as it had in the prior example on the later of wife's death and the children attaining age 25). Instead, it continues in perpetuity for the benefit of wife and all future descendants of husband and wife.[5]

How does this affect investment planning? Assume for simplicity that from an investment perspective a 50% equity allocation 50% bond allocation is determined to be appropriate for the family unit following husband's death. Investment planning would generally be as discussed in the preceding example. However, considering that the bypass trust is now intended to continue in perpetuity, a longer time horizon and perhaps more aggressive equity holdings might be appropriate if it is reasonable to expect significant assets to continue in trust.

The impact of the 2001 Tax Act changes on this type of planning is not always clear. Once trusts are formed, if the increase in the exclusion in future years makes the likelihood of an estate tax insignificant on the second death, then it would become irrelevant how investments are allocated between the various trusts for estate tax purposes.

NOTE

The husband died in the previous example in 2002. The combined estate is $2,250,000. By 2009, $3,500,000 of assets can be bequeathed free of estate tax. As such, no estate tax will be due at the wife's death. Therefore, there is no need to allocate equities to the bypass trust to remove growth from the surviving spouse's estate. Instead, a balanced portfolio could be held in each form: the bypass trust, the QTIP, and the wife's own assets.

If the estate tax is scheduled to be reinstated in 2011 and few advisers are yet confident that repeal is real, the prudent message may be to continue the tax-oriented investment planning to minimize future transfer taxes.

MODIFICATION OF GIFT TAX

Contrary to the initial understanding of many taxpayers, the gift tax has not been eliminated as part of estate tax repeal. The gift tax has simply assumed a somewhat modified role as a backstop to prevent taxpayers from using gift transfers to abuse the income tax system. If there were no gift tax, taxpayers could, at will, transfer assets among themselves to effect an unlimited assignment of income.

EXAMPLE

Fred Father has stock in a closely held business with negligible basis about to be sold for $1,500,000 million. He gifts 10% of the stock to each of his nieces and nephews. They will then own the stock when sold, realize a gain at their low tax brackets, and then gift the net proceeds back to Fred. To prevent this type of transfer tactic, the gift tax remains in effect with a $1,000,000 exclusion.

Gift Exclusion Increased

The 2001 Tax Act increased the then current applicable exclusion (which applies for both gift and estate tax purposes) from $675,000 to $1 million on January 1, 2002. The gift exclusion (in contrast to prior law which pegged the gift and estate exclusion at the same amount) retains the gift exclusion at a fixed $1 million figure.[6] This $1 million exclusion is referred to as the "lifetime gift exemption."

The manner in which the lifetime gift exemption is calculated is based on the "applicable credit amount" determined as if it were a maximum of $1 million, less the amounts allowed as credit in preceding periods against the tax.[7]

Gift Tax Rate Reduced

The gift tax rate continues at the same rate as the estate tax, as reduced by the 2001 Tax Act through the year 2009. After 2009, when the estate tax is repealed, the gift tax rate is reduced to the top individual income tax rate, intended to be a maximum rate of 35 percent. The graduated rates begin at 18 percent on gifts over $10,000 and increase to the maximum 35 percent rate on gifts over $500,000.[8]

This minimal level of change means that all prior gift planning techniques, particularly the use of annual gift tax exclusions to avoid use of the lifetime exemption, can continue to be used (see Chapter 6).

Congress made it appear that the estate tax is to be eliminated, and hence the tax laws simplified. Meanwhile, all the complex rules to qualify gifts for the annual $10,000 gift exclusion remain in place. As a result, many taxpayers will be lulled into not planning. After all, why bother with the headaches of qualifying a gift for the annual exclusion if eventually there won't be an estate tax? This attitude is precisely how most estates that paid estate tax under the pre-2001 law ended up having to do so. They ignored the effects of inflation and time and didn't plan. Although the new exclusion amounts that permit increasing distributions of more assets at death tax-free sound large, they are not certain to occur. Even if they do, the effects of inflation could mitigate their benefit. Therefore, use the cautious approach, just as under prior law: Endeavor to qualify gifts for the annual exclusion, and leverage gifts that use up the lifetime exemption to preserve as much as possible given the uncertainties of what will eventually happen with the estate tax laws.

Annual Gift Rules Unaffected

Taxpayers have been able to gift each year $10,000 to any number of donees without the diminution of their lifetime exclusion (or without incurring a gift tax if their exclusion has been exhausted). In 2002, the amount of annual gift exclusion was increased to $11,000 as a result of inflation indexing. These rules remain unchanged by the 2001 Tax Act.

Planning with the annual exclusion is explained in Chapter 6.

 Many durable powers of attorney authorize agents to make gifts up to only $10,000. Taxpayers should revise these documents to use more specific language to permit maximum gifts to the indexed amount of the annual exclusion.

Transfers to Nongrantor Trusts Deemed Completed Gifts

For the gift tax to apply, the gift must be a completed gift. After 2009, a gift transfer to a trust will be treated as a completed gift, and hence gift tax will be assessed unless the trust is treated for income tax purposes as wholly owned by the donor (as fully a grantor trust).

NOTE

The objective of this rule is consistent with the new use of the gift tax as a backstop to prevent income tax shifting through gifts. This provision demonstrates the proven ability of so-called sprinkle (discretionary) trusts to be used to shift income among various beneficiaries to maximize the income tax benefits (see later discussion). This rule prevents taxpayers from transferring assets to defective trusts structured to be incomplete gifts for gift tax purposes (hence not triggering gift tax) but complete for income tax purposes (so child beneficiaries who are in lower tax brackets than the grantor can realize income in their lower tax brackets).

 When the estate and GST tax are eliminated, testamentary transfers can, and perhaps often should, be made to perpetual sprinkle trusts to facilitate circumventing the gift tax issues for later generations, and to provide income-shifting flexibility.

Planning Highlights

The gift tax post-2001 Tax Act will have the following significant effects on planning. (The specific techniques are explained in more detail in Chapter 6.)

- Despite the scheduled increases in the exclusion to $3,500,000, lifetime gifts will trigger tax on amounts above $1,000,000. This will encourage taxpayers to use all leveraging techniques used under prior law when making large gifts, such as sales to defective grantor trusts, grantor retained annuity trusts (GRATs), family limited partnerships (FLPs), limited liability companies (LLCs), and discounts for lack of control and marketability.

- Annual exclusion planning ($10,000 gifts, as indexed for inflation) to as many donees as acceptable will continue to be a common and advisable planning technique. The significant increases in the exclusion amount, however, will affect planning. As noted previously, many taxpayers will be lulled into ignoring annual gifts believing their estates will never be subject to tax. For some, this may be true, for others it will be a costly mistake.

- The increase in the exclusion from $675,000 to $1,000,000 presents a planning opportunity for increased gifts for taxpayers who may not survive the repeal of estate tax, or for taxpayers who believe the structure of the new law is such that the estate tax will never be repealed.

- Wealthy families will be constrained from making large lifetime transfers because of the continuation of the gift tax. This means that for lifetime transfers the use of qualified personal residence trusts (QPRTs), GRATs, FLPs/LLCs, discounts, sales to intentionally defective irrevocable trusts (IDITs), and other transfer tax leveraging techniques will still be useful.

- The objective of the new gift tax can be circumvented with traditional income shifting techniques. A parent can still form an FLP, gift interests to a child, and eventually distribute income to that child, subject to the family partnership rules.[9]

QUALIFIED FAMILY-OWNED BUSINESS INTERESTS DEDUCTION REPEALED

Prior law has provided for a deduction from the value of the decedent's gross estate for the adjusted value of qualified family-owned business interests (QFOBI).[10] The maximum amount that can be deducted is $675,000.[11] However, the full value of this maximum deduction will not always be realized because of the interplay of the Code Section 2057 deduction and the applicable exclusion (unified credit) amount.[12] If the full $675,000 deduction is claimed, the applicable exclusion amount available to the estate of the closely held business owner will be limited to only $625,000.[13] If the deduction for the closely held business interest is less than the maximum $675,000 allowable, then the applicable exclusion amount (unified credit) will be increased, to the extent it exceeds $675,000, over the amount of the deduction allowed.[14]

--- **EXAMPLE** ---

Assume the deduction claimed under IRC § 2057 for a qualifying family business interest is $550,000. The difference between this deduction amount and the $675,000 deduction, or $125,000 [$675,000 – $550,000], is added back to the amount of the applicable exclusion as limited by IRC § 2057(a)(3)(A). Thus, the applicable exclusion would be $750,000. However, this amount cannot exceed the actual applicable exclusion amount available in that year under the general applicable exclusion provision, or $1 million in 2002 and 2003.[15]

As a result of this coordination of the QFOBI deduction and the exclusion amount, the QFOBI deduction is eliminated as the exclusion amount increases. Specifically, the QFOBI deduction will not be available for decedents dying after December 31, 2003.[16]

IRC § 2057(j), the recapture provision, appears to remain in effect. The result is that if businesses that benefited from a QFOBI deduction in the past cease to meet the many QFOBI requirements, recapture of that deduction will still be triggered.

The recapture provision operates as follows: If the qualifications are met, but later fail, recapture rules apply. If within ten years of the date after the taxpayer's death any of the following events occur, a portion or all of the tax savings may have to be repaid (recaptured):[17]

- None of the heirs materially participate in the business.[18]
- The heirs dispose of any portion of their interests in the business to other than a member of the qualified heir's family or through a conservation easement.[19]
- The heirs lose their U.S. citizenship and don't comply with other provisions to assure the IRS that any future tax due will be paid by meeting requirements similar to a QDOT (qualified domestic trust).[20]
- The principal place of business of the enterprise ceases to be in the United States.[21]

If any of the preceding recapture events occur, an additional estate tax will have to be paid.[22] The amount of the additional estate tax is the applicable percentage of the adjusted tax difference attributable to the QFOBI. The applicable percentage is shown in Exhibit 1.2.

If the recapture event occurs in the year indicated in Exhibit 1.2, then the additional estate tax is equal to the applicable percentage multiplied by the adjusted tax difference attributable to the qualified family-owned business interest.[23] Also, interest will be charged on this additional estate tax for the period from the date the estate tax was originally due (nine months following taxpayer's death) until the date this additional estate tax is due.[24] Obviously, if this additional estate tax is paid late, another interest charge will apply to that late payment.

Exhibit 1.2   Recapture Calculations

Year Following Taxpayer's Death in Which Recapture Event Occurs	Applicable Percentage for Recapture Calculation
1	100%
2	100
3	100
4	100
5	100
6	100
7	80
8	60
9	40
10	20
After year 10	None

GENERATION-SKIPPING TRANSFER TAX CHANGES

The generation-skipping transfer (GST) tax is an expensive and complicated transfer tax that affects taxpayers making transfers by gift or at death to a grandchild or other person the tax laws consider to be two or more generations beyond the donor (called a "skip person"). The GST tax is charged on every gift or other transfer of property that meets the requirements of being a generation-skipping transfer.[25] The GST tax is calculated as a flat 55 percent tax rate on the taxable amount of a generation-skipping transfer. The 2001 Tax Act reduces this rate, as the estate tax rate is reduced, to 45 percent

The purpose of the GST tax is to equalize intergenerational taxation of property transfers where planning is attempted to avoid the estate tax. The GST tax was designed to prevent the very wealthy from passing assets through many layers of generations, transfer tax free, often through the use of trusts.

Until the GST tax is actually eliminated, it remains a costly, almost confiscatory, tax that must be planned for. Overall, the 2001 Tax Act makes such planning somewhat easier. To understand the changes made by the 2001 Tax Act, some background about the GST is necessary. First, it is essential to know what types of transfers are subject to the GST tax. Second, it is necessary to recognize that a lifetime exclusion is a key way to avoid the GST tax and to know how the exclusion (the GST exemption) is allocated to different transfers.

Transactions Subject to GST Tax

Three events can cause the GST tax to apply: (1) a direct skip, (2) a taxable distribution, and (3) a taxable termination.

Direct Skip

A direct skip is a transfer of an interest in property, which is subject to the estate or gift tax, to a skip person (or to a trust for the benefit of a skip person).[26] For example, a direct skip occurs if the decedent's will leaves an asset to any skip person, such as a grandchild. If a trust is created and all trust income is accumulated for a number of years without distribution, but eventually the trust benefits only skip persons, a direct skip occurs and a tax is assessed. The GST tax for a direct skip, when no trust is involved, is to be paid by the person making the transfer (the donor, or if it is a bequest under the decedent's will, the estate).[27] If the transfer is made from a trust, then the trustee will have to pay the tax.[28] A direct skip is a "tax-exclusive" calculation. This means that if the donor pays the GST tax on a gift of assets (a direct skip) to a grandchild, the amount of GST tax paid will not be considered an additional gift for GST tax purposes. The recipient of the property may qualify for an increase in the tax basis of the property. The tax basis is increased by the portion of the GST tax attributable to the appreciation of the property given above the donor's tax basis.[29]

There is a special exclusion from GST taxation as a direct skip where a child has died. If the donor's child dies and the donor then makes a gift to the child of the deceased child (the grandchild), no GST tax will be assessed.[30] The 2001 Tax Act has broadened this exception, as explained later in this chapter.

Taxable Distribution

Where there is a distribution of property or money from a trust to a skip person (e.g., a grandchild), the GST tax may apply.[31] The GST tax on a taxable distribution is based on the fair value of the property transferred, reduced by any expenses incurred in connection with determining the GST tax.[32] If the GST tax is paid out of a trust, the amount of tax paid is treated as an additional distribution subject to the tax.[33] The GST tax on a taxable distribution is charged against the property that was given, unless specific provisions are made for a different treatment.[34] The transferee (e.g., a grandchild), however, is liable to pay the GST tax.[35]

If income from a trust is distributed to a skip person, the GST tax as a taxable distribution will apply. However, the recipient can deduct the GST tax paid on the income distribution on his or her personal income tax return.[36]

Taxable Termination

A taxable termination is a transaction subject to the GST tax when the interests of a beneficiary of a trust (the person entitled to receive income from a trust) terminate and a skip person (e.g., a grandchild)[37] then receives the principal. This could occur as a result of a death, lapse of time (e.g., the trust is only until the child-beneficiary reaches age 60, at which time the trust ends and the grandchild receives the money), or release of a power (right). Such an occurrence is considered a taxable termination resulting in a GST tax.[38] If, however, someone other than a skip person receives some portion of the trust, then the termination would not entirely be a taxable termination.

Three exceptions can prevent incurring the GST tax: (1) Immediately after the termination, a nonskip person has an interest in the property; (2) no distribution can be made to a skip person;[39] or (3) a general power of appointment can be given to a nonskip person (this will cause the assets to be included in that person's taxable estate, thus avoiding the need for GST to be imposed).

The GST tax on a taxable termination is payable by the trustee of the trust.[40] The amount of tax is calculated based on the value of all property[41] to which the taxable termination occurred, reduced by expenses, debts, and taxes.[42]

GST Exemption Increased

Under prior law, the GST exemption was $1,000,000, inflation adjusted. The inflation adjustments increased the exemption to $1,060,000 for 2001 and $1,100,000 for 2002. Under the 2001 Tax Act, the exemption is to increase to equal the unified credit, beginning in 2004 (see Exhibit 1.3).

The figures for the year 2012 are listed as unknown because it is uncertain what the ultimate impact of the repeal in 2010 and the reinstatement as a result of the sunset in 2011, will mean. Will Congress confirm the repeal and make it permanent? Will budget problems and the tremendous skewing of the 2001 Tax Act toward the wealthy result in a backlash and the reinstatement of the estate and GST taxes?

Exhibit 1.3   GST Exemptions

Year	GST Exemption	Comment
2002	$1,000,000	Inflation adjusted ($1,000,000).
2003	$1,000,000	Inflation adjusted (to be determined).
2004	$1,500,000	Consider additional dynasty trust gifts.
2005	$1,500,000	
2006	$2,000,000	Consider additional dynasty trust gifts.
2007	$2,000,000	
2008	$2,000,000	
2009	$3,500,000	Consider additional dynasty trust gifts; (note pronounced back-ending of benefits).
2010	–	Taxes repealed. (Call Jack Kevorkian?)
2011	$1,000,000 (inflation adjusted?)	Sunset provision effective.
2012	Unknown	

Get it while you can. If the estate and GST exclusion increases, taxpayers should consider making permanent irrevocable gifts to dynasty or domestic asset protection trusts to secure the estate and GST benefits in the event that the taxes are not completely phased out or repealed (see Chapter 6). Based on the law as enacted, a person could safeguard $3.5 million (substantially more by using gift leveraging techniques) in 2009 from gift, estate, and GST taxes forever. It would be wise to take advantage of this (or whatever the exclusion is in any given year) before a future Congress lessens the benefits. Presumably, any completed gifts made before a change in the law will be respected ("grandfathered") in the event the law is later changed, although there is no guarantee.

How to Take Maximum Advantage of GST Exemption

The changes in the GST tax, the increase of the exemption, the disparity of the GST exemption and the estate tax exclusion, and the one-year repeal of the GST tax in 2010 before its reintroduction in 2011 make planning to take maximum advantage of the GST exemption complicated, to say the least. Further, since the maximum gift tax exclusion remains at $1 million after 2002, taxpayers cannot take maximum advantage of the GST exemption without triggering a gift tax. Thus, implementation of some portion of GST planning (e.g., funding of generation skipping or perpetual trusts) has to be deferred until death. Because of variable, complex factors, the taxpayer may realize different transfer tax results depending on the year he dies.

To take maximum advantage of the GST benefits, the taxpayer will need a different provision in his will for various years. Consider the following guidelines.

- 2001. The GST exemption of $1,000,000 inflation adjusted, or $1,060,000, considerably exceeds the $675,000 estate tax exclusion. To secure this difference, a bypass trust can be established for

$675,000 and with the GST exemption allocated to it. The remaining $385,000 ($1,060,000—$675,000) of GST exemption can be secured by establishing two marital or QTIP trusts. The first QTIP will be GST exempt and will be funded with $385,000. The remaining QTIP will be non-GST exempt and will be funded with the remainder of taxpayer's assets. This approach defers all estate tax on his death until the death of the surviving spouse. It also ensures maximum GST benefits so assets can be passed on to skip persons, such as grandchildren, or perpetual trusts.

- 2002–2003. The maximum GST exemption is $1,000,000 inflation adjusted to $1,100,000 in 2002. In 2003, it is somewhat higher. The differential between the GST exemption and the $1,000,000 estate exclusion can be bequeathed to a trust as in the planning example for 2001. The cost of a separate trust for this small amount is unlikely to be warranted, but can be done if desired. To use all of the GST benefit if a trust is deemed too costly for the inflation adjustment, consider a bequest of cash to grandchildren for this differential.

- 2004–2009. During these years, the amount of GST exemption is to exactly equal the amount of estate tax exclusion. The planning can be simplified considerably (if the planning described here for bypass trusts could possibly be described as simple) because all taxpayers need to do is fund a bypass trust for purposes of safeguarding the estate tax exclusion and GST exemption; one trust can be funded with the same amount qualifying for each benefit. When analyzing the GST implications for the bypass funding options to be discussed, however, the variations are many. Further, planning to safeguard the GST exemption might encourage the taxpayer to revamp the bypass trust planning he might otherwise prefer.

- 2010. Estate and GST taxes are repealed. At this stage, the taxpayer should consider bequeathing all of his assets to a generation-skipping perpetual (dynasty) trust. This planning technique is discussed in the following subsection.

- 2011. It's back! The estate and GST tax with a $1,000,000 estate tax exclusion and a $1,000,000 inflation-adjusted GST exemption are back. Go back to Step 1 (2001) and plan accordingly. Do not pass "Go."

Effect of Eventual Repeal of GST Tax on Estate Planning

If the GST and estate taxes are in fact eventually repealed permanently, the face of estate planning will change. Tremendous planning opportunities will unfold that had been and still are impractical while these taxes exist.

GST planning requires taxpayers to focus on two planning targets. First, they must plan as if the estate and GST exemptions are going to increase as enacted to be followed in 2010 by a repeal of the GST and estate tax as well as the permanence of such repeal in 2011 if Congress approves the repeal in lieu of the scheduled sunset. However, they should also plan as if the GST and estate taxes will not be repealed and as if the exclusion will never even reach the $3.5 million maximum. The result should be to secure permanent GST planning benefits while they are available. If the GST and estate exclusions increase to $1.5 million or more, take advantage of them while they exist. Don't forget that as enacted in 2011 both exclusions drop back to $1 million.

Wealthy families will continue to be constrained from making large lifetime transfers because of the gift tax with a $1 million lifetime exclusion. However, if the GST and estate taxes are actually eliminated in 2010 as enacted (and should Congress vote to make that repeal permanent), a new type of "post-GST" planning will present a tremendous opportunity to avoid the new gift tax. Through the creative use of trusts, taxpayers can ensure that their descendants will never be subjected to transfer tax. As a bonus, this same type of strategy can circumvent the income tax rules against the assignment of income and obtain a substantial measure of asset protection. The key to obtaining these many benefits, and a focal point of many estate plans, will be the creative use of trusts. The 2001 Tax Act has made planning with trusts more, not less, important for many taxpayers.

Testamentary sprinkle (discretionary), or dynasty, trusts that will continue forever (in perpetuity, hence the name "dynasty" trusts) then become more important. On the death of a family patriarch in a world without estate and GST taxes, significant assets (an entire estate) can be bequeathed to a sprinkle dynasty trust for the benefit of all heirs (or separate perpetual trusts for each family line), and then assets can be distributed to later generations when desired, without triggering the gift tax. This provides an effective means of avoiding the gift tax that the next generation would otherwise be constrained by if children simply received the patriarch's estate as an outright bequest (without a trust). Further, the sprinkle dynasty trust would provide a tremendous income tax planning tool as income could be sprinkled to taxpayers in the lowest tax brackets. Dynasty trusts are discussed in Chapter 6.

The following sample clause illustrates the type of language that might be included in a discretionary (sprinkle) dynasty trust. From an investment perspective, the vagueness of the clause will require more investigation and analysis to determine an appropriate investment strategy. Similarly, the vagueness, which provides planning flexibility, gives no guidance for when distributions should be made. A unitrust or total return approach could be used instead.

SAMPLE CLAUSE

The Trustee shall hold the Trust Estate, in perpetuity unless the Trust Estate is sooner exhausted pursuant to the terms hereof, for the following purposes and subject to the terms and conditions hereof. The Trustee is hereby directed to manage, invest, and reinvest the Trust Estate considering the time horizon, distribution provisions and other terms hereof, to collect the income thereof, and to pay over the net income to, or apply the net income for the benefit of, such one or more of the following persons: the Grantor, Grantor's spouse as such may be from time to time, and the Grantor's Children and the issue of such Children, including issue born or adopted by the Grantor or issue of the Grantor (collectively, the "Recipients"), such amounts of the net income and principal thereof as the Trustee, in the exercise of discretion, may consider appropriate in accordance with the Standard for Payment set forth in this Trust Agreement, and with consideration of the recommendations of the Distribution Committee concerning such distributions.

The Trustee may pay all or none of the income and principal to any one of the Recipients to the exclusion of all others, or in any other manner in the Trustee's discretion. In lieu of paying over income or principal to any Recipient, the Grantor suggests, but does not require, that the Trustee give consideration to instead purchasing assets which the Trustee may permit Recipients to use in order to preserve the asset protection and multigenerational planning characteristics of this Trust.

New Rules for Automatic Allocation of GST Exemption

Prior Law Rules

To recognize the implications of the complex new rules governing allocation of the GST exemption, it is necessary to understand how allocations of a GST exemption were, and generally continue to be, made.

As noted previously, the primary protection from the GST is a lifetime exclusion similar to the use of the lifetime gift ($1 million beginning in 2002) and estate tax exclusion ($1 million in 2002, increasing to $3.5 million in 2009). Up to $1 million (the amount was indexed for inflation prior to the 2001 Tax Act) can be gifted to grandchildren (or other skip persons or trusts) with no GST tax cost.[43] The donor's spouse can similarly make a $1 million transfer to skip persons.

This exclusion must be irrevocably allocated to any property transfers that are made.[44] This was done by completing the appropriate forms on the annual gift tax return to be filed with the IRS. This allocation was often required, and hence a gift tax return filed, even though no gift tax was due. The procedure created much confusion—no need to file a gift tax return for gift tax purposes, but a need to file a gift tax return for GST purposes. Because of the complexity of the GST, this allocation requirement was often overlooked by many taxpayers, who were inadvertently ensnared by the GST. The 2001 Tax Act made changes to these rules to mitigate the problems some taxpayers had with this allocation. But as is so typical, the changes create new complexities and new problems.

The $1 million (indexed) GST lifetime exemption can also be allocated by the executor following the taxpayer's death. Many taxpayers take maximum advantage of this exemption by setting up multiple trusts under their wills and granting their executors the authority to make certain decisions for funding these trusts and allocating the GST exemption. However, the allocation once made cannot be changed.[45]

Once a portion or all of the GST exemption is properly allocated to a particular property transfer (e.g., a sum of money given to a trust) the protection of that allocation will stay with that property. Thus, if the GST exemption is allocated to property given to a trust, that trust will remain protected from GST tax in future years if the allocation is made properly. As with the gift tax reporting requirements, these GST exemption allocation rules created many traps for the unwary. Again, the 2001 Tax Act made changes to these rules to mitigate the problems some taxpayers faced when trusts had an improper allocation (in technical terms, an inclusion ratio of more than zero but less than one). But once again, the changes are perhaps more difficult to implement than prior law.

To understand use of the $1 million (indexed) exemption, the concept of the *inclusion ratio* needs to be understood. The GST tax exemption percentage (the inclusion ratio) is established when the taxpayer makes a gift (or bequest) to a trust, and allocates (or the executor allocates) some portion or all of the available GST exemption. The inclusion ratio is one minus the "applicable fraction."[46] When making the gift to a trust, the applicable fraction is determined as follows:

$$\frac{\text{Amount of GST exemption allocated to trust}}{\text{Value of property transferred to the trust}}$$

The numerator is the amount of the GST exemption allocated to the particular transfer.[47] The denominator is the value of the property involved, reduced by any charitable contribution deduction and any federal or state estate or death taxes.[48] How much of the exemption should be allocated is an extremely important decision, and can be complicated. If any portion of the GST tax exemption is allocated to a trust, that portion of the exemption is considered used, even if a GST tax is never incurred. If no GST tax is ever possible, the taxpayer will have wasted that portion of the exemption. Similarly, the GST exemption is allocated to a trust in the hope that the assets in the trust will appreciate significantly, and if they actually decline in value (that hot dot-com stock), the GST exemption will be wasted.

The 2001 Tax Act provides, as is explained below in more detail, for the automatic allocation of GST exemption to certain gift transfers to trusts that did not receive automatic allocations under prior law. From a planning perspective, these automatic allocations need to be analyzed to determine whether they are really optimal.

Planning for New Rules

A key planning concept to avoid GST taxes before their scheduled repeal is to judiciously allocate the lifetime GST exemption. This is often the most suitable approach for protecting the most assets in trust for the longest period. With respect to the new tax code section Congress enacted that automatically allocates GST exemption for the taxpayer,[49] the tax planner must address the following issues:

1. Does the taxpayer want some portion of GST exemption allocated to protect a transfer to a particular trust?
2. Do the new rules automatically allocate the GST exemption to that trust? If they do, then do nothing if the taxpayer wants the GST exemption allocated.
3. If allocation of the GST exemption is not wanted (or if wanted and the new rules don't automatically allocate it), then complete and file a gift tax return allocating the GST exemption the way the taxpayer requests, or stating that automatic allocation is not wanted.

The decision process is shown in Exhibit 1.4.

Exhibit 1.4   The Decision Process

Rule	Taxpayer Wants GST Exemption Allocated	Taxpayer Does Not Want GST Exemption Allocated
New rules automatically allocate.	Do nothing (Note, under prior law you may have filed gift tax returns to allocate; now you won't).	File a gift tax return and affirmatively elect (state) that you don't want GST exemption allocated to a particular transfer (in the past you did not have to take any action). If you don't take this step, the GST exemption will be wasted.
New rules don't automatically allocate.	File a gift tax return and affirmatively elect (state) to allocate GST exemption to a particular transfer (in the past you also would have had to file—so no change under the new law).	No requirement to file. This doesn't mean do nothing; the trusts and transfers involved may still need analysis to determine whether an allocation is warranted, or whether the new rules may allocate it anyhow.

Automatic Allocation of GST Exemption for Transfers That Are Direct Skips

If a gift is a direct skip (e.g., a transfer to a grandchild or a trust that solely benefits grandchildren), the law (pre- and post-2001 Tax Act) automatically allocates any remaining GST exclusion (i.e., any unused portion) that the taxpayer has to make the inclusion ratio of that skip equal zero (assuming sufficient GST exclusion is available). If the property transferred is worth more than the remaining GST exemption, then the entire remaining amount is allocated to the transfer.

For purposes of these rules, the unused portion of the GST exemption is the maximum available as indicated in Exhibit 1.3. This maximum is reduced by the GST exemption previously allocated on a gift tax return.[50] The GST exemption is automatically allocated to a direct skip[51] and also automatically allocated to an indirect skip under the 2001 Tax Act rules according to the following conditions.[52]

Automatic Allocation of GST Exemption for Transfers That Are Not Direct Skips

The post-2001 Tax Act rules provide that an unused GST exemption will be allocated, in addition to direct skips, to certain indirect skips (transfers). More precisely, some portion or all of the remaining GST exemption will be allocated to an indirect skip that is subject to the gift tax and that is made to a "GST trust." Under prior law, the taxpayer had to affirmatively allocate the GST exemption to such a transfer. The new law will automatically allocate enough of the taxpayer's remaining GST exemption to result in such a transfer having the lowest possible inclusion ratio, if feasible, so that none of the trust assets will ever be subject to GST tax.[53]

To understand these new automatic allocation rules, it is necessary to define the term *GST trust* created by the 2001 Tax Act.

NOTE

In reviewing these complex rules, keep in mind that the lawmakers' objective was to identify the types of trust to which a taxpayer would likely want the GST exemption allocated to protect the trust from GST tax. Although perhaps a noble objective, the draftspersons faced the practical problem of myriad variations of trusts and the unique GST profile presented by each trust and client situation.

Automatic Allocation of GST Exemption to GST Trusts under New Law

A GST trust, which will receive an automatic allocation, is broadly defined as any trust for which a taxable GST transfer may be possible.

More technically, it is a trust that could have a taxable distribution or a taxable termination.

EXAMPLE

Taxpayer sets up a "pot" (discretionary) trust for the benefit of his two children and six grandchildren. If the trustee makes a distribution (for other than qualifying medical and tuition expenses) to a grandchild, there is a taxable distribution. If both of taxpayer's children were to die, only the six grandchildren would remain as beneficiaries of the trust. Since they are all skip persons, the death of the last of the two children would constitute a taxable termination. In either of these cases, a GST tax on the trust would be a possibility, so the new automatic allocation rules would allocate some or all of the remaining GST exemption, unless a special exception applied.

Why would the law need a special exception to an automatic allocation of the GST exemption to the trust described in the example above? Why do the new rules present such complexity? Why would a taxpayer want his accountant to file a gift tax return electing not to have the GST exemption automatically allocated? Before analyzing the actual rules and exceptions provided in the 2001 Tax Act, several hypothetical scenarios based on the preceding example will illustrate the potential problems and set the stage for an explanation of the new rules.

EXAMPLE

Continuing with the example of a pot trust for two children and six grandchildren, consider the following scenarios:

- Assume that the pot trust were to last forever (remain perpetual) unless the funds were exhausted. If neither of the children were particularly wealthy and the father was comfortable helping them extensively, he might well anticipate, with certainty, that the trust would be exhausted during their lifetimes. It would be wasteful to allocate the GST exemption to such a trust because no assets would be distributed to skip persons (grandchildren) needing protection from GST.

- Assume the identical trust, but the children both win the lottery after the trust is established and because they will never have financial need, it is highly unlikely that any funds would be distributed to them. Although the terms of the trust are identical, the facts make the reality of the trust distributions, the time for which the trust will last, and hence the GST consequences completely different.

How can a standard set of rules deal with such divergent situations? It can't. To plan appropriately, taxpayers will have to remain vigilant by affirmatively allocating or electing not to allocate the GST exemption as illustrated in Exhibit 1.4.

The mechanism by which the new rules endeavor to address the complexity of when GST should be allocated is through a series of six exceptions for when GST exemption will not automatically be allocated to gifts to GST trusts. The paradigm has changed—the allocation will be made unless action is taken.

Using a sale to a defective grantor trust (IDIT) is an aggressive estate and GST planning technique (see Chapter 6). A concern of many taxpayers concerning this technique was having to report at least $1 of gift on a gift tax return to allocate a GST exemption to this transaction. It appears that Congress, via the automatic allocation rules, may have eliminated the need to file to make the allocation (see the discussion of IDITs in Chapter 6).

Special Rules When the GST Exemption Isn't Allocated Automatically

The new automatic GST allocation rules include the following six provisions to identify trusts that shouldn't receive an automatic allocation of GST exemption:

1. The trust agreement provides that more than 25 percent of the trust corpus can be withdrawn or must be distributed to one or more individuals who are nonskip persons (e.g., children) before one of three dates:

   (a) Before the date that the beneficiary attains the age of 46.[54]

   (b) On or before the dates set forth in the trust agreement that are before the date the beneficiary attains the age of 46.[55]

   (c) On the occurrence of an event that may reasonably be expected to happen before the date the beneficiary attains the age of 46, which events will be explained in future Treasury Regulations.[56] An example might be graduation from college.

> **NOTE**
>
> Although many trusts split (that is, are divided for EST tax purposes) at stated ages, many trusts also include the spouse as a beneficiary and the spouse may still be alive. The spouse's death may not be an event likely to occur before a child attains age 46.

2. The trust agreement requires that more than 25 percent of trust principal must be distributed to, or may be withdrawn by, one or more individuals who are nonskip persons (e.g., children) and who were living on the date of the death of another person identified in the trust by name or type (or class, such as cousin) who is more than ten years older than the beneficiaries.[57]

The second exception could be interpreted as if it only applies in the event the child survives the death of the spouse.

3. The trust agreement states that if one or more individuals who are nonskip persons die on or before a date or event described in the new rules[58] then 25 percent of the trust principal must be distributed to the estates of one or more of the beneficiaries, or be subject to a general power of appointment exercisable by one or more of the beneficiaries.[59] A general power of appointment is a right granted under a trust agreement that results in the principal of the trust being included in the power-holder's estate. General powers are often granted to nonskip persons (e.g., children) to avoid GST taxation.

   The new allocation rules assume that powers of appointment held by nonskip persons will not be exercised.

4. A portion of the particular trust will be included in the taxable estate of a nonskip person (e.g., a child) if the nonskip person died immediately after assets were transferred to the trust.[60]

5. The trust is a charitable lead annuity trust (CLAT), charitable remainder annuity trust (CRAT), or a charitable remainder unitrust (CRUT).[61] (See Chapter 6.)

6. A gift tax charitable deduction was allowed based on the right to receive annual payments of a fixed percentage of the net fair value of trust assets each year; the trust requires the payment of the principal remaining when the charitable interest terminates, to a nonskip person. There is an exception for a charitable lead unitrust (CLUT) which pays on termination to a nonskip person.[62]

Crummey (Annual Demand) Powers and the New Automatic Allocation Rules

The value of transferred property is not considered to be included in the gross estate of a nonskip person or subject to a right of withdrawal by reason of such person holding a right to withdraw so much of such property as does not exceed the annual gift tax exclusion.[63] This was previously $10,000 but as a result of inflation indexing, was in 2002 $11,000 per year, per donee, to be indexed by inflation. Thus, a transfer to a pot trust for the benefit of children and grandchildren will be more likely to have the GST exemption allocated automatically, because the rules will not assume that the right of a child (nonskip beneficiary) to withdraw an amount equal to the annual exclusion is counted toward the 25 percent tests in the six exceptions to the automatic allocation rule.

If so-called hanging powers are used in a trust (i.e., to qualify gifts to the trust for the annual exclusion), a beneficiary may have the right to withdraw the greater of $5,000 or 5 percent of trust principal that would constitute a limited power of appointment. It is unclear whether the language of the new law causes such a trust to fall within the exception from automatic allocation; if not, then an automatic allocation may be made.

New Automatic Allocation Tied to Estate Tax Inclusion Period

The automatic allocation of GST exemption is not made under the new law unless a special time period called the *estate tax inclusion period* (ETIP) ends. A brief explanation is necessary before this concept can be applied to common trust and gift transactions.

The ETIP concept can be illustrated in the context of a grantor retained annuity trust (GRAT), where the ETIP issue clearly occurs. A GRAT is intended to discount for gift tax purposes the value of assets given as a gift to the GRAT for the ultimate benefit of the GRAT remainder beneficiaries, typically the grantor's children. The GRAT discount is accomplished by the donor retaining an interest in the trust, via an annuity payment, for the term of the trust. The discount for gift tax purposes is based on reducing the value of the assets transferred to the GRAT to reflect the annuity payment retained by the grantor for the term of the GRAT. At the end of the term of years (e.g., five years on a five-year GRAT), the assets of the trust pass to the remainder beneficiaries named. However, if the grantor/donor dies before the trust term ends, the assets of the trust are included, in full, in the donor's estate. This period of time is called an estate tax inclusion period (ETIP), because during the term of the GRAT there remains a risk of all GRAT assets being included in the grantor's estate. For GST purposes, the GST exemption cannot be allocated until this ETIP ends. This occurs at the termination of the trust, when the property is valued fully (without the discount the donor realized for gift tax purposes), as well as any appreciation of the assets during the GRAT term. Thus, the ability to leverage the GST exemption amount using the GRAT technique is limited.

Similar concepts apply to a charitable lead annuity trust (CLAT); thus, just as for the GRAT, the ability to leverage a GST exemption amount using the CLAT technique is limited.

Impact of New Automatic Allocation Rules

The definition of GST trust is so broad that the result might mean an allocation of a GST exemption to many trusts, including a common insurance trust. This is really not the desired result because in many cases you don't want to have a GST exemption allocated to an insurance trust; depending on the trust terms, there are often better ways to use that exemption. Many typical insurance trusts have all assets distributed to the children by some specified age, say 35 or 40, following the second death.

NOTE

If a pot trust eventually distributes all trust assets to a taxpayer's children (nonskip persons), is this situation covered by the exceptions, or must he file a return to state that an automatic allocation is not wanted? Until the new rules are clarified, he may have to file a protective gift tax return stating that GST exemption should not be allocated even if the new rules might appear *not* to allocate GST exemption in the situation involved.

Extension of Time to Allocate GST Exemption

Congress believed that the IRS should provide extensions of the time to make the necessary election to allocate the GST exemption. The

2001 Tax Act authorizes the IRS to grant extensions on the time in which the taxpayer must allocate the GST exemption or elect out of the new automatic GST allocation rules.[64] Thus, the IRS has been directed to create procedures for providing relief[65] for taxpayers who have failed to allocate a GST exemption.[66]

The manner in which the estate tax law is written appears to permit filing for relief now. The taxpayer may have to show factually from written records the intention to file the GST allocation. It will probably be difficult to do. The IRS will issue regulatory guidance on the specifics of how to effect this filing.

When evaluating whether relief should be granted, the IRS must consider all relevant circumstances including the intent set forth in the trust agreement.

Consider including a specific and clear statement in each trust stating the intent of the trust for GST purposes.

Example: "This trust is not intended to be GST exempt and grantor does not contemplate allocating GST exemption to this trust based on the facts existing at the time of the execution of this trust."

Including express language is not necessarily appropriate in many planning circumstances, for example, if it is later determined to allocate GST exemption to the particular trust or if a trust is divided into GST exempt and non-GST exempt subtrusts.

Retroactive Allocation of GST Exemption

The 2001 Tax Act provides yet another liberalization of the GST tax. Now, retroactive allocation to a trust can be made if there is an unnatural order of death. This is defined as a death of a lineal descendant of the transferor before the transferor. The taxpayer can retroactively allocate the GST exemption based on the values at the time of the transfer.[67] This is a generous rule if the property has increased significantly in value.

The rationale for the new liberalization is that taxpayers would not allocate a GST exemption to a trust intended to benefit only nonskip persons, such as children. However, if a child dies and that deceased child's children (the taxpayer's grandchildren) become beneficiaries, it would have proven advantageous to have allocated GST exemption to the trust. More specifically, the new law provides for allocating any portion of the unused GST exemption to the previous transfers, chronologically.

This retroactive allocation is to be made on a gift tax return filed for the year in which the nonskip person died.

Severing a Trust to Secure GST Benefits

The GST tax exemption percentage (the inclusion ratio) is established when the taxpayer makes a gift (or bequest) to a trust, and allocates (or the executor allocates) some portion or all of the available GST exemption. The inclusion ratio is ideally either zero for a trust that is fully GST exempt, or one for a trust that is fully subject to GST tax. When properly planned, the tax preparer would endeavor to use assets in a non-GST exempt trust (the trust with an inclusion ratio of one) first, and only if no other assets remain, to use assets in a trust with an inclusion ratio of zero. This is because the first trust with an inclusion ratio of one is to be fully taxable in the taxpayer's (or another nonskip person's) estate and the trust with the inclusion ratio of zero can be passed on to skip persons (e.g., grandchildren) with no GST tax.

EXAMPLE

In a properly handled GST allocation, the taxpayer sets up a $1 million trust fund for his grandchildren and great-grandchildren. He allocates the entire $1 million (indexed) GST tax exemption to the trust. The assets of the trust appreciate to $10 million before being distributed in a taxable distribution or termination. None of the transfers of the $10 million in trust property to the grandchildren and great-grandchildren is subject to the GST tax. This is because the applicable fraction is 1, and the inclusion ratio, zero. The applicable fraction is 1 because taxpayer allocated $1 million GST exemption to $1 million in assets. The inclusion ratio of zero is the ideal GST result, as it means that none of the assets in the trust will ever be subject to GST tax.

If a trust has an inclusion ratio of other than one or zero, the GST consequences are unfavorable. As a result, many trust documents include provisions authorizing the trustees to divide trusts up in any manner necessary to maximize GST tax planning benefits. If the trust was silent, and the allocation less than optimal, adverse tax consequences could follow, as shown in the following example.

EXAMPLE

To illustrate a less than optimal GST plan, assume the same facts as in the preceding example; however, taxpayer only allocated $500,000 of GST exemption to the $1 million in assets. The inclusion ratio would be 50% and $5 million [50% inclusion ratio × $10 million taxable], and the trust would be subject to GST tax.

The sharply contrasting results of the examples is why Congress sought to provide taxpayers with greater flexibility to properly divide GST trusts by statutorily permitting divisions in situations that would have previously required trust language, or court intervention. Under the post-2001 Tax Act rules, if a trust is divided, then it will be treated as two separate trusts for GST purposes. To obtain this benefit, a trust will likely have to be divided on a fractional basis. This means that if one trust will have 40 percent of assets and a second trust 60 percent, then each asset may have to be divided 40/60 instead of merely dividing the overall value 40/60. The terms of any postdivision trust must have the same succession of interests of beneficiaries as the predivision trust.

Too many situations have occurred where taxpayers have not been able to maintain trusts with a pure zero inclusion ratio. There was a limited ability to rectify this type of problem under prior law. The new law permits taxpayers to sever trusts to achieve a better GST result. They can now split a trust on a fractional basis so that one subtrust is fully included in the estate, and the other GST-exempt subtrust, is not.[68]

The new law raises several issues that may be clarified by future regulations. At present, it is unclear whether you have to divide each asset in the trust or divide (fractionalize) the trust as a whole. Based on other IRS rulings on similar issues, the fractionalization of each asset should not be necessary (you won't have to divide each stock the taxpayer owns between each new subtrust; just ensure that the appropriate values are placed in each subtrust).

It does not appear that the trust can be divided so that the taxable trust terminates with different terms than the nontaxable trust. The new trusts have to have the same succession of interests as the old aggregate trust.

 Despite the leniency and flexibility of the new rules, the cautious approach is still to include powers for the trustees (or trust protector) to divide a trust to maximize GST tax benefits.

How to divide a trust under the new rules can be expected to be addressed in future guidance from the IRS.

Substantial Compliance

The GST tax rules are extraordinarily complex, and it is difficult to fully and properly comply with the reporting and filing requirements. Even so, the GST tax rules never provided that substantial compliance with the GST tax rules would suffice. If the taxpayer can prove his intent to produce the lowest possible inclusion ratio, he may be able, under the new rules, to obtain tax relief by allocating the GST exemption in a manner that produces the lowest inclusion ratio.[69]

STATE DEATH TAX CREDIT REDUCTION

Under the estate tax rules, Code Section 2011 provides a credit against the federal estate tax for a state level estate tax. The result was that states have enacted estate taxes to sop up the allowable federal credit. The state death tax credit is phased out from 2002 to 2004. In 2002, only 75 percent of the credit is allowed. In 2003, only 50 percent of the credit is allowed. In 2004, only 25 percent of the credit is allowed. The credit is fully repealed after 2004.[70] With the 2001 Tax Act, the government has effectively shifted a significant portion of the estate tax reduction to the states by reducing and eventually canceling the state death tax credit.

NOTE

If taxpayer, on death, is domiciled in a state that doesn't set its state estate tax at an amount based on the allowable federal state death tax credit, a larger death tax will be due than the advertised lower federal estate tax.

Special State Tax Considerations

The interplay of the 2001 Tax Act estate tax changes and the estate tax laws of some states creates significant problems. If a state's estate tax is keyed to the federal estate tax rules prior to the recent changes they may not coordinate with the 2001 Tax Relief Act, the state credit then remains at the old level. The result is that a taxable estate in such a state would have a 50 percent federal rate and a substantial state tax rate, less a credit at a lower rate, resulting in a low effective state estate tax rate.

Some states' estate tax law does not recognize an applicable exclusion above $1 million. In 2004, when the federal estate tax exclusion (the amount that can be bequeathed estate tax free) increases above $1 million, if a bypass trust is funded with more than $1 million (more than $1 million is bequeathed in any manner to other than a spouse) the amount in the bypass trust in excess of $1 million then triggers a state level estate tax. The decision the preparer must make in formulating an estate plan, barring a revision of such a state's law, is whether to incur a state estate tax to fund a larger bypass trust. If such a state continues a substantial estate tax, at some point it might be more advantageous to have the taxpayer's will distribute more of the estate to the surviving spouse to avoid the state level transfer tax.

Impact on States Generally

In the past, the state death tax credit has contributed a meaningful percentage of many state budgets. What can the states do? Many states may enact or modify inheritance, estate, or similar taxes. On the other hand, given the tremendous negative press about the death tax, states may be reluctant to do this. The net result may be other state tax increases to offset the revenue losses.

Because the state death tax credit is eliminated after 2004, Congress provided a state death tax deduction. The deduction, however, will not provide the dollar-for-dollar benefit that the credit had.[71] A deduction will be permitted for taxes actually paid and claimed as a deduction on the federal estate tax return.

For a nonresident alien, the deduction for state death taxes is limited to the percentage of the gross estate subject to death tax.[72]

ESTATE TAX DEFERRAL

The 2001 Tax Act has liberalized the special rules enabling qualifying estates to pay their estate tax over a period of years. To understand the changes, they are best presented in the context of an overview of the estate tax deferral rules and Code Section 6166, which includes them. The key Code Section 6166 changes include an increase in the number of partners and shareholders in a qualifying business from fifteen to forty. The new law also includes a look-through rule for a holding company that is not readily tradable, but owns stock in a subsidiary that is readily tradable. Certain lending and finance businesses now qualify for limited estate tax deferral. These are in addition to the businesses that qualified under prior law.

Installment Payment for Qualified Closely Held Businesses

Estate taxes have long been a major bane of the family business. On death, heirs must obtain sufficient cash to pay the estate tax within nine months of death. This financial pressure can ruin a family business. The Tax Code has long provided some flexibility to the closely held business through the mechanism of deferring estate tax payments. Although the federal estate tax is due nine months from the date of taxpayer's death, if certain requirements are met, the estate tax attributable to interest in a closely held business can be paid in two to ten installments and can be deferred for up to four years after the date the tax is due. This is a fourteen to fifteen year deferral. To qualify for the deferral, numerous requirements have to be met.[73]

The tax deferred[74] is the amount of the net estate tax that bears the same ratio to the total net estate tax that the closely held business bears to the adjusted gross estate.[75] The statute allows for the executor to elect to pay the estate tax in up to ten installments, with the first installment being due not more than five years after the date required for the first payment.[76] Only interest needs to be paid for the first five years and the date of the last interest payment is the date of the first installment of tax. The interest on the first $1 million of the value of a closely held business may, in some instances, accrue at the favorable 2 percent rate.[77] The time for making the Code Section 6166 election is no later than the time for filing the estate tax return or on the last date of the extension of time for filing. A protective election may be made on a timely filed estate tax return. This is a statement indicating the intent to make use of the estate tax deferral benefits.

Requirements to Qualify for Deferral

To qualify for the deferral, numerous requirements, the threshold requirements, must be met.[78] The 2001 Tax Act liberalized some of these technical requirements, and these changes are noted in the following discussion.

Citizenship

To qualify, the taxpayer must have been a U.S. citizen or resident alien at the time of death.[79] This prior law rule remains unchanged. Noncitizens who are not residents will have to take other actions to address the estate tax due on nonliquid business interests.

Interest in a Closely Held Business

Only interests in a closely held business may qualify for the deferral of estate tax. As noted previously, an important liberalization of the estate tax deferral provisions is the extension of the number of partners and shareholders permitted to own interests in an entity qualifying as closely held for purposes of estate tax deferral from fifteen to forty-five.[80] An "interest in a closely held business" is defined as:

- A proprietor in a trade or business carried on as a proprietorship
- A partner in a partnership carrying a trade or business, if 20 percent or more of the partnership value is included in the decedent's gross estate, or there are less than fifteen partners. This number is increased by the 2001 Tax Act to forty-five after 2001[81]
- Stock in a corporation carrying on a trade or business if 20 percent or more of the voting stock of the corporation is included in the gross estate or there are less than fifteen shareholders, regardless of class of shares owned.[82] This number is increased by the 2001 Tax Act to forty-five after 2001[83]

In applying the preceding tests, stock or partnership interests held between husband and wife as community property, joint tenants, tenants in common, or tenants by the entirety are treated as though they are owned by one shareholder or partner for purposes of determining the number of shareholders or partners.[84] Stock or a partnership interest held by a trust, corporation, estate, or partnership shall be considered being owned proportionately by those having an interest, provided, in the case of a trust, the beneficiary has a present interest.[85] Stock and partnership interests held between decedent and members of his family are treated as having been held by the decedent.[86] A family is defined as siblings (whole or half blood), spouse, ancestors, or lineal descendants.[87]

Active Trade or Business Required

The IRS has given strict interpretation to the trade or business requirement. Although real estate activities are allowed as trade or business under different sections of the Tax Code, these interests may be disregarded for the purposes of determining qualification for estate tax deferral if the level of active involvement set by the IRS is not met. When evaluating the likelihood of an estate qualifying under the trade or business requirement when real estate is involved, the overall activities of managing, developing, trading, leasing, and otherwise dealing in various real estate assets must be considered. Brokerage and other ancillary activities also should be considered. The more active and integrated the overall real estate and activities are, the more likely the pure real estate assets will qualify. In allowing estate tax deferral, the IRS has focused on the fact that a business was actively involved in negotiating the leases, advertising for tenants, maintaining the buildings, and collecting the rent monies.[88] In contrast, the mere passive direction of management and operations of real estate investments may not be sufficient activity to qualify for the estate tax deferral.[89]

Qualifications for a Lending and Finance Business under the 2001 Tax Act Amendments

Under prior law a lending or finance business may not have qualified for estate tax deferral benefits. The 2001 Tax Act addressed this. Installment payments of estate tax have been liberalized, somewhat, by an extension to include certain qualifying lending and finance businesses. This appears to be a special interest provision designed to perhaps benefit specific taxpayers or a special interest group. Extremely detailed provisions for qualification are provided for.[90]

The installment payment of estate tax will now be available to pay estate tax attributable to the value of a lending and finance business included in the decedent's taxable estate. However, instead of the estate being able to pay the deferred estate tax over ten years as the general estate tax deferral rules provide, the estate will only have a five-year period over which to pay the tax.[91]

For purposes of this new rule, a qualified lending and finance business meets one of two alternate tests:

- *Test 1.* The business, based on the facts and circumstances existing before the decedent's death, exhibited substantial lending and finance business activity.

- *Test 2.* The business meets all three of the following requirements: During at least three of the five years prior to the decedent's death, the business had (1) at least one full-time employee substantially all of whose services were in the active management of the lending and finance business; (2) at least ten full-time employees substantially all of whose services were directly related to the business, but who were not owners of the business; and (3) $5 million or more of gross receipts from lending and finance activities. These include making loans, purchasing or discounting accounts receivable, rental and leasing of tangible personal property, and certain related activities.

Percentage Test

The interest in the closely held business must exceed 35 percent of the adjusted gross estate. Adjusted gross estate is defined as the gross estate reduced by debts, administration expenses, and casualty losses.[92] The deductions need not actually be used to offset the estate tax.

The value of the active business assets are considered for the 35 percent rule. Any closely held business assets that are passive are excluded from the qualifying value of the interest. Passive assets are assets other than assets used in a trade or business. Stock in another corporation is considered a passive asset.

The value of the interest used in determining whether the 35 percent test is met is the value used for federal estate tax purposes. This is the value on the date of death or on the alternate valuation date.[93]

If the closely held business is farming, then for purposes of the 35 percent test, the interest includes the residential buildings and related improvements that are occupied by the owner or lessee or employees on a regular basis.

 If a taxpayer plans on taking advantage of the estate tax deferral benefits if he should die before the estate tax is repealed, then he should exercise caution in taking advantage of the increased lifetime gift exclusion of $1 million beginning in 2002. If he makes large gifts of the business interests as a result of this increase in the exclusion, he could reduce the business interests to less than 35 percent of the estate and thus fail the deferral test.

Aggregation of Interests in Different Business Entities

If a taxpayer has structured business in several different partnerships, corporations, or other entities, how can these tests be applied? If they were applied on a company-by-company basis, many otherwise qualifying estates would lose out on this important benefit. The tax laws therefore permit adding together the figures from different businesses if minimum ownership and other requirements are met. These requirements are generally designed to ensure that the taxpayer has a significant interest in an active business. These rules are complex but can be essential in ensuring that your closely held business will successfully pass to your heirs.

Two special elections (choices for an estate tax return) can help qualify additional business interests for estate tax deferral. Both of these elections require action by the executor and will result in a scale-back of the estate tax deferral benefits. The executor may make an election to have a portion of stock of a holding company that directly or indirectly owns stock in an active trade or business treated as stock in an active company.

Partnership interests and stock that is not readily tradable that are treated as owned by the decedent at the time of death after applying the attribution rules regarding family members (stock or partnership interests owned by family members will be treated for purposes of this test as if owned directly by the decedent) will be included for purposes of the 20 percent test described earlier. If the executor makes either of these elections, the special 2 percent interest rate does not apply. Also, the estate will not qualify for the five-year deferral of estate tax. What's left is a ten-year payout of the estate tax with interest at regular rates.

For purposes of the 20 percent rule, the stock in the holding company will be deemed voting stock, to the extent that voting stock in the holding company owns voting stock in the business company.[94]

Generally, as noted previously, the value of passive assets is excluded in determining whether an estate meets the 35 percent rule. Stock in another corporation is a passive asset. However, a corporate subsidiary will be ignored if the following apply: (1) The executor makes the special election with regard to a holding company; and (2) the stock qualified as an interest in a closely held business.[95]

The value of stock in an active corporation will be included for purposes of the 35 percent rule if (1) the corporation owns 20 percent or more in value of the voting stock of another corporation or such corporation has 45 (previously 15) or less shareholders; and (2) 80 percent or more of the assets of each corporation consists of assets used in carrying on a trade or business.

The estate can aggregate interest in two or more closely held businesses, if with respect to each, 20 percent or more of the total value of each business is included in the gross estate. To determine the 20 percent rule, the estate can aggregate interest of the decedent's spouse and, within the limitation described previously, the decedent's family.[96]

Holding Company Owning Stock in a Traded Subsidiary

The 2001 Tax Act provides that if the stock of a subsidiary is actively traded (and thus not closely held) the estate tax deferral benefits won't be completely lost. To salvage some estate tax deferral benefit from the holding company stock (the shares in the holding corporation owning the interests in the actively traded subsidiary stock held by the decedent's estate), the executor may elect to have five, not ten, annual installment payments of the estate tax attributable to this interest. If the stock of the holding company is readily traded, this new exception won't apply, so no deferral would be possible under prior or current law.[97]

Acceleration of Deferred Payment

The estate tax deferred under the Code Section 6166 estate tax deferral provision will become due immediately if any of the following three events occur:[98]

1. The qualifying business is disposed of or liquidated, and the disposition or liquidation exceeds 50 percent of the value of the interest.
2. Interest or installment payments are not made within six months of the due date.
3. There is undistributed net income; then the acceleration may occur to the extent of such income.

NOTE

A redemption of corporate stock to pay estate taxes and expenses under IRC § 303 does not cause an acceleration of estate taxes. Thus, a portion of the stock can be redeemed under that provision, and the estate tax on the remaining portion of the stock can then qualify for the estate tax deferral benefits.

Other changes are also excluded from the preceding acceleration of deferred estate tax. Certain prescribed reorganizations of the business entities will not cause an acceleration of the deferred estate taxes. There is no acceleration if the transfer is due to the death of the decedent (under will, intestacy, or pursuant to the terms of a trust).

 It appears that the estate tax deferred under IRC § 6166 before estate tax repeal may not have to be recognized if the requirements of IRC § 6166 are not met after repeal. However, caution should be exercised pending the IRS issuing definitive guidance in this regard.

PRIVATE FOUNDATION RULES EXTENDED TO CERTAIN TRUSTS

Split interest trusts are to be subject to the private foundation rules if a deduction is claimed under Code Section 642(c). This rule is to take effect after 2009.[99]

RELIEF FROM RECAPTURE TAX ON SPECIAL USE VALUATION

If recapture tax was paid on a special use valuation of farm or business property, a refund claim may be permitted where it would have otherwise been time barred.[100]

NOTE

Taxpayers whose family had claimed estate tax deferral and paid a recapture tax should review with their accountant the possibility of pursuing a refund claim.

To understand the implications of the preceding change, a brief overview of the special use valuation rules as well as the recapture of the tax benefit provided is necessary.

Special Use Valuation Rules

To minimize the estate tax burden on estates, including certain interests in closely held business or real estate assets, the Tax Code provides special valuation rules. These rules are an exception from the general valuation rules of valuing assets at their fair market value under the standard of a willing buyer and a willing seller. For estate tax purposes, assets owned at death are generally valued at their fair market value at the date of death (or six months later at the alternate valuation date). Fair value is the price a willing buyer would pay and a willing seller would accept. It is generally at the highest and best use value of the asset. Thus, land used as a farm can be valued at its land value as a farm, even if a shopping center developer might pay substantially more for the property to develop it. These rules permit qualifying property to be valued at its current business or farming use. The maximum reduction permitted from using the special valuation rules is a reduction in the gross estate of up to $750,000.[101] Thus, the maximum savings is approximately $450,000 at the pre-2001 Tax Act maximum 60 percent estate tax rate, and approximately $375,000 at the lower 2002 tax rates. The reduction in the marginal estate tax rates will continue to make this benefit of less value and the increases in the applicable exclusion will render fewer estates able to use or in need of this benefit.

Requirements to Qualify

Nine complex requirements must be met for an estate to qualify for the benefits of special use valuation:

1. The real estate must be used as a farm, in a qualified farming activity, or in a closely held active trade or business other than farming on the date of the taxpayer's death.[102]

2. To qualify, during the eight-year period ending on the date of death, there must have been periods totaling five years or more during which the decedent or decedent's family materially participated in the operation of the farm or business.[103]

3. The qualified use of the property must have been by the decedent or a member of the family.

4. The decedent must have been a citizen or resident of the United States.[104]

5. The real property to be valued must be located in the United States.[105]

6. The executor must elect to have this provision apply to the estate.[106] The election must be made on the estate tax return and is irrevocable.[107]

7. Each heir or other person who has an interest in the property must sign an agreement to pay the estate tax saved and respect the related rules if the qualified use of the property ends, heirs cease the required activities, or any other event triggering recapture occurs.[108]

8. The adjusted value of the real or personal property used by the decedent or a member of the family and that was acquired from or passed from the decedent to a qualified heir must be equal to at least 50 percent of the adjusted value of the gross estate.[109]

9. The qualified real property must pass from the decedent to a qualified heir. The phrase *pass from the decedent* is defined to include more than a direct bequest to a qualified heir. It also includes property received by a qualified heir as a result of a qualified disclaimer.[110] *Qualified heir* is defined as members of the decedent's family, including an ancestor, a spouse, parents, siblings, children, stepchildren, a lineal descendent of the decedent, a lineal descendant of the decedent's spouse, a lineal descendant of the decedent's parents, or a lineal descendant of the spouse's parents.[111]

Recapture of Tax Benefit

If the property that qualified for the special use valuation is sold or qualified heirs cease to materially participate within ten years of the taxpayer's death, part or all of the tax savings must be repaid to the government.[112] Each beneficiary who receives an interest in qualifying property becomes personally liable for the recapture tax. If this recapture of tax was paid, the 2001 Tax Act may be of benefit. Specifically, a surviving spouse or a lineal descendant of the decedent is not treated as failing to meet the qualified use requirements solely because the spouse (or lineal descendant) leased the property on a net cash basis to a family member. An adopted child is treated as family for purposes of this test.[113] Prior to this provision being added to the tax laws by the 1997 Taxpayer Relief Act,[114] there was no exception from recapture for the net cash basis lease to a family member. If a lineal descendant had already paid the recapture tax, the liberalization of the 1997 Taxpayer Relief Act would not have helped. The 2001 Tax Act permits affected taxpayers to file refund claims even if they would otherwise be prohibited from doing so because of the length of time that has passed.

CONSERVATION EASEMENTS

The 2001 Tax Act liberalized the requirements to qualify for this potentially valuable estate tax benefit. To understand the changes, an overview of the conservation easement tax benefit is necessary.

A taxpayer may be able to obtain valuable charitable contribution deductions for donations of a preservation, facade, historic development, or scenic easement.[115] The "donation" is really an easement that prevents the owner and any future landowner from modifying the exterior of the property involved. This restriction on modifying the property reduces the value of the property because the owner and any future buyers will be severely restricted in what they can do to the property. The charitable contribution deduction received is equal to the decrease in the value of the property as a result of this restriction. This is estimated by subtracting from the fair market value of the property before the perpetual easement was granted the fair market value of the property after the perpetual easement was granted.

The recipient charity must also meet certain requirements for the taxpayer to obtain a tax benefit. The charitable organization, among other requirements, must have a commitment to protect the conservation purposes of the easement donated and the resources to carry out this objective.[116]

Estate and Gift Tax Consequences under Prior Law

A charitable contribution deduction is allowed for both gift and estate tax purposes if the taxpayer donates a qualified interest in real estate to a charity organized exclusively for conservation purposes.

The executor may exclude up to an applicable percentage (the maximum being 40 percent) of the value of any land that is subjected to a qualified conservation easement from the estate. The value of the property for purposes of this calculation is determined after the qualified conservation easement (restriction) is placed on the property. If the estate retained any rights to develop the property, the value of these retained rights must be excluded in determining the value of the property that qualifies for the exclusion. The applicable percentage is determined by subtracting from 40 percent (the maximum percentage) 2 percent for each percent or partial percent interest by which the value of the conservation easement involved is less than 30 percent of the value of the land involved (after reduction for the value of the conservation easement). There was some uncertainty as to the date at which these values had to be determined. The 2001 Tax Act clarifies this, as shown in Exhibit 1.5. The exclusion is limited to a maximum exclusion.[117]

Granting a conservation easement will not constitute a disposition of the property involved for purposes of the special estate tax

Exhibit 1.5   Phase-In of Maximum Conservation Exclusions

Year	Maximum Conservation Property Exclusion
1998	$100,000
1999	200,000
2000	300,000
2001	400,000
2002 and later years	500,000

valuation provisions available to farms and closely held business property under Code Section 2032A.

EXAMPLE

Property in taxpayer's estate is valued at $630,000. Taxpayer retained certain mineral rights worth only $30,000. The net value of the property is $600,000. The executor donates a qualifying conservation easement valued at $180,000. Thus, the value of the land after the conservation easement (and ignoring retained mineral rights) is $420,000. The value of the conservation easement is $100,000 divided by the $420,000 value of the land after the donation of the easement. This ratio is 23.81% [100,000 ÷ 420,000]. The applicable percentage is reduced by the percentage determined by multiplying the difference between this ratio (rounded up) and 30% by 2, or 12% [(30% − 24%) × 2]. Thus, the applicable percentage is 28% [40% − 12%]. The value of the estate exclusion is thus $117,600 [28% × $420,000].

Estate Tax Exclusion Requirements and Related Rules

To qualify for the conservation easement exclusion, the following six requirements must be met:

1. The executor must make an irrevocable election to have this exclusion apply on the estate tax return.

2. The decedent, or his or her family, owned the land for three years or more ending on the date of death.

3. A conservation easement or contribution[118] had been granted by the decedent, or his or her family.

4. Under prior law, the property had to be located within twenty-five miles of a national park, metropolitan area, national forest, or wilderness area, or within ten miles of an Urban National Forest. This rather restrictive requirement was eliminated by the 2001 Tax Act.

5. Mortgaged property is only qualified for this exclusion to the extent of the equity (value less debt) in the property.

6. The easement must be a qualified conservation easement.[119] This means that the easement must be exclusively for conservation purposes.[120] The preservation of historic sites or structures is not deemed to qualify as being for conservation purposes.

In planning for the estate tax considerations of a conservation easement, it is important to briefly review the income tax issues and related legal questions. Generally, except for certain transfers in trust, no deduction is permitted for a charitable contribution of less than an entire interest (i.e., all of ownership) in a property.[121] For example, a contribution of the right to use property is a contribution of less than an entire interest, which will not qualify for a deduction. There are four exceptions where this limitation will not apply:

1. The partial interest is the entire interest of the donor. So, if the taxpayer only owns one-third of a property, the contribution of that entire one-third would qualify. If ownership is two-thirds of the interests in a property, the contribution of one-third will not qualify.

2. An undivided part interest in property can qualify for a charitable contribution deduction (e.g., a donation of 10 acres of a 35-acre parcel, or 40 percent of an income interest in a property if taxpayer has no other interests in the property).[122]

3. The conservation, façade, or scenic easement is made to a qualifying charity (the subject of the estate tax change discussed earlier).

4. The remainder interest is a personal residence or farm.[123]

As noted previously, the 2001 Tax Act liberalizes the definition of "land subject to a qualified conservation easement" by eliminating the requirement that the land had to be within a specified distance of a national forest and so forth. Now the land may be any land located in the United States or a possession. The date on which the land must comply with the requirements of the law is the date of the donation. This rule has a retroactive effective date for estates of decedents dying in 2001 and later.[124]

SPECIAL RULES FOR NONCITIZENS

As stated, the estate tax is scheduled for repeal in 2010. However, special rules continue the potential for a tax applicable to noncitizen spouses of decedents dying prior to repeal. The estate tax will continue to apply to property held in a qualified domestic trust (QDOT) established by a decedent to qualify a bequest to a surviving noncitizen spouse for the estate tax marital deduction.[125] This continued tax will terminate January 1, 2021.

> **NOTE**
>
> This rule appears to be just another "hidden" way Congress endeavored to make the estate tax repeal budget numbers work.

Estate tax will be levied on distributions of principal (corpus) from the QDOT other than annual income distributions. The tax will be calculated as if the amount distributed had been included in the estate (i.e., the first to die, the citizen spouse). The calculation adds all prior distributions from the QDOT to the taxable estate to push the tax on the QDOT distributions into the highest federal estate tax brackets. The calculation and tax requirement also will somewhat complicate the administration of the QDOT. An exception is provided for certain hardship distributions.[125] In addition, a tax will be assessed on the property remaining in the QDOT on the death of the noncitizen spouse. This tax is calculated in the same manner.

YEAR-BY-YEAR CHANGES IN ESTATE TAX

The complexity and number of changes made to the estate tax rules make a year-by-year analysis helpful for understanding what the new planning environment will be. The following digest of changes probably should have been written in erasable ink, as few tax experts believe that the ten years will play out as written.

2002

- The federal estate tax rate falls to 50 percent from 55 percent.
- The estate and GST exclusion increases to $1 million.
- The state death tax credit provided under Code Section 2011 falls to 75 percent of the pre-2001 Tax Act level.
- Liberalization of the estate tax deferral rules under Code Section 6166 becomes effective.

2003

- The federal estate tax rate falls to 49 percent.
- The estate and GST exclusion remains at $1 million.
- The state death tax credit falls to one-half of the pre-2001 Tax Act level.

NOTE

When factored into the revenue to the federal government, the amount increases as a result of the reduction in the state death tax credit exceeding the reduction in federal estate tax rates.

2004

- The estate and GST exclusion increases to $1.5 million.
- The qualified family-owned business interests (QFOBI) deduction under Code Section 2057 is repealed.

NOTE

This had been an extremely complex benefit for modest relief. Because of the tie-in of the QFOBI benefit and the applicable exclusion in 2004, the benefit is no longer of use.

- The state death tax credit is reduced to 25 percent of the pre-2001 Tax Act level.

2005

- The estate and GST exclusion remains at $1.5 million.
- The state death tax credit disappears and new Code Section 2058 permits state death taxes to be deducted.

NOTE

Under prior law, the state death tax credit served to displace some of the applicable exclusion amount. With a deduction, this does not occur. It would be similar to a Code Section 2053 expense amount.

2006

- The federal estate tax rate falls to 46 percent.
- The estate and GST exclusion (not gift taxes, for which the exclusion remains at $1 million) increases to $2 million.

2007

- The federal estate tax rate falls to 45 percent.
- The estate and GST exclusion remains at $2 million.

2008

- All the estate tax rules remain the same as in 2007.

2009

- The federal estate tax rate remains at 45 percent.
- The estate and GST exclusion increases from $2 million to $3.5 million.

NOTE

This increase will distort estate planning, especially for smaller estates. Bypass and marital trust funding formulas will have to be reviewed if not addressed previously.

2010

- The federal estate tax is repealed completely.
- The new Code Section 1022 modified carryover basis applies and replaces existing Code Section 1014 step-up in basis.
- Under Code Section 684, gain on a death-time transfer by a U.S. decedent to a nonresident alien individual triggers tax.
- Code Section 1040 becomes more generally applicable. If taxpayers fund a pecuniary disposition of property, they will only recognize postdeath appreciation for gain.
- The new gift tax system becomes operative with a gift tax rate set to equal the maximum individual tax rate of 35 percent.

NOTE

The gift tax is not repealed. A concern of Congress existed about income tax shifting in a situation with no gift or estate tax. They wanted to prevent shifts of assets between various taxpayers to minimize income taxes and hence tax avoidance. Thus, the gift tax stays in place with a $1 million exemption equivalent.

- Under Code Section 2511(c), any transfer to a trust is a completed gift unless the trust is wholly a grantor trust as to the transferor.

NOTE

This is directed at the creation of a trust that would have beneficiaries in a lower income tax bracket but would not be a completed gift. This was again part of the concern in Congress about taxpayers shifting income. This rule appears to make gifts complete that might otherwise be incomplete gifts under prior law. This new rule is not intended to affect the Crummey or annual demand power concept currently used for gift tax purposes.

- Code Section 1022 becomes operative. It provides that a transfer at death of property subject to liability in excess of basis is not a realization event.

NOTE

This is different from the gift tax rule specifying that a gift of an asset subject to a liability in excess of basis is deemed a realization of the liability. There is an exception for transfers to tax-exempt entities to prevent taxpayers from mortgaging or financing property, bequeathing the property subject to the liability to the charity and the cash to the heirs, so that the charity can sell the asset without income tax, pay off the debt, and the heirs receive the cash without a basis issue.

- Code Section 121 provides an exemption of $250,000 for the sale of a principal residence. It also allows taxpayers to tack the decedent's holding period to that of the heirs for this purpose. This is another exception to the new carryover basis rule.

- Large transfers occurring at death, defined to be those of $1.3 million or more, will have to be reported to the IRS.

2011

- If a taxpayer has a qualified domestic trust (QDOT), there is a tax based on the estate tax deferral created. For ten years, distributions from the QDOT will continue to be taxable.

- The estate tax repeal sunsets, so that the tax, with a $1 million exclusion and 55 percent rate, becomes effective. Red sky at night, a sailor's delight. Sunset in 2011, an estate planner's heaven.

The many changes made by the 2001 Tax Act to the gift, estate, and GST taxes are complex, and most advisers question whether all the deferred changes will even come to pass. Nevertheless, planning must be reevaluated for every taxpayer in light of these changes. Continued monitoring of estate plans will be necessary and especially so if Congress, as many experts anticipate, again acts to modify the rules enacted as part of the 2001 Tax Act.

2

NON-ESTATE TAX CHANGES AFFECTING ESTATE AND RELATED PLANNING

The 2001 Tax Act is long and comprehensive with myriad provisions. Many of the non-estate tax provisions can affect estate planning. This chapter highlights some of these changes and indicates their likely impact on the estate planning process.

REDUCTION IN INCOME TAX RATES

One of the most talked about, and easiest to understand, changes has been the reduction in income tax rates. The objective is to benefit all taxpayers by reducing the marginal or maximum tax rates paid on any different level of income. The law has created a 10 percent tax rate bracket and triggered the highly publicized advance-refund checks that were issued in the amount of $300 or $600 to many taxpayers by October 2, 2001. The intent was to provide an immediate and timely boost to the economy, although it is questionable how lasting is the effect of a one-time tax cut of that nature and amount. Other individual income tax rates, excluding the lowest 15 percent tax bracket, were reduced by ½ percent for the year 2001.

The tax rate cut and the reduction of the so-called stealth tax (involving the phaseout of itemized deductions and similar measures) are at the core of the tax benefits for high-wage earners. Once phased in by 2010, these changes result in substantial income tax reductions for the highest income taxpayers. However, the alternative minimum tax (AMT) must be factored into any analysis of these purported benefits.

Illusory Tax Chart Simplicity

Congress has again resorted to its old tactic of trying to imply to taxpayers that it has simplified the tax system by simplifying the tax rate brackets. The concept is absurd because taxpayers who prepare their own returns merely use their filing status and income level to look up the tax on an IRS table in the instruction booklet for Form 1040 Personal Income Tax Return, and persons who pay professional tax preparers generally have the amount generated by computer. Although to some the changes may sound great in the headlines, in reality they accomplish nothing for simplifying tax planning. The relevant issues are simply the effective rates of the revised tax brackets and how they affect an individual's tax status.

Smoke and mirrors are a big part of the game of this tax law. And the purported simplification of tax rate brackets is only one of several areas characterized by illusion. In fact, the structure results in an additional tax rate bracket.

A 10 percent lower tax bracket is added at the bottom of the rate schedule, which will apply for the first $12,000 of income for married couples and $6,000 for single individuals. These amounts are increased to $14,000 for married couples and $7,000 for singles for tax years after 2008, and thereafter are inflation indexed.

NOTE

The constant integration into the tax system of more and more inflation adjustment factors is helpful to taxpayers because it keeps the tax system more in line with the consequences of inflation and prevents benefits being eroded over time. However, the result is also a greater degree of complexity. It becomes impossible to determine many key tax benefit figures without looking them up in a source that reflects the current inflation-indexed data.

The new lower rate bracket, as well as the 2001 advance tax refunds, should provide some stimulus to the economy, perhaps especially to

Exhibit 2.1 Tax Rate Reduction Schedule

Calendar Year	Prior Law Tax Rate				
	15%	*28%*	*31%*	*36%*	*39.6%*
2002–2003	Partial 10%	27	30	35	38.6
2004–2005	No change	26	29	34	37.6
2006 and later	No change	25	28	33	35

retailers and others where lower-income consumers can immediately spend such modest additional cash flow (see Exhibit 2.1).

Reduced Limitations on Itemized Deductions and Personal Exemptions

High-income taxpayers have been subject to a complex array of phase-outs of the personal exemption and itemized deduction tax benefits. The result has been that, over certain amounts, these tax benefits were effectively eliminated. Not only did this have an adverse tax effect on certain income taxpayers, it also made planning complex. The 2001 Tax Act proposes to reduce these overall limitations and thus eventually eliminate what has really been an increased tax rate applicable to high income taxpayers.

The limitation on itemized deductions is to be reduced by one-third in the years 2006 and 2007, by two-thirds in 2008 and 2009, and completely eliminated in 2010. Similarly, the phaseout of personal exemptions based on tax rate status is also being reduced and eliminated.

NOTE

These changes are yet another example of the back-ending or prolonged phase-in of tax benefits. It is wonderful for Congress to offer and advertise great benefits for taxpayers, but these don't take effect for a number of years. Thus, there is no immediate tax benefit or implication for current planning other than how these phaseouts affect the ability to accelerate deductions. As explained in some of the following planning ideas, it will be beneficial for many taxpayers to accelerate discretionary tax deductions to early years, while they are in higher tax brackets, and similarly to defer income to later years, when they should be in lower tax brackets. For higher income taxpayers subject to the itemized deduction limitations, acceleration of deductions that would appear on their Form 1040, Schedule A, itemized deductions, may have no impact. Thus, these taxpayers would have to focus on deductions that appear "above the line" (on the front of their Form 1040, such as those for rental property), that are reported on Schedule E, or for a home-based business, that are reported on Schedule C.

It should be evident from the preceding discussion that although lower income taxpayers are to receive important benefits—at least important relative to their earnings—the bulk of the tax savings inure to higher income taxpayers.

 The result of these changes is that taxpayers should endeavor when feasible to defer income and accelerate deductions to take advantage of declining tax rates. This can be done by negotiating deferred compensation arrangements, maximizing the advantages of stock options and timing their exercise, contributing the maximum to retirement plans, and evaluating annuities, IRAs, and other tax-advantaged programs. Historically, these have made up the standard arsenal of tax strategies every time there has been a reduction in tax rates.

Reduced Benefits of Capital Gains Favored Tax Status

For most years of the income tax system, capital gains (the sale of stocks, bonds, and real estate held for investment) have generally received favorable income tax treatment with lower capital gains rates. This has contrasted favorably with the higher income tax rates on ordinary income. Rate differentials continue after the 2001 Tax Act but are less pronounced.

> **NOTE**
>
> The tax rate differentials for taxpayers are approximately 5%, 8%, 13%, or 17%, depending on their tax bracket.

Past rate differentials encouraged tax planners to jump through hoops to plan or restructure transactions so that they would qualify as generating capital gains income rather than ordinary income, which was taxed at higher rates. The same strategies might continue, but with a lower payoff, and financial advisers must question more vigorously whether it is worth the effort.

Examples of this past capital gains-oriented strategy abound. A stock option structured for an employee as an incentive stock option could provide capital gains treatment when ultimately sold, whereas a nonqualified stock option (NQSO) might generate ordinary income. If a real estate investor subleased property, the income earned would be ordinary rental income. In contrast, if the same real estate investor assigned all rights and interest in a lease to a new tenant, the payments would be characterized as capital gains.

The consequence of all these efforts has been the greatly increased complexity of both income tax planning and the tax laws. In 1993 Congress tried to eliminate the favorable tax status of capital gains to simplify the Tax Code. What Congress failed to do then it may have accomplished to some degree now through the rate reductions. To the extent the marginal difference in tax rates between capital gains and ordinary income is reduced, the incentive to get the coveted capital gains treatment is also reduced and will simplify tax planning. If any tax rate benefit can be achieved, however, undoubtedly many taxpayers will still endeavor to reach the capital gains reward even though the payoff is somewhat less.

Expanded Marriage Penalty Relief

Historically, the tax laws have contained an income tax bias against married couples. However absurd and unfortunate, this has been a reality of the tax system. The system's unfairness has been the topic of much discussion for many years as politicians have talked about removing this disincentive to family life. The 2001 Tax Act finally includes a provision to repeal this inappropriate and unfair tax detriment, but the changes only begin to be made in the year 2005. The risk is that if budget deficits occur and a new administration is in office (does that have something to do with when the phasing begins?), these changes may never be enacted. Given the back-ended approach of this change, probably no planning can be done by affected married taxpayers other than to sit, wait, and hope some tax benefit arrives.

Two changes do help mitigate the marriage penalty contained in the prior tax laws. Filers of joint income tax returns now are to have a standard deduction that is twice the amount of the standard deduction for single taxpayers, a significant and fair improvement over prior circumstances (although the cost of a mortgage for a two-adult home versus a one-adult home is unlikely to be double, so the equities of this change are not entirely clear). The income taxed at the 15 percent bracket is now doubled for joint filers. Further, the income level falling under the 15 percent tax bracket is increased to twice that of single taxpayers. The result will lessen the likelihood of marriage pushing lower income taxpayers into higher tax brackets. As with so many of the tax breaks provided in the 2001 Tax Act, these benefits are phased in.

Shifting Income to Family Members in Lower Tax Brackets

A common tax planning strategy used by many families has been to plan investments, in particular when large gains to be realized on the sale of the investments are involved, so that the earnings are realized by family members in lower tax brackets. If a child over the age of fourteen is in the lowest tax bracket and the parent is in the highest tax bracket, there has generally been a substantial incentive to have the income earned by the child.

The tax laws contain a veritable arsenal of rules and traps to prevent taxpayers from achieving these benefits. The family partnership rules of Code Section 704(e) limit the use of family limited partnerships (FLPs) and limited liability companies (LLCs) to transfer income to children and others. A prime tool of the Internal Revenue Service has been the "assignment of income" doctrine, which prevents a parent from simply transferring over income really earned by the parent to the child's name, and hence reporting it on the child's tax return.

NOTE

Pot and dynasty trusts, which are discussed in later chapters, can achieve the flexibility to assign income to the lowest bracket taxpayers.

Successful planning for such transactions is often based on the parent making a gift to the child of an asset that appreciates in value after the date of the gift, with the income then being realized by the child. A simple and common example is the gift to the child of interest in an LLC owning investment real estate or stock in a closely held family business, and the later sale by the child of interest in that business, or even realization of income or other distributions at the child's lower tax bracket.

For children under age 14, the "kiddie tax" would apply, and income shifting would have no benefit: The child would be taxed at the parents' tax rate. These strategies continue to apply, and planning tips in later sections describe how best to take advantage of these tax-shifting techniques.

Even when the 2001 law is fully implemented with the many tax rate reductions, there still will be a substantial 25 percent difference between the lowest 10 percent tax bracket and the highest 35 percent tax bracket. A 25 percent savings would enhance any investment return on any transaction, and thus it certainly will remain a viable planning strategy. State income taxes may enhance planning benefits further.

Tax-Free Investments

Tax-exempt bonds (e.g., muni bonds) have always been a favorite investment vehicle for well-to-do taxpayers. The change in tax rates will have a profound impact on the analysis of investment in tax-exempt bonds. Taxpayers should reevaluate their investment holdings in light of their tax status under the 2001 law. For some taxpayers, the marginal tax brackets may be reduced sufficiently to make the holding of tax-exempt bonds no longer as appropriate. As illustrated in Exhibit 2.1, income tax rates are declining. As they do, the tax incentive of tax-exempt bonds will erode. Also, during times when historically low interest rates exist in the economy, the desirability of tax-exempt bonds as an investment is substantially reduced.

Deferring Income to Lower Tax Bracket Years

A traditional planning technique whenever tax legislation prospectively reduces future income tax rates is to defer the recognition of income for tax purposes. There are many ways to effect this planning, including stock options, deferred compensation plans, Rabbi trusts, sale on installment method, and simply deferring the sale of a stock, bond, or real estate property. The advantage of such techniques is that a taxpayer who is subject to a high effective tax rate may thereby defer income to a later year when the income tax reductions illustrated in Exhibit 2.1 become effective.

NOTE

Taxpayers and investors often get so focused on the changes of marginal tax rates that they forget the reality of the investment world. Holding on to a high-tech stock for another year may be devastating if the market drops significantly and the 5% hoped-for tax savings becomes a 50% reduction in economic value.

NOTE

A major problem emphasized throughout this analysis of the tax legislation is the tremendous back-loading of all tax benefits. Will the future rate reductions and other back-loaded tax benefits all be realized, or will Congress have to act in the future to address budget deficits or other societal needs by increasing tax rebates through greater tax rates and tax increases, or alternatively through freezing, or even repealing, the forthcoming tax rate cuts?

The entire process is further complicated for high-income taxpayers by the phaseout of itemized deductions and personal exemptions. To determine whether the change of marginal rights will be really effective for a person, the impact of these phaseouts and when they occur has to be considered.

Finally, the alternative minimum tax (AMT) makes matters even more complicated, and perhaps worse. For many taxpayers, the result will be that the AMT will be the tax that applies, and no marginal shift in tax rates will occur for this type of tax planning.

Changes in Tax Rates for Corporations and Other Entities

Through much, but far from all, of recent history, corporations have been taxed at lower tax rates than individuals. Regular corporations (not S corporations or tax option or tax favored corporations, which have a flow-through tax structure) are taxed at rates from 15 percent to 38 percent. Professional service corporations (e.g., law, accounting, and medical corporations) are taxed at a flat 35 percent rate. Under the income tax rate structure introduced with the 2001 Tax Act, corporations will probably be taxed at higher rates than individuals. Thus, a planning strategy for many will be to try to distribute income out of the corporations in a tax-deductible manner (such as salaries) so that the income will be realized at the individual rates rather than retained in the corporate entity. Also, limited liability companies and family limited partnerships (and other flow-through entities) will be highly preferred, which largely had already been the case before the 2001 Tax Act.

THE ALTERNATIVE MINIMUM TAX

The alternative minimum tax (AMT) is a nefarious tax that attacks many taxpayers with devastating and unexpected results. Under the 2001 Tax Act, the tax will likely apply to even more taxpayers, thus eliminating the intended or expected tax benefits. No planning for any type of investment or business transaction should be undertaken without first considering the potential impact of the AMT.

Planning for the Alternative Minimum Tax

This tax was initially intended to disallow certain preferences and itemized deductions (which are phased out as income gets higher) and so that income is then taxed at a flat 28 percent tax rate. If the AMT is higher than the regular tax, AMT applies. With the reduction of regular tax rates, the AMT calculation has remained constant, resulting in many taxpayers with high itemized deductions paying AMT. This has become common for high-income taxpayers residing in high income tax states since the state income tax deduction has not been allowed as an AMT itemized deduction.

The AMT will not change, other than a minor increase in the exemption, through 2010. The "change" concerning the AMT is the increased importance it is assuming in determining the actual tax paid by more and more taxpayers. The result of this growth in the applicability of the AMT will be increased pressure for change in the AMT system.

Basic AMT planning remains similar to that in prior years. Financial planners should endeavor that their clients shift income to minors and other lower bracket (lower than the effective AMT rate) taxpayers or try to defer income to lower tax years. In most if not all cases of AMT planning, financial planners and/or accountants should make firm projections to ensure that their initial estimate as to the impact is accurate.

2001 Tax Act Changes

The AMT creates a floor or minimum tax rate that applies to a broad array of income items and sets a minimum tax that initially was intended to ensure that the wealthiest taxpayers paid some level of tax. Over many years, the changes in the regular as well as the AMT laws, the inflation of income, and other factors have resulted in many taxpayers who would not consider themselves wealthy being nailed by an expensive AMT. The 2001 Tax Act makes an effort to address this problem through making the child credit a permanent offset to the AMT, repealing the AMT offsets as refundable credits so that the refunds can in fact be received, and increasing the AMT exemption amount by $4,000 for joint filers and $2,000 for single filers for the tax years 2001 through and including 2004.

These changes are modest at best, and as previously noted, the result remains that the AMT will plague a greater number of taxpayers. Demand for real AMT reform is likely to increase once the tremendous impact on the income tax is realized as many more people are subjected to the AMT.

> **NOTE**
>
> Efforts at ATM reform are already happening. At the time of this writing, Congress was considering proposals to completely overhaul the income tax system or to enact a flat or consumption tax to replace it. Perhaps they can do as clear and good a job on the income tax laws as they've done on the gift, estate, and GST laws!

CHILD-RELATED BENEFITS

Child Tax Credit

A tax credit was available under prior law of $500 per qualifying child under age 17. This credit is increasing, over a ten-year period, to $1,000.

Adoption Tax Credit

The adoption tax credit increases to $10,000, with the current credit being $6,000 for all children. Under prior law, it had only been $5,000 for non-special-needs children. The phaseout range over which this credit has been eliminated has increased from $75,000 to $150,000.

Dependent Care Tax Credit

The dependent care tax credit rate is increased to 35 percent from 30 percent under prior law. The amount of eligible employment expenses that can qualify for the credit is increased from $2,400 to $3,000 and, if there are two or more children, from $4,800 to $6,000. The phase-out range has been changed as well.

Child Care Facilities Provided by an Employer Tax Credit

Employers are to be given a credit of up to 25 percent of qualifying expenditures for child care provided to employees. A 10 percent credit is to be provided for qualified expenditures for child care referral or resource service. The maximum credit is $150,000 per year.

EDUCATION PLANNING

Stipulations for Education IRAs

Taxpayers can establish an Education IRA, also called an Education Investment Account, and contribute annually to that account. The maximum contribution had been $500.[1] This limit has been increased by the 2001 Tax Act to $2,000 starting in 2002. These Education IRA contributions are not deductible on income tax returns (as a regular IRA contribution may be). However, the accounts will grow without being subject to income tax.

An Education IRA cannot purchase life insurance. Assets of an Education IRA must be maintained separately; they cannot be commingled, except for investments in mutual funds and related fund vehicles. Within 30 days of the death of the beneficiary, the Education IRA balance must be distributed to the estate of the beneficiary. The trustee will likely have to be an institution.

Contributions can be made only until the beneficiary reaches age 18; however, the 2001 Tax Act permits contributions beyond that age for families with special needs children.

Distributions from Education IRAs

Distributions that are made to pay for qualifying higher education expenses will avoid tax at that time as well. Under prior law, qualifying education expenses had included undergraduate and graduate tuition, room, board, and books. This list has been expanded to include elementary and secondary school expenses. Distributions for any other purpose will be, proportionately, subject to tax and a 10 percent penalty. The penalty is not assessed if the beneficiary is disabled, or if the beneficiary dies and the distributions are paid to the estate of the designated beneficiary.

NOTE

Forms with the bank or brokerage firm where these monies are invested should provide an option of payment to the beneficiary's estate in the event of death in order to effect this kind of distribution.

Another means of avoiding the 10 percent penalty is to have the undistributed Education IRA funds distributed into an Education IRA for another family member.

The distribution penalty can be at odds with estate-tax planning by well-meaning grandparents. For example, parents save the maximum possible in an Education IRA. By the time junior reaches college, grandparents are feeling generous and desire to reduce their estate tax. They gift $10,000 each to a trust for Junior, and then offer to pay tuition for him. Their goodwill gesture could trigger the 10% penalty. However, the parents can still use their Education IRA to fund room, board, and books. The grandparents can only gift money for tuition directly to the institution. Thus, coordinating family estate planning and reading the fine-print distinctions between the various tax rules is important for maximum savings.

Phaseout of Education IRA Benefits

The ability to fund the Education IRA is phased out as the taxpayer's income (technically, modified adjusted gross income, or AGI) exceeds $190,000 for a joint return ($150,000 under prior law). The benefit is completely eliminated on a joint income tax return when the modified AGI reaches $220,000 ($160,000 under prior law). For single taxpayers, the benefit is phased out from $95,000 to $110,000. For this calculation, AGI is modified by adding non-U.S. income excluded from gross income.[2]

As a result of the 2001 Tax Act, contributions can now be made until April 15 of the year following the year the contribution is for. Under prior law, contributions had to be made by December 31 of each year, which was difficult for some taxpayers.

Coordination with HOPE or Lifetime Learning Credits

Taxpayers no longer will have to choose between the tax credits available in the HOPE credit and lifetime learning credit programs and the Education IRA, because beginning in 2001 they will be able to exclude Education IRA distributions and claim both tax benefits in the same year as long as they are not used for the same educational expenses. In addition, the 2001 Tax Act further liberalizes the Education IRA by permitting taxpayers to make contributions during the year to a qualified state tuition program (Code Section 529 plan) and still make gifts to an Education IRA for that beneficiary in the same year.

Excess Tax on Excess Contributions

If more is funded in an Education IRA than permitted, an excess tax is imposed.[3] The excess subject to penalty is generally the amount in excess of the maximum amount permitted, reduced by the previously mentioned income limitations.

Integrating Education IRAs into Planning

The $2,000 Education IRA could be a useful financial planning tool. It is unlikely to have significant estate planning benefits, because the income phaseouts ensure that many taxpayers with net worth at the level sufficient to justify estate-tax planning will not qualify. Except for the small dollar limits, however, it could be a good planning tool in some circumstances. Any taxpayer with modified AGI past the phaseout ranges cannot make a contribution to an Education IRA on behalf of any other taxpayer.

Code Section 529 College Savings Plans

The 2001 Tax Act has made Code Section 529 college savings plans one of the best income, gift, estate, and educational planning techniques. Many families can contribute to state-run college education programs to fund educational costs for heirs. The definition of qualified education expenses that can be funded through such a program includes not only tuition but also expenses associated with room and board. The definition of a family member qualifying for the benefits involved includes sons, daughters, grandchildren, brothers, sisters, nephews, nieces, certain in-laws, and spouses.

When the contribution exceeds the annual gift tax exclusion amount, which is presently $10,000 per person (inflation indexed), the excess can, by election of the contributor, be treated as if made over a five-year period. Thus, it is possible to give five years of Code Section 529 education contributions at one time: A married couple can fund $100,000 free of gift, estate, and GST tax in a single year. Grandparents and parents undertaking education planning should give consideration to this.

 Taxpayers should consider revising their durable powers of attorney to expressly authorize their agents to make maximum Section 529 plan gifts.

Many states have plans to assist investors and families in taking advantage of these benefits. The investment allocation models of the various plans, the flexibility of investment options, and other factors can vary from state to state. Further, with the tremendous enhancements made to the Code Section 529 plans under the 2001 Tax Act, more states are likely to sponsor programs, and others will expand and enhance existing programs.

NOTE

Financial planners should shop the various state programs to determine which are the best for clients' needs, and which programs provide investments consistent with their objectives. For a detailed discussion of the IRC § 529 plans, see the website www.laweasy.com for an audio clip. There are also several audio clips reviewing investment allocation and diversification.

The earnings on the Code Section 529 plan assets will never be subject to income tax as long as they are used for higher education expense. This is a tremendous liberalization of the tax benefits in that under prior law the distributions were taxed at the beneficiary's income tax rate. For lower income taxpayers, the savings might be 10 to 20 percent or more. However, for heirs in wealthy families who may at a young age have sufficient assets to be in a maximum income tax bracket, this could be a tremendous savings.

NOTE

Tax-free earnings and other 529 plan benefits should be carefully weighed if a decision is being made to fund trusts for children or grandchildren. If the trusts will be funded with cash that will have to be invested, the 529 college savings plan can present a great tax, investment, and administrative opportunity (without the costs or complexity associated with a trust). However, if the trusts are intended to hold interests in closely held businesses or other assets that cannot be invested in a college savings plan, the approach of using a trust will remain the preferable option.

When evaluating the choice of a Code Section 529 plan versus a trust, consider the funding options, rates of return, and other factors. For example, what rates of return have been realized on the investment portfolio in past years? If the investor has done remarkably well and has top-notch money managers, a Code Section 529 plan may not prove better. If the time horizon is long enough and funds are managed for tax efficiency, the rates of return outside a Code Section 529 plan may be better than inside such a plan. However, many investors have realized rates of return that are far less than the return that many of the professionally managed and diversified college savings plans would be anticipated to realize. Estate planners have to weigh the considerations net of tax returns under both options. The tax-free payments from a Code Section 529 plan can be an excellent deal, especially if it is likely that the amounts can be used to fund qualifying education costs. When analyzing the options, also consider the benefits of the front-loading of five years of gifts into a Code Section 529 plan.

The 2001 Tax Act has made Code Section 529 plans more flexible. Tax-free rollover rules and tax-free transfers between plans have been liberalized. As such, if the balance cannot be used by the particular beneficiary for education costs, then the plan benefits can be transferred to another beneficiary until they are used appropriately. The definitions of family members and qualified higher education expenses have all been expanded. Thus, these plans provide for even more significant income and estate-tax savings than under prior law.

Student Loan Interest Deductions

To help taxpayers who borrowed money to pay for college and other higher education costs, special rules have existed for a long time providing favorable deductions for the interest on those loans. Qualifying expenses could have been incurred for the taxpayer, the spouse, or any dependent. An interest expense deduction could be claimed under prior law for up to $2,500 of student loan interest "above the line." An individual cannot be claimed as a dependent on another taxpayer's tax return (e.g., the parent) and obtain this deduction.

This benefit, after the changes enacted as part of the 2001 Tax Act, are being phased out at income levels of $50,000 to $65,000 for single taxpayers and $100,000 to $130,000 for married taxpayers filing joint returns.

Under prior law, deductions were only permitted during the first 60 months for which interest payments are required to be made. This restriction has been eliminated.

Higher Education Expense Deduction

The 2001 Tax Act permits taxpayers, beginning in 2002, to deduct qualified higher education costs up to a maximum $3,000 in 2002–2003, $4,000 in 2004–2005 (for adjusted gross income under $130,000 on a joint return or $65,000 on a single return).

This deduction is available for expenses paid for academic-related costs during the first two years of postsecondary education. Also, the institution must be eligible to participate in the U.S. Department of Education student aid program. These are the same definitions that apply to the HOPE credit.

PENSION AND RETIREMENT SAVINGS

The 2001 Tax Act has provided considerable new incentives for retirement savings. These include, among many complex and sweeping changes, an increase in IRA and 401(k) benefits.

Individual Retirement Accounts

Contributions to regular individual retirement accounts (IRAs) are deducted in calculating adjusted gross income (AGI) if the taxpayer making the contribution was not an active participant in an employer-provided plan, or if the taxpayer's income was sufficiently low. Once the taxpayer's income has exceeded a specified threshold, no deduction for the IRA contribution is permitted. If the taxpayer's income is in the indicated phaseout ranges, then a portion of the maximum deduction is permitted. The maximum annual contribution (whether deductible or not) was $2,000 under prior law. The 2001 Tax Act increased the limit as shown in Exhibit 2.2.

If the taxpayer is over age 50, a special catch-up rule may allow additional contributions.

Roth IRA Requirements and Contribution Limits

The general rules affecting a Roth IRA are the same as those applicable to a regular IRA, described earlier, with a few critical differences.[4] For example, the Roth IRA has been described as a back-ended IRA. Although there is no income tax deduction for the

Exhibit 2.2   IRA and Roth IRA Limits

Year	Maximum for Age 50 and Older ($)	Maximum if Under Age 50 ($)
2000	$2,000	$2,000
2001	2,000	2,000
2002	3,500	3,000
2003	3,500	3,000
2004	3,500	3,000
2005	4,500	4,000
2006	5,000	4,000
2007	5,000	4,000
2008	6,000	5,000
2009 and later	6,000*	5,000*

*Inflation indexed in $500 increments.

contribution, distributions are generally not subject to income tax. The tax free withdrawal of funds, including appreciation, is a tremendous tax benefit.

The 2001 Tax Act has increased the limits for contributions to Roth IRA accounts in the amounts set forth in Exhibit 2.2 for regular IRA contributions. Taxpayers may continue to make contributions to a Roth IRA until death. A purpose of the Roth IRA is the tax-free growth of contributions over time. After the contributor's death, however, the executor cannot make a final contribution on the decedent's behalf.[5]

To avoid income tax and penalties on Roth IRA distributions, several requirements must be met (the language of the statute is that the distribution must be a "qualified distribution").[6] The funds must be invested in the Roth IRA for five tax years. The term *tax* year means the calendar year for which the investment is made. If the taxpayer makes a contribution to a Roth IRA for the year 2001 during 2002 (but on or before April 15), the first tax year is still 2001 and the fifth tax year is still 2005. The funds must be distributed for a specified purpose or in specified situations: The taxpayer is 59½ or older, has died, has become disabled, or is using distribution for a qualifying special purpose (e.g., a first-time home buyer for qualifying expenses)[7]. If the requirements are met, the distribution will be treated as a tax-free withdrawal from the Roth IRA.

The minimum distribution rules applicable to regular IRAs do not apply to Roth IRAs.[8]

As regular income tax rates are reduced, the benefits of the Roth IRA will be modestly reduced but not sufficiently for most taxpayers to stop endeavoring to take maximum advantage of IRAs.

Employer Retirement Plans

The 2001 Tax Act changes the contributions that employers can make to plans. The deferral limits for employee participants and the deductibility limits for employer deductions have been increased. As with IRA plans, special catch-up provisions for taxpayers over 50 have been provided. The limits have been increased for participants under age 50 from $10,500 in 2001 to $15,000 in 2006. The limits have been increased for participants age 50 and older from $10,500 in 2001 to $20,000 in 2006. In years after 2006, the limits are to be inflation indexed for all participants.

SIMPLE Plans

Employers with no more than 100 employees, each earning at least $5,000 per year, can set up a SIMPLE plan if they do not have another employer retirement plan. A SIMPLE plan (the acronym for savings incentive match plan for employees, also known as a SIMPLE IRA) is a retirement plan for employees with a matching contribution from the employer. All employees with more than $5,000 of earned compensation must be eligible to participate. Under prior law, an employee could contribute, through deferral of salary, up to $6,000 a year. These contributions to the SIMPLE plan are not subject to income tax until they are withdrawn. The sponsoring employer must match the employee elective contributions according to an established

Exhibit 2.3   SIMPLE Plan Limits

Year	Maximum for Age 50 and Older ($)	Maximum if Under Age 50 ($)
2001	$ 6,500	$ 6,500
2002	7,500	7,000
2003	9,000	8,000
2004	10,500	9,000
2005	12,000	10,000
2006	12,500	10,000
2007 and later	12,500*	10,000

*Inflation indexed.

formula. Generally, the employer matching must be dollar-for-dollar up to 3 percent of compensation, or alternatively, the employer can make a nonelective contribution of 2 percent of compensation on behalf of each employee permitted to participate (regardless of what the employee actually contributes).

The 2001 Tax Act has increased the limits for SIMPLE plans (see Exhibit 2.3).

Flexibility in Retirement Plan Transfers

The intent of many changes has been to make retirement plan balances more flexible (portable) in the event of job changes. These include the ability to roll over IRA contributions into employer-sponsored plans and similarly to roll over employer-sponsored plans with more flexibility into IRAs.

COMPREHENSIVE TAX PLANNING

The 2001 Tax Act has made changes to income and retirement planning that affect estate planning as well. Income tax changes likewise affect trust planning. The Code Section 529 college savings plans present an important alternative to trusts for children and grandchildren. Retirement asset-related changes, especially since such assets represent a substantial portion of so many estates, will affect planning. The key point is to carefully consider ancillary tax implications when engaging in comprehensive estate planning.

3
KEY ISSUES BEYOND TAX CONSIDERATIONS

Non-estate tax planning objectives have always been vital. Perhaps one benefit of the increasing exclusion will be the shifting of focus to these other important issues because many taxpayers will no longer face estate taxes. But what is more likely to happen is that taxpayers will ignore these vital personal issues because it was only the hoped-for tax savings that pulled them into an estate planner's office in the first place.

A major newspaper article reported that the estate tax exclusion increase from $675,000 that can pass free of tax in 2001 to $1 million in 2002 will remove 40 percent of those estates filing estate tax returns from the estate tax rolls. Before the 2001 Tax Act, only about 2 percent of decedents filed estate tax returns, perhaps less. Of those who filed, fully one-half of the total estate taxes collected were paid by the largest 5 percent of filees! So the vast majority of estates never had to be concerned with estate taxes, and now even fewer will. It remains a tax of the wealthiest of the wealthy. So if there is no concern about estate taxes, what is left to worry about? Plenty. Personal issues, income tax considerations, business succession planning, and asset protection are among many non-estate tax questions that need to be addressed.

IMPORTANT NON-ESTATE TAX CONSIDERATIONS

The discussion in this chapter highlights some of these non-estate tax problems to alert planners and those individuals planning their estates that even if the estate tax were repealed (and it certainly wasn't!) people still need to plan. Although the issues will vary dramatically from person to person, all clients need to consider the relevant non-estate tax issues that affect them and their loved ones. Financial advisers and estate planners should direct their clients' attention to the following matters.

Emotional Aspects: Minimizing Family Disputes

During estate planning highly emotional issues inevitably surface and have to be addressed. For example, the reaction of children to wealth or perceived differences in treatment can have a tremendous impact on a family.

It is not uncommon for parents to have distribution schemes favoring a particular child, or in some instances even to pit one child against another, whether on purpose or as a result of an oversight. It is essential to address these risks any time one child (or other heir) is named, and not another, or one child is appointed as an executor and not the other. Try to be cognizant of what may develop and review alternative suggestions. If the client is not comfortable with a particular child as an executor, the estate planner might suggest listing that child's name at the end of a list of several other executors. The odds of the person at the end of a list serving may be almost nil, but for the child involved, being named on the list is a tremendous positive compared with the potential slight of not being on the list of executors at all.

 Can fiduciaries be appointed in a manner to minimize disputes? Instead of naming one of two children as an executor, perhaps naming a third party, such as a friend, cousin, or bank, might avoid insult to the child not named.

Minimizing Legal Fees

Limiting legal and other professional fees is a goal of many people undertaking the estate planning process. In many cases, this means not being penny-wise and pound-foolish. Encourage people to take the time and spend the money to think through the planning and dispositive provisions, to understand the documents, and to ensure

---
EXAMPLE

If taxpayer has a closely held business, having a specialist address issues relating to the structure of the business entity, buyout provisions, liquidity, investment clauses in wills and trusts, and S corporation income tax requirements will ultimately save substantial costs and taxes. A non-estate planning specialist may not have sufficient expertise to address these and other complex issues.

---

that they are tailored to their individual needs. Careful planning in the beginning can save substantial sums in the end.

ESSENTIAL GUIDELINES

Financial advisers should present the following advice to all their clients insofar as the six broad areas covered below are closely allied with many of the aims and objectives of estate planning.

- *Disability Planning*   Minimizing the difficulties you and your loved ones might have if you unexpectedly become ill or disabled is an essential part of estate planning, regardless of estate taxes. You must have a durable power of attorney authorizing someone, called an agent, to make legal, tax, and financial decisions if you can't. Similarly, appoint and authorize an agent (health care proxy) to make health care–related decisions on your behalf if you cannot do so. Long-term care insurance ensures not only the financial security of future health care related needs but also emotional security for loved ones. Purchasing your own insurance to provide for your care is a clear message to loved ones that they need not sacrifice their entire lives during your illness or infirmity.

- *Emergency Planning*   Stuff happens. It's like the *Candid Camera* line ". . . somewhere where you least expect it . . ." Minimize the difficulties you and your loved ones will face in an emergency (not just death or disability, but casualty loss, burglary, and so on). Collect and organize key financial and legal data. Disseminate key emergency data. Compile a list of key family members, neighbors, and advisers (telephone and cell phone numbers, e-mail addresses, and so forth), key financial assets (bank accounts, brokerage accounts), and other important biographical data (Social Security numbers, and so forth). Have sufficient liquidity, lines of credit, and liability insurance. Cash reserves should exist for emergencies. Available home equity lines, personal lines of credit, and overdraft privileges on checking accounts can all be extraordinarily important to address financial and other emergencies. Adequate property, casualty, medical, disability, malpractice, and other insurances are similarly essential to any comprehensive estate and financial plan. These precautions should always be part of an overall estate plan.

- *Probate Costs* Minimizing probate costs, time delays, and complications are admirable goals for every estate plan. This may include using a revocable living trust and will certainly include having a will and other appropriate documents prepared with sufficient clarity, planning, and proper execution. It also includes organizing your records and might require one or more letters of last instruction to heirs and fiduciaries. It always includes reviewing and properly planning for the title (ownership) of the assets you own and identifying the heirs for the particular assets involved. You need to plan to minimize or avoid ancillary probate (probate in a state other than where you reside) and estate taxes (e.g., fund a bypass trust or take maximum advantage of the new modified carryover basis rules after the repeal of the estate tax).

- *Investment Planning* Who needs an investment plan? Just buy a couple of hot growth stocks. Well, maybe not. If clients don't properly plan and diversify their investments now, and coordinate that plan with your cash flow needs, time horizon, and risk profile, they will only achieve financial and estate planning goals by luck. Luck may be helpful, but it's best not to rely on it. Many an estate tax problem has been prematurely eliminated by lousy investment planning. Plan investments and estate matters, not just one or the other. The investment provision of every will and trust should be reviewed in light of the testator's or grantor's goals, needs of loved ones, and asset mix (e.g., stock portfolio, closely held business, real estate, and so on).

Investment planning is also more than just what an investor does with his financial planner or money manager. Any trusts should address investment issues. An investor might want (especially in light of the uncertainties created by the 2001 Tax Act) to name a trust protector for trusts to provide greater flexibility. The taxpayer could give the trust protector the authority to replace trustees and hence change the investment policy of the trust. If the taxpayer opts to have an investment committee appointed for a trust, then he might give the trust protector the right to hire and fire the members of that committee.

- *Religious Issues* Religious issues have generally been ignored in estate planning. They should not be. Whatever religion you are affiliated with, it is likely to influence the stipulations of a living will and charitable giving. You should address these matters, regardless of the status of the estate tax.

- *Charitable Giving* Charitable giving should remain a cornerstone of every estate plan. Everyone able to make a contribution back to society should do so and seek guidance through the many options regardless of the status of the estate tax.

Common charitable giving techniques, such as charitable lead trusts (CLTs) may have lost some of their appeal given the increase in the exclusion and the eventual elimination of estate tax. However, the CLT can provide important personal benefits such as deferring when a child or other heir receives money and setting an example of philanthropy.

Charitable remainder trusts (CRTs) will remain a popular technique for avoiding capital gains taxes. As the estate tax and basis carryover are eliminated, reducing income tax will become the focus of income planning and CRTs will increase in popularity.

NON-ESTATE TAX BENEFITS OF TRUSTS

For many taxpayers, the increased exclusion amount, $1 million in 2002 with annually scheduled increases thereafter, makes the estate tax an unlikely event. If those taxpayers can be sure that the estate tax won't apply to them, do they no longer need to consider trusts in their planning? Hardly. Trusts have always had important non-estate tax benefits. Trusts are a highly useful and flexible estate and financial planning tool that can accomplish the following goals:

- Provide income for the taxpayer and loved ones in the event of sickness and disability
- Bridge the gap between life and death by continuing to care for the taxpayer's family after his death
- Ensure management expertise and continuity for the taxpayer's business or investments in the event of illness or disability
- Achieve significant income tax savings by enabling a trustee to allocate income to lower bracket taxpayers
- Protect assets from creditors, malpractice claimants, and divorce actions
- Manage business or other assets
- Protect children or other heirs while managing assets for their benefit
- Minimize or avoid probate
- In accomplishing all of these important goals, remaining confidential, thus protecting the taxpayer's privacy

INCOME TAXATION OF TRUSTS

A trust can be structured to give the trustee the flexibility to allocate distributions between various beneficiaries. This is referred to as a sprinkle, pot, or discretionary trust. To the extent that different beneficiaries are in different income tax brackets, this flexibility can provide income tax savings. The key to this savings is the distribution to beneficiaries that carries taxable income to them. In simple terms, when the trustee makes a distribution to a particular beneficiary, that distribution can carry out trust income to be taxed to that recipient beneficiary. The discretionary trust structure offers a potential asset protection benefit as well. If one of the several beneficiaries is in the midst of a lawsuit, divorce, or other problem, the trustee can direct distributions to other beneficiaries. With the changes made by the 2001 Tax Act, income tax planning for trusts should receive renewed attention as gift and estate tax concerns wane for many taxpayers.

Calculating Trust Income

When a trust is required to report its income on its own tax return, it usually will be taxed in a manner that is similar to the way in which an individual taxpayer is taxed. The gross income of a trust is generally determined in the same manner as the gross income of an individual.[1] Then several modifications are made. Trust income determined under the trust's accounting methods includes all income received by the trust during the tax year: income accumulated in the trust; income that is to be distributed currently by the trustee to the beneficiaries; and income that, in the trustee's discretion, may be either distributed to the beneficiaries or accumulated.[2] One of the most important concepts of trust taxation is that the trust will generally only pay tax on income that it accumulates. When the trust distributes income to its beneficiaries, the trust will be treated as a conduit for tax purposes. It will not pay tax on distributed income. Instead, the income and deductions will be taxed to the beneficiaries to the extent the income is passed out of the trust to them. This result is achieved by giving the trust a tax deduction for the income actually distributed (or required to be distributed) to the beneficiary.

A trust, however, is not a perfect conduit, because several items are affected by special trust tax rules. For example, all losses do not generally pass through the trust to the beneficiaries until the year in which the trust terminates.[3] Capital losses are not deducted in the calculation of a trust's distributable net income (DNI). Thus, where a trust has a capital loss (e.g., from selling stock) but no capital gain, the loss is not passed through the trust to be reported on the beneficiaries' income tax returns. Capital losses, however, can be offset against capital gains of the trust.

The determination of the extent to which the trust or beneficiary bears the actual tax liability on any income depends on the calculation of a complex tax concept called *distributable net income* (DNI). DNI is explained later in this chapter.

Deductions and Losses Available to Trusts

Trusts are entitled to certain tax deductions in calculating their income. Generally, trusts are allowed the same tax deductions and credits as are individual taxpayers.[4] Trusts are not, however, permitted to claim the standard deduction to which individual taxpayers are entitled.[5] The 2 percent floor on miscellaneous itemized deductions applicable to individuals is similarly applicable to trusts, which will be favorably affected by the phaseout of this so-called stealth tax in the 2001 Tax Act.[6] Trust expenses that may be subject to this limitation include tax return preparation fees, safe deposit box rentals, legal and accounting fees, and investment counsel fees. A trust must make special calculations to determine its adjusted gross income. For example, the expenses paid or incurred to administer the trust and make distributions are deductible in arriving at adjusted gross income.

A trust is permitted to deduct ordinary necessary expenses incurred in its business, expenses incurred in the production of income, and expenses to determine its tax liability.[7] Where a trust owns a house occupied personally by a beneficiary, the trust may not be able to deduct maintenance and similar costs.[8] Instead, these personal expenses may be treated as a distribution to that particular beneficiary.[9] Reasonable amounts incurred for trustee fees are deductible. The deductions, however, are only allowed for items that are obligations of the trust.

A trust is not permitted to claim any deductions for the expenses allocable to tax-exempt income.[10] The rationale for this rule is simple: If the trust is not taxed on the income, it should not be able to deduct expenses incurred to generate that income.

Depreciation deductions are allowed but may have to be allocated between the beneficiaries and the trust based on the allocation of trust income.[11] Bad debt deductions, net operating losses,[12] and casualty losses[13] are also permitted, but may not all pass through to the beneficiary in each tax year.

Charitable contribution deductions are permitted for amounts paid to recognized charitable organizations under the terms of the trust.[14] The rules for trusts are more generous than those for individuals. Individual taxpayers are only permitted deductions for contributions up to certain percentages of their income. These rules do not apply to trusts.[15] The contributions, however, must be made in a manner that is consistent with the terms of the trust agreement and must be paid out of trust income (not principal).[16]

Trusts, like individual and certain other taxpayers, are subject to the complicated passive loss rules, which can limit the ability to deduct losses from rental real estate and other passive investments.[17] The passive loss limitations are applied to beneficiaries on the passive income or deductions distributed to them and to the trust on the passive income or deductions that it does not distribute.

Special Deductions for Trusts

Trusts are entitled to several special deductions that differ from those available to individual taxpayers.

Simple or Complex Trusts

The rules for determining the deductions available to a trust vary, depending on whether the trust is characterized as simple or complex. A simple trust is required by the trust agreement to distribute all of its income currently, make no distributions other than of current income, and has no provision for charitable contributions.[18] The fact that the trustee may not distribute all of the income as required will not affect the characterization of the trust.[19] The fact that capital gains must be allocated to principal rather than income, under applicable state law or the trust provisions, will also not affect the characterization of the trust as a simple trust.

Any trust not characterized as a simple trust under the preceding rules is characterized as a complex trust. A complex trust includes any trust not required to pay out all of its income currently.

The rules for complex trusts are more difficult because complex trusts may accumulate income (when a trust doesn't pay out all of its income currently, that portion is "accumulated," or kept by the trust for distribution in later years). Where income is accumulated, then some portion of the distributions in any year may be made from principal amounts. This can be principal from the original assets given to the trust, or from accumulations in prior years.

Exemption Deduction

Every trust is entitled to an exemption deduction. Simple trusts are entitled to an exemption of $300, complex trusts, $100.[20]

Distributable Net Income (DNI) Deduction for Trusts

This is the key deduction enabling trustees to plan to minimize income taxes. The most important deduction available to a trust is the deduction for distributions to beneficiaries. This deduction is the key to avoiding double taxation of the same income to the trust and its beneficiaries. It is also the basis of a trust being characterized as a conduit for income tax purposes. To understand these rules, it is necessary to grasp a tax concept unique to the taxation of trusts: distributable net income (DNI).

DNI accomplishes three purposes: (1) It determines the maximum amount that a beneficiary of the trust will be taxed on in any year,[21] (2) it determines the maximum amount that can be deducted by a trust for distributions it makes to beneficiaries in any year,[22] and (3) it provides for the character (e.g., tax-exempt income or non-tax-exempt income) of the income that the trust passes to a beneficiary.[23]

In the simplest terms, DNI is roughly equivalent to the trust's taxable income (rather than its income determined under trust accounting concepts), although there are modifications and adjustments. The rules for DNI are different for simple and complex trusts (not that the rules are simple for "simple" trusts).

The trust's deduction for distributions is limited to its DNI.[24] The DNI also limits the amount taxable to the beneficiary. Distributions to a beneficiary in excess of DNI are generally subject to income tax.[25] Also, the DNI concept preserves the character of income distributed out of the trust.[26]

For a domestic trust, DNI is calculated based on modifications of the trust's taxable income. The modifications include the following:

1. Any deduction claimed for distributions to beneficiaries is added back.[27]
2. The personal exemption is added back.[28]
3. Tax-exempt interest, less deductions allocated to it, is added back.
4. Capital gains that are allocated to the principal of the trust and are not paid or required to be distributed to a beneficiary are subtracted.
5. Capital losses that aren't used to offset capital gains are subtracted.[29]

Calculating DNI Deduction for Simple Trusts

A simple trust is generally entitled to deduct the lesser of DNI or the amount of income required to be distributed currently to the beneficiaries of the trust.[30] The concept behind a deduction for the trust's DNI is that a trust, when it distributes current income to its beneficiaries, is treated as a conduit, passing tax consequences to those beneficiaries. For a simple trust, the DNI deduction is available even if the actual distribution is made after the close of the tax year.[31]

Calculating DNI Deduction for Complex Trusts

Where complex, as opposed to simple, trusts are involved, two different categories of trust distributions must be considered. The first category is distributions of current income of the trust that must, by terms of the trust instrument, be distributed to the beneficiaries in that year. This is similar to the concepts discussed for simple trusts.

The beneficiaries are taxed on this first category of income to the extent of DNI.

The second category includes all amounts, other than those included in the first category, that are paid, credited, or required to be distributed by the trust to its beneficiaries.[32] These beneficiaries will only be taxed on the amount they receive if the distributions to the first category of beneficiaries do not use up all of the trust's DNI for that year.

A complex trust may deduct the amount of income that is required to be distributed during the year. This can include any amount that is required to be distributed, whether paid out of income or principal, to the extent that it was actually paid. Where different types of income are distributed, the deduction available to the trust for the distribution is allocated in the same proportion as each type of income bears to the total DNI, unless state law or the trust instrument provides for a different allocation method.[33] Rules for allocating the different deductions and classes of income to the amounts received by the beneficiary are also provided.[34]

For a complex trust, the trustee can elect on an annual basis to treat any distribution made to a beneficiary within the first sixty-five days after year end, to be treated as if made in the prior year.[35]

ASSET PROTECTION

Asset protection planning is the process of structuring, in advance, investments, business interests, and activities to minimize, as much as possible, the ability of malpractice claimants, creditors, or others to reach assets to satisfy their claims. It is not a process of taking illegal action, thwarting existing claimants, or engaging in inappropriate conduct. Every corporation was organized primarily to prevent business claimants from reaching shareholders' personal assets. So asset protection is practiced by many people.

Where the transfer to a trust, limited partnership, limited liability company, or other entity, is deemed fraudulent, the transfer can be set aside and the purported asset protection benefits reduced or eliminated. A fraudulent transfer also can be subject to additional penalties. Therefore, careful planning is essential to ensure the proper selection of the structure for the transaction, appropriate timing, careful drafting of the appropriate documents, and implementation.

Transferring some portion of the assets to an offshore trust may secure the assets so transferred from a suit or other claim. Similarly, assets transferred to a family limited partnership can secure those assets. These transfers should be made of the portion of assets that are not needed for daily living expenses. Transferring all of the assets may taint the transaction as an intent to avoid creditors. (Some taxpayers may attempt to transfer nearly every asset they own—other than assets deemed exempt under state law—to foreign situs trusts, family limited partnerships, or other protective arrangements.) Where the nest egg approach is used, asset protection planning is probably an appropriate objective for almost every estate plan. Fraudulent conveyance and other issues are less a concern where this approach is used since substantial assets will remain in the taxpayer's hands.

The greater the number of entities, the more components into which various interests and rights in an asset have been divided, the more layers of entities and contractual relationships, the more difficult it is to pierce the transfer. Planners should address the option of transferring assets to limited partnerships, limited liability companies, or other entities to insulate each property, investment, or business from the others as well as from the personal assets of the principals. A single limited partnership owning several real estate assets can insulate partners' personal assets from claims, but it results in all partnership assets being attacked if a liability or claim occurs to one property. The division of a single partnership into multiple partnerships can minimize this risk.

Despite the 2001 Tax Act, trusts will remain a cornerstone of planning to protect assets. Assets owned by a properly established trust can be safeguarded from claims. If the assets of the trust are distributed to the beneficiary at a certain age, a lawsuit or divorce after that age will reach those assets. If assets stay in trust longer, they stay protected longer. This can require a more comprehensive approach to preparing the terms of the trust. Instead of simply distributing money from the trust to enable a child to purchase a house, a better approach in a longer term GST or dynasty trust may be to have the trustee loan the child or grandchild money to buy the house, or even to buy the house in the trust and permit the beneficiary to use the house. This keeps the assets protected. This more comprehensive approach is rarely used for a trust that will make substantial distributions when a beneficiary reaches age 30 or so.

EXAMPLE

The Delaware Qualified Dispositions in Trust Act § 3572(b) provides that a creditor's claim shall be extinguished unless the creditor's claim arose before the qualified disposition to the trust was made and the action was brought within the Delaware statute of limitations (§ 1309 of Title 6), or the creditor's claim arose concurrent with or subsequent to the qualified disposition and the action was brought within four years after the qualified disposition to the trust was made. The creditor must prove such matters by clear and convincing evidence. In § 3573, exceptions are provided for alimony and child support, and in the event of certain claims for death, personal injury, or property damage.

SUCCESSION PLANNING

The most difficult aspect of planning for any family business is that in addition to complex employee/employer, business, economic, regulatory, and other matters, superimposed over all is the family relationship. Will child and parent get along? What about siblings? However difficult these two relationships may be, more distant family ties can increase the difficulty of planning succession, as is demonstrated by the limited longevity of most family businesses. The ties that may have bound parent and child or siblings may not bind nieces and nephews, who want job security and wealth, but may not have sufficient family loyalty to make necessary sacrifices or compromises that would preserve family and business harmony.

Where sons-in-law or daughters-in-law are involved, the dilemmas of split loyalty can destroy a business. Should daughter side with her father, the patriarch of the family business, or her husband, who is a junior executive to the father? The implications and complications are endless. Some families believe their businesses have survived by religiously adhering to the strategy of "Blood Only." They do not allow any person with an in-law in their relationship description to work in the business. Some families go further and have an unwritten law against in-law persons spending any significant time in the business, even if unpaid and unofficial. Although there may be merit to this in some situations, it is certainly not an appropriate golden rule. Many family enterprises would not have survived had it not been for a son-in-law's or daughter-in-law's involvement.

All these problems play heavily in a key issue for every family business: succession planning to get the business to the next generation. The favorable changes of the 2001 Tax Act, liberalizing the estate tax deferral rules, increasing the exclusion, and so forth will make the estate tax aspects of achieving this goal easier. However, no tax change will solve the tremendous nontax challenges of succession planning.

NEED FOR BROAD-BASED PLANNING

Although the focus of this book is estate tax planning after the 2001 Tax Act, every plan must address many non-estate tax issues. Planning should always be broad based and include relevant personal, investment, income tax, and business issues. Achieving estate or gift tax savings at the expense of violating personal wishes is never appropriate. The client's personal goals and objectives should govern tax planning, not vice versa.

PART II

Specific Techniques and Planning Strategies

4

PLANNING FOR DIFFERENT TYPES OF TAXPAYERS

The uncertainties of the 2001 Tax Act suggest that taxpayers should plan cautiously. It is impossible to predict what will happen in future years with the substantial deferred effective dates for many of its provisions, the complexity of the changes, and the unknown actions of a future administration. This chapter examines special issues or planning considerations that may affect different taxpayers.

GENERAL CONSIDERATIONS FOR ALL TAXPAYERS

The evil death tax never affected most taxpayers, and it will be even more unlikely to affect them now. Does that mean that they should ignore planning? No. Often the estate tax was avoidable if only the taxpayer had engaged in a modicum of planning. As demonstrated in Chapters 2 and 3, there are a plethora of non-estate tax matters to plan that affect almost everyone. Also, it is uncertain what future changes Congress will make to the estate tax system. Finally, no one can know what the value of their estate will be at some future unknown date of death. Thorough planning remains critical, as the example below illustrates.

--- **EXAMPLE** ---

A young couple with modest net worth went to a general practice attorney for a cheap estate plan. They had simple wills and standard form powers of attorney and living wills drafted. Both of them

> were killed in a tragic car accident. Although they were certain that they could never face an estate tax, their estate was $1.8 million and a tremendous estate tax was due in 2003. The young couple had neglected to realize that although they had only about $100,000 of assets alive, they had substantial, inexpensive term life insurance policies and additional insurance through each of their employers. A simple irrevocable life insurance trust would have kept the life insurance proceeds out of their estates and would have solved the estate tax problem. This same trust would have protected the insurance proceeds from mismanagement, a new spouse if only one of the couple died, and many other risks and problems.

A large number of estates paying estate tax only fell into the estate tax trap because, on the death of the first spouse, all assets were simply bequeathed to the survivor outright and without a trust. The passage of time and inflation alone could have moved many of these estates to a point of paying significant estate tax. All that had to be done was include a bypass trust in the will of both spouses so that on the death of the first spouse assets would be held in trust to benefit the surviving spouse, but these assets would never be taxed in the surviving spouse's estate no matter how much they grew. Taxpayers looking to ignore the estate tax should learn from this costly lesson many families have faced.

MODERATE ESTATES OWNING INSURANCE

Insurance can create an instant estate. This is exactly why many people should, and do, purchase insurance. If a taxpayer has small children and dies prematurely, a moderate estate will not be worth enough to support the family and put the children through college. Insurance is often the logical answer. Before the 2001 Tax Act, an insurance trust has often been called for to ensure that the insurance proceeds are available to fund expenses and are not dissipated on estate taxes. As the exclusion increases, moderately wealthy families may opt for the simplicity of having insurance payable to their estates instead of using insurance trusts, as was more effective under prior law.

EXAMPLE

A taxpayer is a single parent. She has a house worth $300,000, $250,000 of stock, and purchases a $500,000 insurance policy. Under prior law, an insurance trust would have been called for to avoid estate tax since the estate would have exceeded the exclusion by $325,000 [($300,000 + $250,000 + $500,000) = $1,050,000 − $675,000]. In 2002 with a $1 million exclusion scheduled to increase she might opt to forgo the trust.

Another approach for married couples is to use a bypass trust under the will to effectively shelter the insurance proceeds from taxation in lieu of an irrevocable life insurance trust (ILIT). The advantages this can provide are simplicity, avoidance of the legal costs of establishing an insurance trust, and no Crummey powers (a technique used to qualify gifts to trusts for the annual gift tax exclusion).

ELDERLY OR INFIRM TAXPAYERS WITH LARGE ESTATES

Taxpayers who are elderly or infirm having significant estates cannot await the increase in the exclusion or possible repeal of the estate tax. Planning should continue as usual, with the possible exception of incorporating more flexibility in planning documents.

To aggressively reduce the estate tax, a combination of charitable lead trusts, sales to defective grantor trusts, grantor-retained annuity trusts (GRATs), and family-limited partnerships with discounted gifts should all be evaluated. If the age or health status is such that the time frame is short, quick estate tax benefits can often be obtained by

EXAMPLE

Assume that taxpayer's age is 78. His assets are worth about $8.2 million. He has four children from a first marriage. He is currently married to Wife #2 and has a prenuptial agreement whereby husband must create a $2.2 million QTIP trust for Wife #2 if she survives. Wife #2 has $950,000 in assets on her own, which have a $720,000 tax basis. Husband has an existing will complying with the prenuptial agreement. All remaining assets not needed to satisfy the prenuptial agreement will be distributed outright to the four children.

Husband could maintain the status quo. But what if he won't be competent to execute a will in two or three years? Does it make sense to anticipate long-term estate planning issues now? Unless he is willing to assume the risk, he needs to incorporate long-term planning considerations into the current will. This means addressing what happens if he is alive when the new increased exclusions apply and when the modified carryover basis rules come into effect.

When the exclusion goes from $1 million to $1.5 million and Wife #2's property remains at $1 million, husband will have the opportunity to gift $500,000 to Wife #2 in a lifetime QTIP to enable her to take advantage of the increased exclusion. This creates a problem, however. If Wife #2 dies before her husband, and the modified basis carryover rules are in effect, the $3 million basis increase won't be available if the assets of the QTIP come back to husband for his lifetime (e.g., through a bypass and/or QTIP trust for his benefit formed under the inter vivos QTIP set up for Wife #2). The only way to qualify would be to have a power of appointment or invasion power to remove the assets from the inter vivos QTIP.

When the estate tax exclusion increases to $2 million, the GST exemption is set to increase as well. This raises the question as to whether taxpayer really wants to leave all of his property outright to his children instead of in trust for his grandchildren. The GST exemption is scheduled to increase to $3.5 million in 2009. He should reevaluate the plan and dispositive scheme in light of a consideration of dynasty trusts and other planning techniques (see Chapter 6).

restructuring assets to create minority, noncontrol positions that can qualify for discounts for estate tax purposes. The time period for a GRAT or the time for which a sale to defective grantor trust transaction should be allowed to continue can be shortened to reflect the facts at hand. If the anticipated time frame is short relative to the taxpayer's life expectancy (but is more than one year), a self-canceling installment note transaction may be preferred to a GRAT or other transaction that the taxpayer won't survive long enough to effect (see Chapter 6 for detailed discussion of GRATs).

HIGH-NET-WORTH TAXPAYERS WHO ARE NOT ELDERLY OR INFIRM

High-net-worth taxpayers who are not reasonably worried about their immediate demise might feel they should wait out the potential repeal of the estate taxes. There are several problems with this approach. If the tax is not repealed, substantial time will have been lost that could have generated considerable estate tax savings had planning been pursued. There is no assurance that a revenue-hungry future Congress won't repeal estate tax planning benefits and create a more costly situation. The mere repeal of the discounts on family-limited partnerships and family-limited liability companies could add a substantial amount to the estate tax bills of many wealthy families. Another fallacy is that estate tax planning can be addressed in the future. Even the best planners cannot be certain of the date of their death. Try calling the psychic hotline. Will they live long enough after future estate tax changes to complete the planning that is being put off today?

A dilemma with planning for many estates is to determine how complex a will and other documents should be made to address the possibility of repeal or no repeal of estate tax, and the possibility of the modified carryover basis rules actually coming into play. If, as an estate planner, you knew with certainty, you could draft documents accordingly. Not only can't you know when the documents will be used, but it is impossible to know if the client will be competent after

> future changes to sign new documents. The question is then, can people really afford the risk of taking no action now or signing a simplistic will if they might not be able to sign a new will in the future when the state of the tax laws is more certain?

Gift programs should be pursued. A major advantage of gift programs is the removal of future appreciation from the estate. This benefit remains, and high-net-worth taxpayers should carefully consider this even in light of the proposed increase in the exclusion. What will appreciating assets be worth relative to the exclusion in the year of death?

For high-net-worth but young taxpayers, a domestic asset protection dynasty trust of which they remain a beneficiary is potentially an ideal planning tool. If the estate tax is not repealed, they will have secured discounts and locked in estate planning benefits and removed appreciation from their estate. If the tax is repealed, they have not lost, because they can still benefit from the assets that they have transferred, and they have realized asset protection, asset management, and other objectives. Taxpayers can remain a discretionary beneficiary of an Alaska or Delaware trust, yet have the assets removed from their estate. All the growth in the assets transferred to the trust after the date of the transfer will be removed from the taxable estate.

 Considerable risks still are associated with these trusts as they have not been fully proven in court cases since their relatively recent development.

ELDERLY WIDOWS AND WIDOWERS

The increased exclusion may solve the tax problem of many widows and widowers. A common problem with the estate tax system has always been the complexity that ensnared unsuspecting couples in a tax that really shouldn't have applied to them. A typical scenario of many estates that paid tax was the following. One spouse would die. Their simple two-page will would bequeath everything to the surviving spouse (referred to as an "I love you will"). Simple inflation often pushed the surviving spouse's estate into a taxable position. Often a house purchased decades earlier for a modest amount increased so substantially in value that the unsuspecting widow never imagined she was wealthy and could be subject to an estate tax. On her death, a tax of several hundred thousand dollars was due. It is estimated that the increase in the exclusion from $675,000 to $1 million alone will remove 40 percent from the system of the estates that would have filed estate tax returns. This change, which will be further enhanced as the credit increases, will solve the estate tax problems for many widows and widowers.

 If the estate is close to the exclusion amount, don't risk having inflation push it above the filing and tax paying threshold of the exclusion. Often a basic gift program or a QPRT (see Chapter 6) for the family home can suffice to secure the estate.

UNMARRIED, GAY, AND LESBIAN COUPLES

The increase in the exclusion will help nonmarried couples transfer greater amounts of assets to their partner and help many such couples avoid the tax. The estate tax system, however, continues, and in many ways enhances, the bias against nontraditional couples. The unlimited marital deduction available to traditional families is still not available. This means that the amount that can be transferred to a partner free of estate tax will be limited by the amount of the exclusion.

Further, under the modified carryover basis system scheduled to become law in 2010, the bias against gay, lesbian, and other nonmarried couples is increased. This is not exactly reflective of the growing diversity of American society. The basis adjustment of $3 million that will effectively eliminate the capital gains tax any heirs will pay, other than the wealthiest sliver of society, won't be available to nonmarried couples. The special exception for deathbed transfers (gifts within three years of death) that is available to married couples enabling them to more easily plan for the new modified carryover basis rules, is not available to nonmarried couples. (For an explanation of these rules, see Chapter 6.)

The unlimited gift tax marital deduction that enables married couples to transfer assets freely between them is not available to nonmarried couples. This will make it more difficult for nonmarried couples to restructure assets to equalize their estates, give assets to each other for nontax reasons, and so forth.

EXAMPLE

A taxpayer is a physician and his partner is a college professor. The physician is extremely concerned about malpractice exposure. His estate is substantial. His lawyer advises him as to the benefits of using a limited liability company (LLC) to own assets, transferring the physician's house to his partner, and taking other steps to protect assets from potential claimants. The physician will be limited in the transfers that he can make as a result of the gift tax exclusion. A qualified personal residence trust can leverage the gift of the house to use up less exclusion.

A grantor-retained interest trust (GRIT), which is similar to a grantor-retained annuity trust (GRAT), can leverage gifts of a limited liability company. Don't be mislead by the increase in the exclusion available to estates. The gift tax exclusion remains at $1 million. In the example above, if the physician transfers more to his partner, a substantial tax will be due.

FOREIGN TAXPAYERS

The 2001 tax law includes many provisions creating additional traps and costs for noncitizens, such as the continuation of the qualified domestic trust (QDOT) tax and other technical changes. Foreign taxpayers also should consider the impact of their country's laws and treaties.

TAXPAYERS MAKING CHARITABLE CONTRIBUTIONS

The 2001 Tax Act through the decrease in income tax rates, the increase in the estate tax exclusion, and other changes significantly reduces the tax incentives for the wealthy to give to charity. For many, the nontax reasons of contributing back to society—such as helping those in need and encouraging children and others, by example, to be philanthropic—will become in effect the only reasons to make charitable contributions. And, for many, this won't be sufficient enticement.

Charitable remainder trusts (CRTs) will remain a valuable planning technique and will perhaps be more commonly used if the estate tax is repealed and the basis step-up with it. This is because the CRT has primarily been used as a tool to minimize capital gains, not save estate taxes. Insurance funding to replace the assets given to the CRT, which was a common technique under prior law, will remain popular (see discussion in Chapter 6).

Charitable lead trusts (CLTs) are likely to be used less since a primary purpose was to minimize estate and gift taxes on large transfers. However, inter-vivos CLTs to reduce gift tax on large gifts (since the gift tax has not been repealed), testamentary CLTs to reduce estate tax in the event of death when the estate is larger than the exclusion, or CLTs to defer heirs' receipt of assets while teaching the values of charitable giving, remain relevant (see Chapter 6).

As discussed in Chapter 1, conservation easement donations have been enhanced.

TAXPAYERS CONCERNED ABOUT MEDICAL CARE COSTS

Taxpayers who want to remove assets from their estate may have more flexibility in doing so in light of the increase in the exclusion to $1 million in 2002. There have always been many taxpayers who might be labeled as rich by virtue of the estate tax to which they may be subject, but who can be quickly made poor by the burden of costly nursing home and related care needed by a family member with Alzheimer's disease or other illnesses. These taxpayers could be caught in the bind of wanting to protect assets from medical care costs (a major focus within the specialty of elder law planning) while at the same time having to deal with potential estate tax costs. For these taxpayers, the increase in the exclusion will make it easier to gift away assets to protect them from medical and nursing home costs without incurring a gift tax cost.

LOW-NET-WORTH TAXPAYERS

Why would a book about estate planning mention low-net-worth taxpayers, who will probably never pay an estate tax? Because the 2001 Tax Act has made changes that adversely affect a much larger portion of society than the tiny group that will benefit from the substantial tax breaks enacted, and few lawmakers seem to have considered the larger consequences. The real issue is how these changes will impact the fabric of society over coming decades.

The estate tax changes, if they remain permanent, can be expected to result in much greater concentrations of wealth in the richest segment of society. The reduction of income tax rates serves to enhance the earnings of the wealthiest as well. A $300 rebate check for a typical worker pales beside the tax benefit of a moderate drop in income tax rates for someone earning seven figures. Furthermore, the repeal of the state death tax credit may force many states to find other sources of revenue. This will likely come, in many instances, as an increase in sales or other taxes that are regressive and fall disproportionately on the poor. Likewise, the reduction in charitable giving caused by the estate tax changes will affect the charities that assist those of lower economic means. Is this really what the taxpayers want for their grandchildren?

5
PLANNING FOR DIFFERENT TYPES OF ASSETS

The 2001 Tax Act is a complex web of tax changes. The estate tax rate is reduced and the exclusion amount for estate tax purposes increased. Eventually, the estate tax is eliminated entirely, but only for one year and then it's back (just as in that famous horror movie, *Poltergeist*, "I'm back!"). This book presents planning from different perspectives to help estate planners identify the best options for various circumstances. Chapter 4 identified common taxpayer profiles and highlighted planning techniques appropriate for each. This chapter examines planning techniques for specific types of assets. Later chapters describe overall planning techniques. Reviewing all of these different perspectives will give readers a better understanding of planning post-2001 Tax Act.

ASSETS LIKELY TO APPRECIATE SUBSTANTIALLY

If an asset is likely to have substantial appreciation in a short time, planners should use techniques such as a grantor retained annuity trust (GRAT), a sale to a defective grantor trust (IDIT), an outright gift, discounts, and perhaps gifts to a dynasty trust to remove that asset (or at least a significant portion of it) from the taxpayer's estate. This planning can safeguard a significant value outside the estate in the event the estate tax is never eliminated. These same techniques will help protect the value transferred from ever reaching creditors and claimants. Pursuing such planning is important because

---
EXAMPLE

Taxpayer holds stock in a closely held business that he confidently believes will soon have a new and significant patent that could generate tremendous growth. He anticipates a real home run with this holding. Since the patent has not yet been applied for, considerable risks remain, and a business and patent appraiser might not value the interests in the business at much. This may be an opportunity to gift a portion or all of the equity in the business outside the estate at a nominal value. If taxpayer waits until the next year for the patent to be proven, the equity in the business might be so valuable that a substantial estate or gift tax would be incurred to consummate a transfer.

Why should he take a risk in not planning? It would be wiser to make the gift before the appreciation becomes so likely that an appraiser would value it at a high amount. If taxpayer is worried about losing access to the assets, the transfer could be made to a domestic asset protection trust of which he remains a beneficiary.

---

a tremendous opportunity may be forever lost if not acted on before the asset increases in value.

ASSETS THAT HAVE DECLINED SUBSTANTIALLY IN VALUE

Taxpayers who own stock that has declined in value should check with their accountant about selling the losers and realizing the losses. They should try to time the losses with gains and income for maximum advantage. It generally won't pay to contribute losing investments to charity.

 Once the new modified carryover basis rules come into play in 2010, there might be an incentive for taxpayers to sell the losers on their deathbed and obtain a tax deduction on their final returns. This is because carrying over a low basis for an asset, such as a stock that declined, won't provide the taxpayer's heirs any tax benefit. However, selling losers and triggering a loss on the soon-to-be decedent's income tax return may provide an income tax benefit.

MARKETABLE SECURITIES

Securities can be used to fund annual gifts using the annual gift tax exclusion with little extra effort. Several techniques are available for highly appreciated securities. To increase cash flow from those securities while the taxpayer is alive, a charitable remainder trust (CRT) could be a valuable technique. The securities can be gifted to a charity that can then sell them without reporting any taxable income. The charity could diversify the holdings and pay the donor an annuity for life.

 As income tax rates are lowered, taxpayers can enhance their benefits by structuring the charitable contribution deduction from a CRT in tax years when rates are higher and plan to receive annuity or unitrust payments in later years when tax rates are lower. See Chapter 6.

An alternative would be to contribute the securities to an exchange fund, a type of managed fund structured to achieve diversification free of income tax. If the estate is large, the exchange fund might also convert a full marketable security into a nonmarketable limited partnership interest that would be ideal for gifts at discounts to remove the future appreciation from the estate.

For clients who want to benefit school-age heirs by means of a securities portfolio, the newly enhanced Code Section 529 college savings plans is something to consider for appropriate heirs.

NOTE

For gains on capital assets purchased after the year 2000 and held for more than five years before sale or exchange by taxpayers in the lowest tax bracket the maximum capital gains rate is 8%. If a taxpayer has such investments and gifts them to an heir, the proceeds may qualify for taxation at this very low 8% rate.

REAL ESTATE INVESTMENTS

Real estate always has a significant liability exposure. To protect an estate (i.e., the assets other than those of a particular real estate property), real estate attorneys should review transferring the taxpayer's real estate to separate limited liability companies for each property. This technique can prevent a domino effect in the event of a lawsuit or claim originating from one property. For estate tax purposes, multiple entities can facilitate a gift program, the securing of discounts for lack of marketability and control, and the avoidance of ancillary probate. Given the uncertainty of estate tax repeal, these holding entities can then be used to fund grantor retained-annuity trusts, sales to defective grantor trusts, self-canceling installment note sales, outright gifts, and other techniques to minimize potential estate taxes. Even after the repeal of the estate tax (if it really becomes effective), this type of planning will facilitate the making of gifts qualifying for the annual gift tax exclusion to avoid using any of a taxpayer's $1 million applicable exclusion. If the applicable exclusion, or some part of it, is used, these techniques can help leverage the use of the gift tax exclusion for maximum benefit.

Succession planning issues may have to be addressed, especially if the real estate will require active management that should be handled by the family and not outside management companies. These might include buy-sell provisions and restrictions on transfer. As the applicable exclusion increases so that fewer taxpayers' real estate holdings will be subject to estate tax, the planning will be easier to address.

As long as an estate tax remains in force, planning an estate with significant real estate holdings will include planning to qualify for the estate tax deferral provisions of Code Section 6166, if the real estate meets the requirements of an active business. The special use valuation provisions of Code Section 2032A are discussed in Chapter 1.

Because real estate investments, unlike marketable securities, are difficult to value, taxpayers have long sought lower values to reduce gift and estate taxes, and they will continue to do so as long as an estate and gift tax remains, with one exception. As the exclusion amount increases, fewer estates are going to be subject to estate tax.

The incentive for estates not subject to tax might change with the changes enacted by the 2001 Tax Act in that many taxpayers will have an incentive to value assets at the highest, not the lowest, value. There will be no estate tax cost for many in doing so and the benefit will be a higher tax basis to minimize future capital gains costs.

 Be certain that the partnership (for a limited partnership owning the real estate) or an operating agreement (for a limited liability company owning the real estate) has a provision ensuring that heirs can take advantage of the IRC § 754 election to adjust the inside basis in the assets. If not, the step-up in tax basis to fair value on the taxpayer's death will not enable heirs to avoid later capital gains or obtain greater depreciation deductions. This will be just as important for the vast majority of estates following 2010 and the imposition of the modified carryover basis rules. Without the appropriate clause being included in a partnership or operating agreement, the $1.3 million/ $3 million spousal basis adjustments may not help heirs (see Chapter 6).

CLOSELY HELD BUSINESS INTERESTS

The interests of closely held business owners and farmers led the battle cry for the reform, if not repeal, of the death tax. As a result, these taxpayers stand to benefit handsomely from the estate tax changes, or so it would appear. The increase in the exclusion creates substantial benefits for closely held business owners by reducing the estate tax on such businesses. The liberalization of the estate tax deferral technique under Code Section 6166 mitigates the problems caused by an estate tax on estates larger than the exclusion. Although the qualified family owned business interest (QFOBI) deduction is being phased out, the increase in the exclusion should mitigate the loss of this benefit for the few estates affected.

All is not roses, however. Many, if not most, closely held business owners seek to transfer interests in their businesses to heirs during their lifetime to encourage participation in the business, to develop loyalty, and to test a succession plan. The 2001 Tax Act, as explained in Chapter 1, leaves a gift tax in full force. This will be so even after the repeal of the estate tax. Thus, closely held business owners may, for the foreseeable future, have to use techniques like grantor-retained annuity trusts, sales to defective grantor trusts, and discounts to shift assets to their heirs. A tremendous planning alternative, as discussed in Chapter 6, is to fund perpetual or dynasty trusts, especially at death. Assets held in properly drafted irrevocable trusts forever may be passed to future generations and circumvent the tough gift tax laws.

PERSONAL RESIDENCE

As long as an estate tax exists, qualified personal residence trusts (QPRTs) will remain a tremendously beneficial estate tax minimization tool (see Chapter 6). Even as the increase in the exclusion makes the estate tax applicable to fewer and fewer taxpayers, the QPRT may remain a viable planning tool for special circumstances.

EXAMPLE

A large and unique farm/vacation property has belonged to the family of taxpayer for several generations. He wants to ensure that it will be passed on to the next generation. If the estate will be subject to the estate tax, a QPRT can be a valuable technique to minimize the estate tax attributable to the value of this asset. Apart from the estate tax benefits, a QPRT can avoid ancillary probate if the farm/vacation home is in a state other than where taxpayer resides: it can avoid probate in the state of residence, it can ensure that the home will be passed on while taxpayer is alive, and it might minimize the possibility of a successful will challenge (this assumes the transfer is being made while taxpayer is alive and before aging raises questions about his competency to make a large gift).

The liberalization of the home sale exclusion rules will present new planning issues if the world of modified carryover basis ever comes into being. This type of planning and the relationship to the $1.3 million/$3 million spousal basis step-up are discussed in Chapter 7.

VACATION HOME

As noted in the preceding section, to keep a vacation property in the family, a qualified personal residence trust (QPRT) to transfer the house to the taxpayer's children or other heirs at some future date— even if the increased exclusion at some point might obviate the need for estate tax planning—may still be appropriate.

If the vacation home is in a state other than the state in which the taxpayer resides, ancillary probate (a second probate proceeding in that other state) may be necessary. As a result of the repeal of the state death tax credit, the 2001 Tax Act might affect the taxation of that vacation home. The repeal of the credit will reduce state revenues from the sharing of the federal estate tax collections. States will have to recoup that lost revenue and may do so via an increased state inheritance or estate tax, or perhaps through increasing other fees. There may not be much anyone can do to avoid these costs, but the same techniques used to avoid ancillary probate (e.g., having a revocable living trust own the property) might help. Estate planners should check with a tax adviser in the state where the vacation property is located as the laws develop.

LIFE INSURANCE

Life insurance is a key asset in many estates. There are two bottom line points on life insurance planning post-2001 Tax Act. First, if the taxpayer has and will retain any significant insurance, it should be owned by an irrevocable life insurance trust unless the estate planner confirms another option is satisfactory. A trust is not necessary if the following conditions are present: the taxpayer is not concerned about the surviving spouse's use and investment of the money or about creditors, claimants, or future spouses affecting the assets; and the aggregate estate inclusive of insurance is sufficiently less than the increased exclusion, so that it will never trigger an estate tax. However, even if all these conditions exist, if there is a significant death benefit, or likely future cash value, the protection a trust offers is likely to be worthwhile.

Second, if there is existing insurance, the insured should think very carefully before terminating it, given the reinstatement of the estate tax in 2011.

 Taxpayers cannot be sure that they will live until the estate tax is repealed (or at least until the exclusion exceeds the size of their estate). Health concerns might make it impossible to obtain coverage that might be needed in the future. So consider steps now that will secure coverage.

Encourage clients who have inadequate insurance coverage for current and future needs (in 2011 when the estate tax is back) to consider securing more insurance. Depending on their need for asset protection and so forth, they might purchase a permanent policy now, or instead use a combination of permanent and term insurance along with guaranteed insurability riders (a feature that enables the insured to obtain additional insurance coverage in the future without a medical exam; see Chapter 6).

NEED FOR CAREFUL REVIEW OF ASSETS

The 2001 Tax Act is going to affect estate planning for specific types of assets in many ways. The breadth of the changes requires careful consideration of the effect on any significant assets. The analysis should include the interplay of the estate tax changes, the possibility of the repeal or reinstatement of the estate tax, the possibility of modified carryover basis rules, and the income tax rules.

6

RECONSIDERATION OF TRUSTS AND OTHER PLANNING VEHICLES

The 2001 Tax Act has a significant impact on virtually every estate planning technique. Any generalizations are subject to the facts of the specific situation and when and how the estate planner used or plans to use the particular technique. The passage of this sweeping tax act and the uncertainty of future changes require that advisers reassess what, if anything, to do with planning techniques already in place (in many instances, little can be done since the techniques are often irrevocable once set into motion). In other instances, the flexibility built into the options of the trust or other planning documents might provide an opportunity to unwind or modify the existing planning techniques. If the planning has not yet been implemented (e.g., in the case of a trust under the will of a person still alive), how should the documents be revised or should they be revised at all? This chapter reviews these issues for many common planning techniques and also provides brief background information for each technique.

TERMINATING AN EXISTING TRUST BECAUSE OF 2001 TAX ACT CHANGES

If the trust involved is revocable, then there will generally be no problem terminating it. Unfortunately, most trusts, such as insurance trusts, children trusts, and indeed most tax minimization-oriented trusts, are irrevocable. The real issue arises with respect to

SAMPLE LANGUAGE

The Grantor has been advised with respect to the difference between revocable and irrevocable trusts and hereby declares that any trust formed under this Trust Agreement, and the Trust Estate created hereby, are to be irrevocable. The Grantor has no power to alter, amend, revoke, or terminate any Trust provision or interest, whether under this Trust Agreement, or any rule of law.

irrevocable trusts, which generally, under the terms of the trust (as the sample language above illustrates), cannot be changed after being formed.

Nevertheless, there are several ways to eliminate a trust after the 2001 tax law:

- *Stop additional gifts to the undesirable trust.* If the trust is an insurance trust, it might be possible to stop making additional gifts, convert the policy into a paid up policy (or have the different options available under the policy used to eliminate or minimize payment for a few years while congressional intent becomes clearer), and effectively freeze the policy as is. This approach may not be as desirable as a complete termination, but it may come close to meeting the taxpayer's needs. Many trusts, such as children and grandchildren trusts, are set up to receive annual gift exclusions of $10,000 from the primary donor, and perhaps from other donors as well. Stop making any additional gifts and form a new trust with provisions reflecting more flexible options to deal with law changes. Freezing the current balance of an existing trust will mitigate the concerns about it.

- *Change revocable documents to eliminate pourover provisions.* Revise wills and other revocable documents that would otherwise pour over additional assets into an undesirable irrevocable trust. This is yet another way to minimize the assets of that trust. Since the taxpayer can't really change the trust, he minimizes what gets paid to it.

- *Maximize discretionary distributions.* Another approach may be to increase distributions. If a trust has a broad distribution standard that permits the trustees to distribute assets to different beneficiaries, especially if the distributions can be made without any significant restriction (e.g., for the "comfort and welfare" of the beneficiaries), then simply liberally applying the distribution standards may, over a period of time, reduce, if not eliminate, the trust assets until the trust document becomes irrelevant since it will not affect any assets.

- *Terminate the trust based on trust language permitting termination.* As noted above, whether it is possible to terminate the trust will depend on the language in the trust. If the will or trust agreement that established a bypass trust, for example, provided for its termination in the discretion of the trustee or included language to permit a trust to be terminated, perhaps the trust can be terminated. For example, some trusts include language permitting a trustee or trust protector to terminate the trust and distribute assets to current beneficiaries if the trust purpose is no longer relevant or if the trust becomes uneconomical to operate.

- *Seek court approval to terminate the trust.* It might take a court action in which the trustees and beneficiaries all petition the court to permit the termination of the trust on the basis that the purpose for which the decedent established the trust is no longer served. This argument may not be an easy sell given the nontax benefits of so many irrevocable trusts. It might be difficult to convince a court to terminate the trust if minor children are future beneficiaries. Also, if the trust agreement included a spendthrift clause, a court might be hesitant to terminate the trust on the basis of a change in the estate tax laws alone.

   Spendthrift language similar to the following sample can prevent beneficiaries from alienating trust assets and thus can protect the trust estate. A court might well find that such protection was an integral purpose in creating the trust and that such purpose is not affected by changes in the tax laws. That would not be an unreasonable finding. Termination or acceleration of a trust will not be ordered where the donor's general plan of disposing of the assets will be defeated.

——————————————— **SAMPLE LANGUAGE** ———————————————

Spendthrift Clause

Except as may be otherwise provided in this Trust Agreement, no transfer disposition, charge, or encumbrance on the income or principal of any trust created under this Trust Agreement by any beneficiary by way of anticipation shall be valid or in any way binding upon the Trustees. The right of any beneficiary to any payment of income or principal is subject to any charge or deduction which the Trustees make against it under the authority granted to them by any statute, law, or by any provision of this Trust Agreement. No beneficiary shall have the right to transfer, dispose of, assign, or encumber such income or principal until the assets shall be paid to that beneficiary by the Trustees. No income or principal shall be liable to any claim of any creditor of any such beneficiary.

- *Have the trustee terminate the trust.* The role and obligations of the trustee could conflict with the beneficiaries' desires to terminate the trust. The trustee has a generic duty to administer a trust by doing what is necessary for the good of the trust and those interested in it. The general duty to administer is the source of other trustee duties, including the duties of loyalty and impartiality. The general duty to administer could conflict with the request for a termination or an acceleration of the trust since the termination or acceleration eliminates the need to administer. If the purpose of administration is found not to be of continued relevance, the duty to administer should not then matter. The key issue is how a court reading the trust would interpret the language.

NOTE

An argument to be stressed to a court in such a situation is that but for the estate tax the trust would not have been formed or funded. This might be an easier argument to demonstrate if the trust was formed based on a tax formula (e.g., a bypass trust). It might be easiest with a trust, such as a grantor-retained annuity trust, that is typically a pure tax-oriented transaction. It might be harder to demonstrate such a point for an inter vivos trust formed to hold insurance. In all cases, however, a consideration of all the other facts and circumstances and terms of the trust will be essential.

- *Beneficiaries may be able to consent to the trust's termination.* Consent of all beneficiaries (assuming they are adults—*sui juris*), if no material trust purpose is defeated by the trust's termination, may be another approach. State law might provide some flexibility in this regard. If state law permits, the beneficiaries of a trust may all agree to terminate a trust even if it is irrevocable. Typical rules may require that all the beneficiaries be adults and that they unanimously agree in writing to terminate the trust. If the trust provides that minor children of the adult beneficiaries may also be beneficiaries of the trust, it may still be possible to terminate the trust if either the trust agreement or state law provides for virtual representation. This legal concept may enable an adult beneficiary to sign off for and bind a minor claiming under him (e.g., if the beneficiary dies, his children claim his share).

BYPASS (CREDIT SHELTER) TRUSTS

The bypass (credit shelter) trust has been a basic building block of most estate plans. It will remain so after the 2001 Tax Act. However, the decisions that must be made, the options of how to fund the bypass trust, the manner in which it will be structured, and how it will be used (e.g., who will be the trustees and what distribution standards will be provided for) all become far more complex under the 2001 Tax Act.

The classic zero estate tax plan for the first death has been to establish a bypass trust to safeguard the amount that can be transferred free of estate tax, the exclusion. The general concept is that assets on the first death should be segregated in a trust to avoid inclusion in the surviving spouse's estate. Failing to do this (e.g., by instead bequeathing assets outright to the surviving spouse) would result in doubling up assets in the survivor's estate and eventually triggering a larger, and avoidable, estate tax. This trust is referred to as a bypass trust because the assets in it (no matter how much they appreciate) are sheltered from estate tax in the surviving spouse's estate—they bypass the survivor's estate. The assets bequeathed to the bypass trust then grow outside the taxable estate of the surviving spouse, yet remain reasonably accessible to the surviving spouse to protect him or her economically. As noted, this type of planning will remain the cornerstone of many estate plans.

The question is, what approach should be used to take advantage of this benefit? The 2001 Tax Act increases the exclusion amount so substantially, and there is the possibility of the tax being repealed; how does this change basic planning?

Planning after the 2001 Tax Act

The maximum amount that could have been transferred, in general terms, to a bypass trust under prior law (year 2001) was $675,000. This was the amount that could be bequeathed free of estate (or gift) tax. Under the 2001 Tax Act, the amount was increased to $1 million in 2002, and eventually up to $3.5 million in 2009, prior to the scheduled repeal of the estate tax. The increases in the exclusion are scheduled to come in phases (see Exhibit 1.1 in Chapter 1).

NOTE

A key planning issue when addressing the scheduled increases in the exclusion is how the will, revocable living trust, and other documents are drafted, and how the assets are owned (whether in the taxpayer's name, joint with a spouse, and so forth).

The increases are so substantial that many taxpayers will fall outside the transfer tax system. But will the increases all occur, or will a future Congress freeze or roll them back? What will be the inflation-adjusted value of the later, larger exclusions? Will taxpayers, thinking they never will have an estate tax, be willing to engage in similar planning to obtain the nontax benefits of a trust: asset protection, control on disposition, professional management, and so forth? The planning is more complicated and hence more expensive because the options and what-ifs have increased.

The current estate tax regime, which may continue in some format until the year 2009, presents a problem similar to that of the prior estate tax laws predating the 2001 Tax Act: When all assets are bequeathed outright to the surviving spouse, those assets might be taxable in the surviving spouse's estate if, on the surviving spouse's death, the tax either has not been fully repealed or the estate exceeds the exemption amount applicable in that year. Many taxpayers may be lulled into taking no action because of the significant increases in the exclusion amount or because of a misconception that the tax has already been fully repealed.

Also keep in mind that the tax savings is only one of myriad reasons to use trusts, including a bypass trust, in estate planning. The planning that could provide a potential tax savings can be worthwhile for the nontax benefits even if the tax savings are never realized because the phaseout and ultimate repeal are allowed to occur.

Ways to Fund a Bypass Trust

For a married couple, the first step of any estate tax plan is to plan to preserve through a bypass trust some portion or all of the exclusion available on the death of the first spouse. The following subsections describe various approaches as an estate planner might present them when discussing these options.

Disclaimer Bypass Trust

Instead of requiring that a specified amount of assets be transferred to a bypass trust on your death, you might not even want to have a bypass trust if the exclusion is large enough. The paperwork (e.g., annual trust income tax returns after the credit shelter trust is funded following your death) might not seem worth it. Alternatively, you might debate having all assets over the credit shelter amount given outright to your surviving spouse versus holding them in trust to protect them from her new spouse. There is an option. Instead of your will or trust forcing the funding of the credit shelter trust, you can have the document give the assets outright to your surviving spouse. If she disclaims them (files required papers in the surrogate's court within nine months of your death declining to accept the assets), your will can then provide that these assets must be transferred to the bypass trust. This mechanism gives your surviving spouse nine months after your death to determine which approach to use.

The uncertainty of the increase in the exclusion (how high will it go before another Congress acts to change it) and the uncertainty of how large your estate will be before you die make the disclaimer approach the most flexible method of addressing how much value should be distributed to the bypass trust. It effectively gives your surviving spouse the ability to complete estate planning up to nine months following your death.

While this might sound ideal, and many estate planners are advocating this approach, consider the issues and requirements raised by the use of disclaimers. The following illustrative language from a disclaimer document indicates some of the technical requirements and issues.

SAMPLE LANGUAGE

Disclaimer Document

The undersigned, surviving spouse, domiciled at 123 Main Street, Any Town, USA, pursuant to Section * of the State Name Statutes Annotated, irrevocably and without qualification does hereby forever irrevocably and for no consideration renounce, disclaim, relinquish, surrender and release, any rights, titles and interests in and to the shares of *Fund-name equal to $*Dollars.

The undersigned has not: (i) accepted or exercised any control as beneficial owner over any of the property disclaimed hereunder; (ii) voluntarily transferred, encumbered, or contracted to transfer any interest in the property disclaimed hereunder; (iii) executed

> this disclaimer in an attempt to defraud any creditors; (iv) made any direction as to how the property subject to this disclaimer shall pass; (v) received, and is not to receive, any consideration in money or money's worth for this renunciation/disclaimer from any person or persons whose interest is to be accelerated or increased, or from any other person or persons.
>
> This disclaimer is executed and filed with the Trustees of the Trust within the required Nine (9) month time period required under Internal Revenue Code Section 2518.

The reality is that it is not always easy to meet all the technical requirements of a qualified disclaimer.

Another key issue that has been the undoing of many a disclaimer estate plan is the emotional trauma. If your life partner of twenty, thirty, forty, or more years has just lost you, will she have the confidence and comfort to give up any control, even for tax savings, over what might be a significant portion of your assets? Many surviving spouses, no matter how much their accountants and attorneys encourage them, simply won't disclaim assets.

Disclaimers can raise an important personal issue. If the surviving spouse disclaims the determination of who will eventually receive assets, that surviving spouse will be governed by the terms of the will of the first spouse to die. If the surviving spouse is not in full agreement with the selection of beneficiaries or trustees, she will not disclaim. Instead she can take an outright distribution of assets and then bequeath them to whomever she wants.

The result is that a disclaimer approach might be the ideal theoretical technique to address the additional uncertainty the 2001 Tax Act has created. However, it may not be the most practical or effective technique.

Minimum/ Maximum Bypass Amount

Another approach is to set a minimum and maximum amount to fund a bypass trust. This approach would ensure (assuming the title to your assets is structured properly so that, whichever spouse dies first, there will be sufficient assets to fund the trust) some minimum amount is being protected by the trust, but would avoid having too large a portion of the estate transferred into trust.

A minimum/maximum bypass trust could be funded in your will or revocable living trust by stating a minimum figure that must be transferred to the trust, no matter the circumstances, but limiting the maximum amount that can be funded. The maximum could be drafted as a specified amount, say $800,000. However, if the maximum funding amount specified is more than the exclusion might be in some years, you will have to limit it to the lesser of the maximum or the exclusion, to avoid unintentionally triggering a tax (see the example below). This two-tier maximum, although a bit more complex, is essential given the uncertainties of the size of your estate, the changes in the exclusion, the year of your death, and what Congress may do in the future.

EXAMPLE

Assume you are married and your combined estate is $4 million, which you divide equally between you and your spouse. You decide that the maximum amount that should be distributed to a bypass trust is $1.5 million so that your survivor will have at least $2.5 million under complete control. If you drafted a provision stating that the bypass trust could be funded up to $1.5 million but you died in 2002 or 2003 when the maximum exclusion was only $1 million, you would trigger an estate tax.

Following is possible sample language for a minimum/maximum bypass trust for a surviving spouse, but many variations on the minimum/maximum approach could be used. For example, you could fund the minimum or a specified dollar maximum limited to, say, a percentage of your estate.

─────────── **SAMPLE LANGUAGE** ───────────

Minimum/Maximum Bypass Trust for Surviving Spouse

I give, devise, and bequeath the greater of:

- Four Hundred Thousand Dollars ($400,000.00) [minimum amount] to my Trustee, in trust, in accordance with the provision below "Disclaimer Bypass Trust," if my spouse should survive me for 180 days.

- The smaller of: (i) The pecuniary sum equal to the largest amount which will not result in any federal estate tax payable after giving effect to the exclusion amount, to which I am entitled, as well as any other credits applicable to my estate; or (ii) One Million Five Hundred Thousand Dollars ($1,500,000.00).

The trust formed, if any, under this provision, shall be known as the "Bypass Trust under *Your Name Will" [*remaining trust provisions not illustrated*].

I give, devise, and bequeath my residuary estate to my spouse, if my spouse should survive me for 180 days.

Hybrid or Two-Tier Disclaimer Bypass Trust

Another approach is to ensure that some minimum amount be mandatorily contributed to the bypass trust, while preserving flexibility to determine how much more than the minimum should be contributed. The remaining assets can then be bequeathed outright to your surviving spouse. She can then have up to nine months following your death to determine if any additional assets, based on her feelings, the size of the estate, the estate tax outlook, and other relevant factors, should be disclaimed to go into that trust. Even if your surviving spouse takes no action, some significant amount of assets will be distributed to that trust. Sample language for such a trust follows.

SAMPLE LANGUAGE

Two-Tier Disclaimer Bypass Trust

Minimum Bequest Disclaimer Bypass Trust for Surviving Spouse

- I give, devise, and bequeath Four Hundred Thousand Dollars ($400,000.00) to my Trustee, in trust, in accordance with the provision below "Disclaimer Bypass Trust," if my spouse should survive me for 180 days.

I give, devise, and bequeath my residuary estate to my spouse, if my spouse should survive me for 180 days. If my spouse shall disclaim and renounce any portion or all of this bequest, then such disclaimed and renounced portion, but not in excess of the amount specified in the following provision, I give, devise, and bequeath to the Bypass Trust provided in the following provision.

Disclaimer Bypass Trust

If my spouse survives me, I give to my Trustee, in trust, the lesser of:

- The amount disclaimed in the preceding provision; or
- The pecuniary sum equal to the largest amount which will not result in any federal estate tax payable after giving effect to the exclusion amount, to which I am entitled, as well as any other credits applicable to my estate, reduced by the Four Hundred Thousand Dollars ($400,000.00) heretofore bequeathed to said Bypass Trust.

The trust formed, if any, under this provision, shall be known as the "Bypass Trust under *Your Name Will" [remaining trust provisions not illustrated].

Bypass Trust Limited to Percentage of Estate

A bypass trust can be provided for in your will, but you might choose to limit it to a percentage of the estate to avoid having too large an amount transferred to the bypass trust. The concept is that as the exclusion increases so dramatically, you may not want to have that large a value of assets held in trust.

SAMPLE LANGUAGE

Bypass Trust Limited to Percentage of Estate

I give and bequeath *Dollars ($*) [*this could be a fixed dollar amount or the maximum exclusion amount*] to the Trustee of my Bypass Trust, as set forth below. However, in no event shall this bequest exceed [*percentage limit*] of my "gross estate," as said term is defined for federal estate tax purposes. The figure for gross estate appearing on the federal estate tax return for my estate shall be determinative. My executor shall, so long as he has acted in good faith, not be required to adjust the figure used for "gross estate" from that reported on the originally filed estate tax return as a result of a tax audit or later amendment.

The sample clause presented here begins to hint at the potential complexity of using a percentage limitation. How should the percentage be determined? A percentage of what figure? What if there is a will contest or estate tax audit? How and when can the trust be funded if the gross estate cannot be finally determined until a lawsuit is settled? How can you ever complete the proper funding of the trust if there is an opportunity to increase or decrease the amount on which the percentage is based because a new asset is discovered, additional accounting fees are paid, or an IRS audit results in a change?

Although limiting the bypass trust under your will to a percentage of your estate has appeal as a commonsense way to limit the assets placed in trust, it presents some practical problems. Before opting for this approach, review these issues with your tax adviser.

Sprinkle Bypass Trust Options

Another approach is to focus not on the amount of assets being contributed to the bypass trust, but on your surviving spouse's access to the funds in the trust. Many people are concerned about having too many assets in the trust. Instead, put in the maximum allowed; just tinker with distribution, beneficiary, and other provisions to ensure the surviving spouse adequate comfort, no matter what portion of the family assets end up in the trust.

This alternative approach is to fund the bypass trust with the maximum amount permitted using a funding formula similar to what would have been used under prior law (this portion of your will might not even have to be changed). To mollify the worries about whether the surviving spouse will have adequate assets within her control, revisit

---

OLD SAMPLE LANGUAGE

Typical Sprinkle Bypass Trust (Under Prior Law)

The Trustee shall hold, manage, and invest the amounts held in this trust. The Trustee shall collect and receive any income and shall pay over or apply any portion or all of the net income or principal, or both, in equal or unequal amounts, at such times as the Trustee shall determine to or for the benefit of such one or more members of a class consisting of my spouse, my children, and other descendants (I recognize that if skip persons are named herein a GST tax may be due upon distribution to or for such persons) living from time to time (collectively, the "Recipients"), as the Trustee shall determine necessary or advisable for the health, support, and maintenance of the Recipients. Any net income not so paid over or applied for the benefit of the persons named in this provision, shall be accumulated and added to the principal of the Trust Estate, at least annually, and thereafter shall be held, administered, and disposed of as a part of the Trust Estate of this Bypass Trust.

NEW SAMPLE LANGUAGE

Sprinkle Bypass Trust with Greater Spousal Protection to Address Larger Amount of Funding

The Trustee shall hold, manage, and invest the amounts held in this trust. The Trustee shall collect and receive any income, and shall pay over or apply, not less frequently than quarterannually, not less than Eighty Percent (80%) of all net income of said trust to or for the benefit of my spouse.

The Trustee may pay over or apply any portion or all of the remaining Twenty Percent (20%) of the net income, or any portion of the principal after reasonable consideration to the future needs of my surviving spouse, in equal or unequal amounts, at such times as the Trustee shall determine to or for the benefit of such one or more members of a class consisting of my spouse, my children, and other descendants (I recognize that if skip persons are named herein a GST tax may be due upon distribution to or for such persons) living from time to time (collectively, the "Recipients"), as the Trustee shall determine necessary or advisable for the health, support, and maintenance of the Recipients.

Any net income not so paid over or applied for the benefit of the persons named in this provision shall be accumulated and added to the principal of the Trust Estate, at least annually, and thereafter shall be held, administered, and disposed of as a part of the Trust Estate of this Bypass Trust.

the terms of the bypass trust. Instead of having your surviving spouse and children all as beneficiaries, with the trustee having absolute discretion as to distributing income and principal between them, revise these provisions to give more comfort to your surviving spouse.

In lieu of directing a specific portion of annual income to your surviving spouse, you could simply state a preference so that your objective is clear.

The following sample language highlights how drafting a will to serve your personal and unique needs often now requires more tailoring and personalization than drafting a bypass trust under prior law. Given the many different variations and each person's unique mix of circumstances, relying on boilerplate (standard) approaches will rarely accomplish your goals.

—————— **ALTERNATIVE NEW SAMPLE LANGUAGE** ——————

Sprinkle Bypass Trust with Greater Spousal Protection to Address Larger Amount of Funding

The Trustee shall hold, manage, and invest the amounts held in this trust. The Trustee shall collect and receive any income, and shall pay over or apply, in the Trustee's discretion, any portion, all, or none of the net income of this trust, to or for the benefit of a class of beneficiaries consisting of my spouse and children then living ("Recipients"). However, my Trustee is directed to give primary consideration to my surviving spouse when making distributions hereunder, even if such consideration results in less or even no distributions to the other Recipients.

The Trustee may pay over or apply any portion or all of the remaining net income, or any portion of the principal after reasonable consideration to the future needs of my surviving spouse, in equal or unequal amounts, at such times as the Trustee shall determine to or for the benefit of such one or more members of a class consisting of my spouse, my children, and other descendants (I recognize that if skip persons are named herein a GST tax may be due upon distribution to or for such persons) living from time to time (collectively, the "Recipients"), as the Trustee shall determine necessary or advisable for the health, support, and maintenance of the Recipients.

Any net income not so paid over or applied for the benefit of the persons named in this provision shall be accumulated and added to the principal of the Trust Estate, at least annually, and thereafter shall be held, administered, and disposed of as a part of the Trust Estate of this Bypass Trust.

Multiple Bypass Trusts with Different Beneficiaries and Distribution Rights

Instead of merely tinkering with the language of the bypass trust, you can create two bypass trusts. One would be a sprinkle trust for your spouse and certain heirs. This type of trust is also called a spray or discretionary bypass trust because it permits the trustee to distribute monies in any portion and to any mix of the named beneficiaries. The rest of the exclusion amount can be transferred into a spouse-only bypass trust. This approach, with equal amounts given to each such trust, is another method of addressing concerns about having too many assets available to children (and other heirs) as well as your spouse.

 Don't assume that a discretionary bypass trust should only benefit your spouse and children. It can benefit any persons you are concerned about. It is not uncommon or inappropriate to name an elderly dependent parent, a sibling in financial need, or others.

This approach can secure the spouse. The following illustrative language could be revised to mandate income distribution to the spouse, or other payments for that matter. The spouse-only bypass trust is illustrated first, followed by the family discretionary bypass trust. You should carefully consider who the trustees are of each trust. Many people name their children as cotrustees with their spouse.

─────────── **SAMPLE LANGUAGE** ───────────

First Bypass Trust: Spousal Bypass Trust

If my spouse survives me, I give to my Trustee, in trust, One-Half (½) the pecuniary sum equal to the largest amount will not result in any federal estate tax payable after giving effect to the exclusion amount to which I am entitled, as well as any other credits applicable to my estate. The trust formed, if any, under this provision, shall be known as the "Spousal Bypass Trust under *Your Name Will."

The Trustee shall hold, manage, and invest the amounts held in this trust. The Trustee shall collect and receive any income and shall pay over or apply any portion or all of the net income or principal, or both, at such times as the Trustee shall determine, to or for the benefit of my spouse only, as the Trustee shall determine necessary or advisable for the health, support, and maintenance [*ask your estate planner about using the phrase "comfort and welfare" to permit broader distribution standards if your spouse is not the trustee being authorized to make such distributions*] of my spouse without consideration of any assets held or available to my spouse under the Family Bypass Trust, below. Any net income not so paid over or applied for the benefit of my spouse shall be accumulated and added to the principal of the Trust Estate, at least annually, and thereafter shall be held, administered, and disposed of as a part of the Trust Estate of this Spousal Bypass Trust. My express intent is that the Trustee should liberally distribute income and principal to my spouse without regard to any remainder beneficiaries.

SAMPLE LANGUAGE

Second Bypass Trust: Family Bypass Trust

If my spouse survives me, I give to my Trustee, in trust, One-Half (1/2) the pecuniary sum equal to the largest amount which will not result in any federal estate tax payable after giving effect to the exclusion amount to which I am entitled, as well as any other credits applicable to my estate. The trust formed, if any, under this provision, shall be known as the "Family Bypass Trust under *Your Name Will."

The Trustee shall hold, manage, and invest the amounts held in this trust. The Trustee shall collect and receive any income and shall pay over or apply any portion or all of the net income or principal,

> or both, in equal or unequal amounts, at such times as the Trustee shall determine, to or for the benefit of such one or more members of a class consisting of my spouse and my children living from time to time (collectively, the "Recipients"), as the Trustee shall determine necessary or advisable for the health, support, and maintenance of all of the Recipients. Any net income not so paid over or applied for the benefit of the persons named in this provision shall be accumulated and added to the principal of the Trust Estate, at least annually, and thereafter shall be held, administered, and disposed of as a part of the Trust Estate of this Family Bypass Trust.

Consider whether an independent bank or trust company should be used with the spousal bypass trust to avoid any conflicts. If the children are named, there is an inherent conflict of interest in that the more they distribute to the surviving spouse (their mother or father), the less they will inherit. Even "good" children can act in a less than ideal manner when money is at stake ("Mom will do fine in that cheap nursing home").

Terminating the Bypass Trust If Estate Tax Is Repealed

If you knew with certainty that the estate tax would be reinstated in 2011, you would plan to maximize your tax benefit. Similarly, if you knew with certainty that the estate tax were going to be repealed, forever, in 2010, you would plan accordingly. Specifically, if you were signing a will today and knew the tax would permanently end in 2010, you could provide for a bypass trust, just in case you and your spouse died before 2010. However, if your spouse survived until 2010, you could provide that the bypass trust would terminate and distribute all assets to your then still surviving spouse. After all, why keep the bypass trust in place if there is no tax?

This concept presents another possible option for planning a bypass trust. You could state in the trust that if the estate tax were permanently repealed, the bypass trust would end and distribute assets to your surviving spouse. This would avoid the need for an annual trust income tax return, separate accounts, dealing with a trustee or cotrustee, and other unnecessary hassles and costs.

 Before redrafting a bypass trust so as to terminate if the estate tax ends, consider the following:

- If you draft a bypass trust to end if the estate tax is repealed, how do you address the possibility of it being reinstated? What if it is revamped and changed but not repealed? What if instead of repeal, some variation of the Democratic-favored plan of a very high exclusion (one that you would be confident your family net worth could never reach) is instead added? How could you draft the trust to address all of these contingencies?
- There are significant non-estate tax benefits of a bypass trust: asset protection planning, professional management, probate avoidance, and so on. These would all be lost at termination of the trust.

Funding All Assets to a QTIP Trust and Letting Executor Decide Non-Marital Part

As an alternative to the preceding option, there are two types of QTIP planning approaches that can be used in lieu of a bypass trust. One approach is to bequeath the entire estate, to the extent it is qualified for the marital deduction and the decedent's executor so elects.

The second approach is to bequeath the entire estate to a marital trust, specifically, to a qualified terminable interest property (QTIP) trust. The executor can then choose the optimal portion of that trust to qualify for the marital deduction. The remaining portion of the trust would then use up a portion of the decedent's applicable exclusion. This QTIP trust can even be further subdivided to take advantage of GST planning. The fiduciaries will have to be given the latitude to effect this type of planning. (A complete discussion of QTIP trusts appears later in this chapter.)

Authorizing a Trust Protector to Terminate the Bypass Trust If Estate Tax Is Repealed

Given the benefits of keeping a bypass trust in place even if the estate tax is repealed, you probably don't want to force the dissolution of the bypass trust. Depending on the legislation repealing the estate tax, it might be a real repeal or just a fake end run. The best way to address the dissolution of your bypass trust would be to empower a trusted person to force the dissolution based on the knowledge available at that time. The person to whom you give such a power is a *trust protector*.

The trust protector role has been commonly used in many foreign situs asset protection trusts and is now making its way more commonly into domestically structured trust agreements. The trust protector is a fiduciary role but as a relatively new function lacks as much case law or other authoritative literature defining its parameters, obligations, and responsibilities as have other trust issues. The trust protector role, typically a limited but powerful and important one, must be clearly defined in the trust instrument since statutory law in most states does not exist to "fill in the blanks," as it would for many trustee powers. As illustrated in the sample language on pages 146 and 147, a typical approach would be to highlight a limited number of powers or rights granted to the trust protector, such as changing or removing an institution or even non-institutional cotrustee or sole trustee, changing the governing law or situs of the trust (this might be important to transfer the trust to a state where there is no restriction on the rule against perpetuities, for example), changing the designated investment advisers, and occasionally adding other limited powers. In light of the uncertainty of the 2001 Tax Act, consider giving your trust protector the authority to direct the trustee to distribute all assets to the then current beneficiaries of the trust.

SAMPLE LANGUAGE

Trust Protector Authority

- The Trust Protector may modify or amend the terms of the Trust in order to: (i) take advantage of opportunities to minimize tax costs for the Trust and/or its beneficiaries; (ii) address significant changes in the estate, gift, GST, or other taxes which affect the intent and purpose of this trust; (iii) respond to changes in the Code and regulations thereunder that the Trust Protector determines adversely affect the administration of the Trust; (iv) respond to changes in circumstances that adversely affect the Trust or the beneficiaries in a manner which the Trust Protector reasonably would not have believed the Grantor to have anticipated, including but not limited to the permanent repeal of the estate, gift, and/or GST tax; (v) facilitate the Trust taking advantage of favorable developments in the tax and other laws occurring after the execution of this Trust; (vi) make any modifications to this Trust necessary to qualify this Trust as a "grantor trust" and to ensure that the transfer to the Trust is deemed an incomplete gift for United States gift tax purposes, as such terms are defined under applicable United States gift and estate tax laws.

- The Trust Protector shall have the right at any time to change the governing law applicable to the Trust. (For example, if the state in which the trust is formed passes unfavorable laws, the Trust Protector could state that the laws of another state apply.)

- The Trust Protector shall have the right to change the situs of the Trust and/or the Trust Fund to any jurisdiction.

- The Trust Protector shall have the power to remove and discharge any then existing Trustee by Notice in writing, whereupon such Trustee shall cease to be a Trustee hereof.

- The Trust Protector shall have the authority to provide a written designation to the Trustee specifying the names of current

> Recipients and/or beneficiaries of the Trust and/or any separate Trust hereunder.
>
> - The Trust Protector may at any time adjust the interests of beneficiaries and/or Recipients at any generational level to facilitate the equitable administration of the Trust Estate.
> - The Trust Protector may direct the Trustee to distribute all trust assets in any proportions to the then current beneficiaries of the Trust as a result of the Trust Protector determining that as a result of a change in tax or other laws, a major objective of Grantor on forming this Trust can no longer be served. (By way of example and not limitation, is the permanent repeal of the estate, gift, and/or GST tax.)

Who should be named trust protector? The trust protector is typically a person named outside the family who is independent of both the trustees and the beneficiaries. In some instances, typically after a succession of trust protectors, a class of beneficiaries may be granted the right to nominate an independent and unrelated person. If the power to terminate the trust is to be given, you must review with your estate planner the possible tax and legal implications this power can create for the trust protector.

Nonfunding of the Bypass Trust

Another variation can be added to the approaches to address the funding of the bypass trust under your will or revocable living trust. You could simply add a clause stating that if the estate tax does not exist at the date of your death, then the bypass trust won't be funded.

You might not even need new language to accomplish this result. The typical language used to fund a bypass trust won't create or fund the trust if there is no estate tax when you die. Consider the following language. If there is no exclusion, there will be no trust.

SAMPLE LANGUAGE

Language Funding a Bypass Trust

If my spouse survives me, I give to my Trustee, in trust the maximum applicable exclusion amount to which I am entitled, after giving consideration to any inter vivos transfers or testamentary transfers above which have reduced the exclusion available.

The nonfunding issue highlights a major planning problem for almost every will and trust. This problem proves wrong all those who have said that you may not need to revise your will. It proves wrong the many estate planners who have focused on avoiding overfunding a bypass trust. It proves that the many jokes about Jack Kevorkian and Tony Soprano taking reservations for December 2010 (the last month scheduled not to have an estate tax before the January 1, 2011, reinstatement) have missed the real point. The opposite problem might be more severe. How so? If you die in 2010, there is no estate tax. If there is no estate tax, your will won't fund a bypass trust. The problem isn't in 2010, because you could leave your estate to your spouse or anyone else, without an estate tax. However, the manner in which most wills are drafted is that your entire estate would then pass to your surviving spouse. If your spouse then dies any time after 2010, there will be a tax. Therefore, even if there is no estate tax in force when you die, unless you are positive that the estate tax will not be reinstated before your spouse dies, you have to take steps to plan. Few if any existing wills do so. The standard language in the typical will would result in an estate tax. Change is necessary.

The point of the following drafting approach is that even if there is no estate tax in force on your death, you might still benefit from funding a bypass trust. If you don't feel comfortable with this approach,

--- **SAMPLE LANGUAGE** ---

Revised Language Funding a Bypass Trust

If my spouse survives me, I give to my Trustee, in trust the maximum applicable exclusion amount to which I am entitled, after giving consideration to any inter vivos transfers or testamentary transfers above which have reduced the exclusion available. However, if there is no estate tax in force at the time of my death, I give to my Trustee in trust the lesser of One Million Dollars ($1,000,000.00) or my entire estate . . . [*add typical bypass trust provisions to complete the clause*].

then leave in a disclaimer to at least enable your surviving spouse to fund a bypass trust if she deems it appropriate. Standard disclaimer language will also have to be revised because it, too, if based on the maximum applicable exclusion, may not permit funding.

Ensuring Proper Distribution of an Estate to a Bypass Trust

Typical bypass trust language might be interpreted as passing all of your estate to the trust. This may be similarly undesirable. Does the following language imply that all of your estate will fund the bypass trust? Or would a court interpret the language to imply that if you die and there is no "exclusion amount" the provision simply cannot apply?

--- **SAMPLE LANGUAGE** ---

Typical Language Funding a Bypass Trust

If my spouse survives me, I give to my Trustee, in trust the pecuniary sum equal to the largest amount which will not result in any federal estate tax payable after giving effect to the exclusion amount, to which I am entitled, as well as any other credits applicable to my estate. . . .

Here are several interpretative scenarios. If the estate tax is in fact repealed, then the transfer of the entire estate to the bypass trust will not trigger a tax. Alternatively, a court may find that if the tax has been repealed, no amount should be transferred to a bypass trust. The best answer is to revise your will so it is clear what your intent is. Without a clear indication in your will, then a court would have to interpret your entire will, and perhaps consider extrinsic evidence and state law to reach a conclusion.

Other Options to Draft Flexibility into a Bypass Trust

There is considerable flexibility in drafting a bypass trust. Adding more flexibility to the trust can provide greater comfort to you and your spouse and provide the option you need to deal with whatever Congress does in the future. Consider the following options:

- The trustee can be given the right to pay income to the surviving spouse but not children. Alternatively, you can include children and a wider listing of beneficiaries if the GST tax won't become a problem.
- The surviving spouse can be the sole benefactor.
- Persons other than the spouse and children (e.g., parents) can be included if you want to provide funds or even just a safety net for them. This could prove helpful if the estate tax is repealed and you want to benefit more people.
- Various principal invasion rights can be provided. Distributions could be limited by an ascertainable standard (e.g., maintaining the surviving spouse's standard of living). An independent trustee (not the surviving spouse) could be given a broad distribution power to maintain the surviving spouse or any other beneficiary's comfort and welfare.
- The surviving spouse (or any beneficiary) could be given the right to demand up to 5 percent of the principal of the trust each year. This can provide her with additional flexibility and access to principal (see sample language).
- The trustee can be provided some rights for terminating the trust (see sample language).

--- SAMPLE LANGUAGE ---

Spouse's Right to Demand Percentage of Principal

My spouse shall have the right to request of the Trustee of this Trust to pay over to such surviving spouse, upon written request, out of the principal of this Trust, in each successive calendar year commencing with the calendar year in which my death occurs, a sum not exceeding the greater of Five Thousand Dollars ($5,000) or Five Percent (5%) of the assets of the principal of this Trust valued as of the date of the receipt of such request, provided, however, that only one such request may be made in any such calendar year, and such right to withdraw sums of principal shall not be cumulative from year to year.

--- SAMPLE LANGUAGE ---

Trustee's Rights to Terminate Trust

Notwithstanding anything to the contrary contained in this Will, if the trustee of any Trust created hereunder (or, if any such trust shall not have been funded) the executor of this Will shall determine that the aggregate value or the character of the assets of such Trust (or the estate assets available to fund such Trust) makes it inadvisable, inconvenient, or uneconomical to continue the administration of (or to fund) such Trust, then such fiduciary may transfer and pay over the Trust Estate (or the estate assets available to fund such trust), equally or unequally, to one or more persons then eligible to receive current distributions from such trust. However, if the executor of my Will shall determine not to fund such trust and the executor of this Will and the trustee of such Trust should not be the same, the executor of this Will shall obtain the consent of the trustee of such Trust before distributing the estate assets otherwise available for funding such Trust.

Multiple Bypass Trusts for GST Purposes

Just in case the many options for planning your bypass trust weren't complicated enough, GST planning adds another twist: You must consider how you would allocate the GST exemption to the various bypass trusts (see discussion of GST planning in Chapter 1). This is important because the GST benefits might encourage you to structure bypass trusts differently than you might without GST planning.

To understand the implications of GST planning and bypass trusts, it will be helpful to first summarize typical GST/bypass trust planning as done under pre-2001 Tax Act law (which will apply for 2001 and 2011 and thereafter when the estate tax is scheduled to be reinstated). A common GST planning approach used through 2001 was to establish two GST trusts to which the $1 million (indexed) GST exemption was allocated. The first trust would have been equal to the amount of the unused estate tax exclusion, $675,000 for 2001. This was the amount that you could bequeath to a trust to benefit your surviving spouse while avoiding taxation in her estate. Your executor would then have allocated that portion of your GST exemption to the bypass trust. This transfer would not have triggered any estate tax because of the exclusion. The assets in this trust would be protected forever from GST tax because of the allocation of the GST exemption amount in a manner to ensure a zero inclusion rate.

A second trust would have been provided under your will to absorb the remaining $325,000 GST exemption amount ($1 million total less the $675,000 allocated to the bypass trust). This trust would be a QTIP or marital trust, which would avoid any estate tax because of the unlimited marital deduction. In 2001 when the inflation-adjusted GST exemption was $1,060,000, this GST-exempt QTIP trust would be funded with $385,000 ($1,060,000 − $675,000). In 2002 the amount of GST exemption increased to $1,100,000.

Finally, this plan would probably have been completed with a third QTIP or marital trust for any remaining assets. The reason to have two QTIP or marital trusts is that one of the trusts would have been GST-exempt and the other would have been entirely subject to GST tax. The GST-exempt trust would be the last to be touched for principal invasion. The non-GST-exempt marital trust would be spent down first. While the GST-exempt trust would waste some GST (e.g., by the requirement of paying income to your surviving spouse), it would waste less by virtue of the trustees first spending down the other marital trust.

Planning for the GST exemption when marital trusts are used presents an important but somewhat confusing opportunity. Assume a husband dies and his will establishes a QTIP trust for his surviving wife. On her death, the trust assets pass to the children. Generally, the surviving spouse (the wife in this scenario) who is benefiting from the QTIP trust would be considered the person transferring the trust assets to the children following her death. The husband who died first, and whose will established the QTIP trust, would not generally be considered the transferor of the QTIP property.[1] Thus, only the wife's $1 million GST exemption can be allocated against this trust. The problem this creates is that the husband's $1 million exemption could be lost. The solution to this is a special tax election that treats the husband as the transferor of the assets in the QTIP trust for GST tax purposes.[2] This election thus permits the husband to allocate his $1 million GST exemption against the trust. This election can be made by the executor of the husband's estate (or by the husband if it is a gift made during his lifetime) for an income-only marital trust. This election is known as a "reverse QTIP election."

Under the 2001 Tax Act, analyzing the interplay of GST planning and bypass trusts is necessary in 2001 and again in 2011 when the tax is back. During the interim period that the GST exemption and the estate tax exclusion are the same, you can fund the maximum bypass trust and simply allocate the GST exemption to it. However, as the preceding detailed analysis of some of the many bypass trust options demonstrates, many taxpayers may not want to fund the maximum bypass trust. Many planners are raising this issue with their clients. But before you opt not to fund the maximum bypass trust, consider that you are forgoing the ideal planning to ultimately benefit your entire family. Maximum funding of a sprinkle dynasty trust will facilitate circumventing the new paradigm for the gift tax, allocating income to lowest bracket taxpayers, avoiding the estate tax if it is reinstated, and more. Thus, the option of underfunding the bypass trust should be avoided. The minimum/maximum, disclaimer, and other approaches are not ideal. The better approach, from a long-term family planning perspective, is to fund the maximum bypass trust and allocate all GST exemption to it. If you believe it is necessary, you can modify the provisions of that bypass trust during the lifetime of your surviving spouse to provide her with additional protection and still achieve maximum long-term planning benefits.

Bypass Trusts and Nonmarried Taxpayers

The purpose of a bypass trust is to benefit a surviving spouse without having assets doubled up in that surviving spouse's estate. If the bypass trust is not used, then the tendency would be to simply rely on the unlimited estate tax marital deduction and to bequeath all assets to the surviving spouse.

For nonmarried, single, gay, or lesbian couples—anyone who is not legally married—the planning concept of the bypass trust may seem irrelevant. It isn't. They don't have the benefit of an unlimited marital deduction. But the same concept can be used in a somewhat different manner.

EXAMPLE

John Smith and his partner each have a $2 million estate. If Smith simply bequeaths all assets to his partner, if he survives, then on his death potentially a larger estate tax cost could be incurred. Instead, Smith should use a bypass trust concept by having each of the wills fund the maximum bypass amount into a trust for the benefit of the surviving partner. It should be structured in a manner similar to that of a bypass trust: Give the surviving partner considerable access to the assets of the trust, but sufficiently limit that access to avoid inclusion of the assets in his estate. The result will be protecting the assets from estate tax and thus preserving the asset for distribution on the death of the last of Smith and his partner to their friends, nieces and nephews, or whomever they choose.

When reviewing any of the planning discussed in this book that does not expressly indicate that a particular planning benefit is only available to a spouse (such as the marital deduction and, after 2009, the $3 million spousal basis adjustment), a modified form of the planning might be useful for nonmarried people as well. The example on the previous page illustrates one such planning opportunity.

Post-2001 Tax Act Planning for Existing Bypass Trusts

What does an estate planner do if a client has an existing bypass trust formed on the death of her spouse, and in all likelihood she will never face an estate tax? Should the planner advise ending the trust? One benefit will be simplicity (separate trust accounts won't be needed); she also will save some financial fees (e.g., money management might be cheaper by consolidating all assets into one account, and the cost of preparing an annual trust income tax return will be eliminated). The taxpayer might avoid some of the cost of the higher graduated trust income tax rates, but, on the other hand, she will lose all the nontax benefits. Trust assets would likely have remained protected without the need for a prenuptial agreement (should that ever come into play). The ability to sprinkle income to taxpayers in a lower income tax bracket (if the language of the trust permitted this) will be lost. If the trust was structured to avoid GST tax by allocating GST exemption, this benefit too will be lost. In many cases, especially if the trust had some built-in flexibility, it won't really be advantageous to terminate the trust.

QTIP/MARITAL TRUSTS

Trusts for a spouse have been popular for many reasons that the 2001 Tax Act will not affect. Their use ensures that assets bequeathed to a spouse will eventually be distributed to the chosen heirs, regardless of the actions of the surviving spouse. If the surviving spouse remarries, the assets are protected from her new husband, whether or not she executes a prenuptial or postnuptial agreement. In addition, marital trusts provide some protection from claimants and creditors of the surviving spouse. The trust may include a spendthrift clause to prevent the spouse from assigning interests in the trust and other provisions to safeguard trust assets. In addition, marital trusts provide an important mechanism to manage assets in the event the surviving spouse is ever disabled, one of the keys being the appointment of successor trustees in case the spouse cannot manage her own assets. Marital trusts can provide for professional management of assets, control of business interests, avoidance of ancillary probate, and so forth. Family units change frequently in American society, whether as a result of divorce or otherwise, ensuring the continued popularity of marital trusts. The Cleaver family is just not as common as some might wish to believe. In fact, marital trusts should probably be used far more often than they are, even post-2001 tax relief.

The tax benefits of marital trusts need to be reexamined in light of the 2001 Tax Act. Under prior law an important benefit of using marital trusts was to allocate and secure the GST exemption on the death of the first spouse. (This concept is explained in Chapter 1 and in the discussion of GST planning and bypass trusts in this chapter.) Discounts on fractionalized business interests were supported by transfers to marital trusts, as seen in the example that follows. This technique will continue to be useful for many taxpayers.

EXAMPLE

Jones owned 100% of the stock in Widget Manufacturing, Inc. Prior to his death, he gave each of his four children 1% of the stock, so he owned 96% of the stock. He then formed an inter vivos marital trust (QTIP trust) and gave 48% of the stock to that trust. On Jones's death, his will bequeathed the remaining 48% of the stock to the bypass trust under the will. By fractionalizing the ownership, so that he did not have control (50% or more ownership) and through the QTIP trust in combination with the bypass trust, so that his spouse will never have control (he fractionalized the ownership interests), Jones will ensure discounts on the value of the stock in the estate and in his surviving spouse's estate.

In 2011 unless Congress acts to reinstate or make permanent the estate tax repeal, the estate tax, with rules similar to those in force in 2001, will be back. Estate planners cannot overlook the importance of the planning previously illustrated. Simply factoring inflation into the analysis shows that the $675,000 taxpayers could give or bequeath in 2001 tax free may be worth more than the inflation-adjusted $1 million they will be able to give or bequeath in 2011!

If the modified carryover basis rules scheduled to become effective in 2010 actual happen, the marital trusts will have to be reexamined in light of qualifying for the $3 million spousal basis adjustment available under that new system (see Chapter 7).

Although there are different ways to qualify for an estate tax marital deduction, the following discussion focuses on the qualified terminable interest property trust (QTIP). Many wills should include a QTIP trust. This trust has traditionally been intended to achieve several nontax objectives noted earlier and some important tax objectives as well. Tax objectives include the ability to defer estate taxes on the death of the first spouse through the unlimited estate tax marital deduction (although special provisions apply if that spouse is not a citizen), to allocate GST tax exemption on the first spouse's death thus preserving this benefit for future heirs, and to secure discounts on business and other assets. To qualify for these benefits, a host of requirements must be met.

On the death of the surviving spouse, the entire value of the QTIP property is included in the surviving spouse's gross estate. These assets will be taxed at the top marginal tax brackets applicable to her estate. The value of the QTIP technique is that the estate (assuming the first spouse's death precedes that of his spouse) can qualify for the unlimited estate tax marital deduction on the assets transferred to the trust without that first spouse having to give up complete control over the assets to his spouse.

The QTIP technique (as would an outright marital bequest) effectively defers all tax until the second death. This is the concept behind second-to-die or survivorship life insurance—insure two lives but only pay once, on the death of the last of them, when the estate tax is due.

Requirements for QTIP Treatment

Where the following requirements are met, the QTIP trust formed under a will should qualify for the unlimited estate tax marital deduction. Estate planners should explain to their clients that the first spouse to die will be able to exert some control over the use and ultimate disposition of the property, subject to these restrictions:

- The surviving spouse must be given a life estate in particular property. She must also have the right to demand that the property be income producing.

- The surviving spouse has the right to all of the income from that property in the trust payable at least annually. This can be affected by how the money is invested, whether, for example, the first spouse wants to address modern portfolio theory by investing for total return and making distributions in a fashion that supports this; by the trust's definitions of principal and income; by state law definitions, and by the interplay of all these factors with the QTIP regulations. These details, which are beyond the scope of this discussion, should be addressed by the estate planner and investment manager (who should be an integral part of the estate planning process if these types of decisions are to be made in the optimal manner).

- The property must pass from the first spouse's estate to the QTIP. There is a similar requirement to qualify for the $3 million spousal basis adjustment under the modified carryover basis system scheduled for 2010. The Treasury Department will have to issue regulations clarifying how this concept will be applied before those rules take effect. These matters may have to be addressed in the language included in the client's will or revocable living trust.

 Much remains unknown, and so many changes are likely. Even the issuance of clarifying regulations may require revisions in planning. Taxpayers should periodically meet with their estate planner to consider the necessary changes.

- No person has a power to appoint any part of the property to any person other than the surviving spouse.
- The necessary election is made by the executor to have the property qualify for the estate tax marital deduction. This simply involves reporting the desired treatment as a QTIP trust on the estate tax return.

Effect of 2001 Tax Act on Surviving Spouse's Access to QTIP Assets

Various principal invasion rights can be provided to the surviving spouse as beneficiary of the QTIP. Distributions could be limited by an ascertainable standard (maintaining the surviving spouse's standard of living). The trustee could be given a broad distribution power to maintain the surviving spouse's comfort and welfare. This is essentially an unlimited standard. The surviving spouse could be given the right to demand up to 5 percent of the principal of the trust each year. Technically, this is referred to as a *5 and 5* power and is the greater of $5,000 or 5 percent of the principal of the trust.

How has the 2001 Tax Act affected this type of planning? As discussed in the context of bypass trusts, the taxpayer might want to give the surviving spouse broader powers to invade than might have been given under prior law. This change is feasible because there is less concern about the estate and GST tax affecting the family in the future; larger amounts are being distributed under the will to the bypass trust as a result of the 2001 Tax Act having increased the exclusion amount.

It is essential for taxpayers to coordinate their overall estate planning. They should not consider altering the terms of a bypass trust, for example, without adequate consideration of the consequences of a QTIP trust, insurance trust, and other planning. It's only by looking at the big picture of what assets and cash flow a surviving spouse will have from all trusts and planning that the taxpayer can properly evaluate what decision to make for any particular trust.

Tax Relief Changes Affecting QTIP Trusts

The 2001 Tax Act includes no significant change directly to the QTIP rules. The most significant indirect change is the scheduled dramatic increases in the estate tax exclusion amount such that the bypass trust may encompass more, and even the entirety, of many estates.

Further, the equalization of the GST exemption and the estate tax exclusion for the years 2005 through 2009 eliminates the need for those dying in those years to have a QTIP trust to "soak up" and secure the portion of the GST exemption that could not be allocated to the bypass trust. This planning won't be necessary in those years. However, in 2011 when the estate tax is back, such complex twists in planning also will return.

All the nontax reasons for QTIPs remain unaffected by the tax changes. These alone will continue to spur the inclusion of QTIP trusts in wills and revocable living trusts.

 The biggest planning problem for QTIPs created by the 2001 Tax Act is that too many taxpayers will mistakenly assume that the estate tax has been repealed (or that because of the higher exclusion it doesn't apply to them) and simply won't plan. These folks will get a general practice attorney to prepare a cheap, short will void of most trusts, including marital trusts. The only ones to benefit from that shortsightedness will be the lawyers specializing in estate litigation, especially when second and later marriages are involved.

The interplay of the various changes is such that estate planners should coordinate the distribution provisions between any QTIP and other trusts and planning techniques included in the estate plan.

Post-2001 Tax Act Planning for Existing QTIP Trusts

Do taxpayers who have an existing QTIP in place really need to keep it? Probably. The trust, presumably formed by the predeceased spouse, is irrevocable and therefore cannot be changed. Further, the remainder beneficiaries of a QTIP are almost assuredly people that the grantor wanted to protect. The GST benefits may continue to help family members in the future. The management, asset protection, and other nontax benefits remain intact. In addition, until the estate tax is permanently repealed, tax benefits such as GST allocation and fractionalization of interests for discount purposes, as discussed earlier, will continue to be beneficial for the foreseeable future.

If, in spite of these factors, a client still wants to eliminate the QTIP trust in the belief that the 2001 Tax Act obviates the need for it, the estate planner should review the discussion at the beginning of this chapter concerning termination of an irrevocable trust. In seeking to find a method that would facilitate termination, the planner should examine the document thoroughly with the idea of a termination or acceleration in mind, check on pertinent state law, and consider the grantor's objectives for the trust.

ANNUAL EXCLUSION GIFT PLANNING

A cornerstone of estate planning has always been to make annual gifts, because there is an annual per donee exclusion of $10,000 (indexed for inflation after the 1997 Tax Act. In 2001, the amount was $11,000 per year).[3] Thus, each year taxpayers can gift $10,000 to as many different people as they wish.

EXAMPLE

Husband and his wife have three married children and four grandchildren. Husband can give each child and grandchild $10,000, for a total of $70,000. Wife can give a similar amount. In aggregate, Husband and Wife can gift $140,000 every year, year after year, without any use of their estate tax exclusion amount.

Problems Presented by Gifts to Trusts

The annual gift exclusion, however, is only available for gifts of a present interest. Specifically, the statute includes in this $10,000 gift provision gifts "other than gifts of future interests in property." A present interest is defined as an unrestricted right to the immediate use, possession, or enjoyment of property or the income from property.[4] The term *present interest* indicates the right to substantial present economic benefit in the gift property. If a barrier exists, causing a substantial delay prior to the donee being able to enjoy the property, the gift is not of a present interest.[5] Gifts in trust, absent special measures or qualifications for limited exceptions, are gifts of future interests.

When a gift is made to a trust, it is the donee, and not the trustee, whose interests must be considered for purposes of determining the annual exclusion.[6] As a general rule, a gift in trust will not qualify for the annual gift tax exclusion if special provisions are not made. Since most trusts tend to have distributions in the discretion of a trustee, there can be no certainty that the beneficiary will receive a distribution, so no gift of a present interest can occur on funding the trust. In limited circumstances, a gift to a trust can qualify as a gift of a present interest. Three rules must be met: (1) The trust should generate an income flow; (2) some portion of the income must be required to be distributed to the trust beneficiaries; and (3) the amount of income the beneficiaries will receive must be ascertainable.[7] For most trusts, this is not likely.

Post-2001 Tax Act Gift Planning

The increase in the lifetime exclusion from $675,000 prior to the 2001 Tax Act (i.e., the amount taxpayer could give away gift and estate tax free in 2001) to $1 million in 2002, and eventually $3.5 million in 2009, may eliminate the need to make annual gifts.

NOTE

It is important not to overlook the personal benefits of an annual gift program. Gifts to children and other heirs teach the recipients fiscal responsibility, help them out when they are in need, and allow the donor to experience the happiness with which gifts are received.

On the other hand, the 2001 Tax Act retains a $1 million lifetime gift tax exclusion. Thus, for families seeking to transfer a business to children or other heirs active in the business, annual gift planning will likely continue. Given this $1 million lifetime gift tax exclusion, the uncertainty of the estate tax repeal ever becoming a reality, the budget problems in Washington that might result in curtailment of the increases in the estate tax exclusion, and other uncertainties of the new legislation, it is prudent that taxpayers continue gift planning if they anticipate any likelihood of being subject to the estate tax in the future. Also, for personal reasons, existing gift programs should not be curtailed. If children have come to expect payments for tuition or annual $10,000 gifts, curtailing those gifts could significantly affect their lifestyles. Finally, gift planning can move assets out of the reach of the donor's creditors and claimants, avoid ancillary probate, and effect a business succession plan, among other possible uses.

QUALIFIED PERSONAL RESIDENCE TRUSTS

NOTE

The 2001 Tax Act introduced a new concept called a qualified revocable trust (QRT). This has nothing to do with the QPRT discussed in this chapter, and the two should not be confused. Chapter 7 provides a more detailed discussion of the new QRTs.

A qualified personal residence trust (QPRT) provides a mechanism through which the donor (grantor) irrevocably transfers a home or vacation home to a special trust. The donor retains the right to live in the home for a period of time (a term interest). At the end of that period, the heirs (typically children but not grandchildren because of GST problems) receive ownership of the home as remainder beneficiaries. QPRTs take advantage of the time value of money to dramatically reduce federal estate and gift taxation on transfer of the home. The residence can be retained in a further trust for those family members at such time if the donor is uncomfortable having them own the house outright. The donor can continue to live in the house after the

QPRT trust ends and the children own the house but will have to pay rent as a tenant. The key benefits of the QPRT technique, thus, include the ability to significantly leverage the estate tax exclusion amount and to remove future appreciation in the home from the estate.

For many taxpayers, yet a further advantage of the QPRT makes it an even more desirable planning tool. A QPRT can enable taxpayers to reduce the size of their taxable estate without the expenditure of investment assets they believe will be needed to support their retirement years.

EXAMPLE

If a residence is worth $1,150,000, a gift of the residence could trigger an immediate gift tax (since the $1,150,000 gift will exceed the $1,000,000 lifetime gift tax exclusion, post-2001. The $150,000 excess will trigger a current gift tax cost. When the transfer is to a QPRT, none of this gift can qualify for the annual $10,000 gift tax exclusion. However, the discounting effect of the QPRT calculation can reduce the current value (for gift tax purposes) of the residence to perhaps $600,000, and maybe even less, thus protecting the transfer from triggering any current tax cost.

EXAMPLE

If the residence in the preceding example appreciates to $1,850,000 at the end of the 10-year QPRT term, the entire appreciation of $700,000 [$1,850,000 − $1,150,000] is removed from the estate. Note, however, that if this planning is not completed and the estate tax is back in full force in 2011, as the law presently provides for, the family could face a substantial estate tax cost.

Tax Relief Changes Affecting QPRT Trusts

The 2001 Tax Act has not made any direct changes to QPRTs. This was not the expectation of many estate planners, because the QPRT technique has been recommended several times for repeal. The Joint

Committee on Taxation Staff Description (JCS-4-98) and Revenue Estimates for Revenue Provisions in President's Fiscal Year 1999 Budget Proposal included a recommendation to repeal the personal residence exception.[8] What the tax changes did do was to make the need for a QPRT appear far less likely as a result of the increase in the estate tax exclusion. The increase from $675,000 to $1 million alone is expected to remove 40 percent of the estate tax filers from the system. As the exclusion increases to greater levels, even more taxpayers will be removed from the reach of the estate tax. This development would make it appear less appropriate for many taxpayers to pursue an irrevocable trust for estate planning purposes. Although this is a reasonable conclusion, it is also a risky one. There is no assurance how much of the proposed increases in the exclusion will actually be realized. The tax is scheduled to return as is in 2011. These considerations make it dangerous to ignore the estate tax benefits of using a QPRT.

Planning for New QPRT Trusts

For taxpayers who are confident that their longevity and the scheduled increase in the estate tax exclusion will ensure that their estate won't be subject to an estate tax, the primary purpose of a QPRT may be eliminated. However, few estate planners are yet confident that the tax is really gone, so it is prudent to do some planning now to ensure that heirs won't face a huge estate tax.

QPRTs can provide important non-estate tax benefits. Because the estate tax leverage this technique provides was the focus under prior law, these other benefits were often overlooked. They should not be. A QPRT can provide an important measure of protection from claimants and creditors. It is an irrevocable trust and might be structured with minor children as beneficiaries. If the house was transferred to the trust when the taxpayer was solvent and minor beneficiaries exist, a court might be very reluctant to let a later claimant reach the asset. A QPRT can avoid ancillary probate as well, as the example on page 166 illustrates.

A QPRT can provide a vehicle for passing on a favorite family farm or vacation property to children. The trust is prepared, signed, and funded while the donor is alive. If the trust continues in force for

---
EXAMPLE

Taxpayer lives in Illinois and has a summer home in Michigan. The estate will be subject to ancillary probate in Michigan. By transferring the house to a QPRT and from the QPRT to taxpayer's children if the parent survives the QPRT term, the Michigan house instead won't be included in the estate on death, and the costs and delays of ancillary probate (a second probate proceeding in Michigan) will have been avoided.

many years before the donor's demise, it may be much more difficult for a disgruntled heir to overturn the transfer ("Mommy and Daddy always promised me their lake home."). Since the transfer was made while the donor was alive and presumably mentally competent, and time passed before death, it will be difficult to challenge that the donor did not understand or desire the particular result.

Planning for Existing QPRT Trusts

The QPRT is an irrevocable trust. However, there are typically important differences between QPRTs and other types of trusts such as a bypass trust, insurance trust, or other pot or discretionary trust. The key difference is that because of adverse GST tax implications, a QPRT is often limited to having adult children as beneficiaries. If this is the case, taxpayer might be in a much better position to encourage a court to accelerate or terminate a QPRT. Estate planners should review the discussion about terminating trusts at the beginning of this chapter and analyze state law about terminating a QPRT. If a client has only adult beneficiaries and provision of state law permits them to consent to a termination or acceleration, perhaps termination will be possible.

Being able to terminate a previously formed QPRT doesn't mean it is the right thing to do. It might, in fact, be if taxpayer's dot-com portfolio went bust and he will never be subject to the estate tax risk he had when the dot-coms were flying high. However, for most people who formed a

> QPRT, terminating it early when there is a risk of the estate tax returning in full force in 2011 is less likely to be prudent.

Before terminating an existing QPRT, taxpayers should review the transaction with a real estate attorney and title company. If the trust is improperly terminated, it could affect the quality of title to the real property, which could have an adverse economic effect.

INSURANCE PLANNING AND INSURANCE TRUSTS

Insurance has always been a cornerstone of many estate plans. Traditional uses of insurance were to create an instant estate if the breadwinner died and left heirs in need of financial help. If estates were not liquid, insurance could provide liquidity to meet a wide range of issues. Although payment of estate tax was perhaps the most cited cash need, it was far from the only one. Insurance can fund a buyout of a deceased (or even disabled) business partner. Insurance can provide the cash flow for a business to hire and train a replacement for the decedent. Insurance can provide cash flow to fund operations of real estate assets pending their sale or retention of a management firm.

After the 2001 Tax Act, insurance will continue to provide all of these nontax benefits; the tax legislation has little impact on them. Thus, insurance will remain an integral part of many estate plans.

However, what of the tax uses of insurance in an estate plan? The effect of the 2001 Tax Act on insurance funding is uncertain. If the increase in the exclusion under the new law ensures that an estate won't be subject to tax, then insurance to fund a no-longer-relevant tax will be unnecessary. However, in many cases, as noted above, taxpayers have intended to use insurance for non-estate tax needs, such as for creating an estate, providing liquidity, and so forth. These needs should also be evaluated.

 In 2010, there will no longer be an estate tax, but there will be a carryover basis system that can assure very large estates with substantial appreciation of a capital gains tax being passed to the heirs. For this limited number of estates, insurance funding might be useful. But then again, in 2011 the estate tax is back with a $1 million exclusion that, on an inflation-adjusted basis, may prove to be worth less than the $675,000 exclusion in 2001. Therefore, the use of insurance during this transition period cannot be ignored.

The only taxpayers who should cancel insurance are those who are certain, after a careful review with their estate planner and financial adviser, that the coverage will not be needed. Given the uncertainty of what will happen with the estate tax, the decision to cancel insurance coverage should be made cautiously. The increase in the exclusion from $675,000 to $1 million in 2002 may eliminate 40 percent of estate tax filings. Those included in this category are perhaps the first taxpayers who should evaluate their insurance coverage. But even taxpayers in this group should be careful not to cancel before the exclusion increase becomes effective, and they should also project their estate to 2011 when the exclusion will again be $1 million and inflation alone may have made their estates taxable.

An irrevocable life insurance trust could provide some important advantages. It could remove the value (proceeds) of any insurance settlement from an estate. Insurance is usually purchased in large amounts; the estate tax consequences of this potentially large figure should be carefully weighed. The insurance trust can provide that the insurance proceeds received on the taxpayer's death can be used to repurchase assets from the estate. This would provide additional liquidity and a ready method of disposing of any nonliquid real estate, business assets, or other nonliquid assets. This is an important benefit if the estate may need cash to make pecuniary (dollar) bequests, to pay taxes, or to cover expenses.

To effectively remove the insurance proceeds from the estate of the insured, the insurance policy and all incidence of ownership of the insurance policy must be transferred to the trust more than three years prior to the insured's death. Alternatively, the insurance trust could purchase new insurance directly (in contrast to existing insurance policies), thereby avoiding the risk of this three-year rule.

Tax Relief Changes Affecting Insurance Trusts

The main changes that the 2001 Tax Act has made to insurance planning and insurance trusts are the increase in the estate tax exclusion, the reduction of rates, and the ultimate elimination of the estate tax. These reductions in the potential estate tax are favorable in that they may enable estate planners to reduce or even eliminate life insurance coverage needed for the payment of estate tax. However, caution is warranted for the many reasons previously noted.

Planning after the 2001 Tax Act

If the taxpayer has an existing life insurance trust, the estate planner should reevaluate the trust and the insurance coverage when reevaluating the overall estate plan after the 2001 Tax Act.

--- **EXAMPLE** ---

Taxpayer purchased $100,000 of life insurance in a trust several years ago when his estate was $900,000 and the estate tax exclusion only $600,000. Say the estate is now $975,000 and he has a $100,000 insurance policy to pay the estate tax. On January 1, 2002, the estate tax exclusion rose to $1 million and the estate no longer faces a tax. Should taxpayer terminate the trust? The answer depends on all the facts and circumstances. What if he lives to 2011 and the tax is back? Inflation might make the estate taxable. What if he cancels the insurance (more technically, stops giving the trust money to pay annual premiums and the trustee has no choice but to let the policy lapse)? If Congress freezes the estate tax exclusion at $2 million, he may have made a good move. What if the exclusion remains at $1 million? What if $950,000 of taxpayer's assets are risky high-tech start-up companies? Perhaps the insurance is all heirs will receive. If the estate is comprised of risky assets, insurance could be retained regardless of the tax. Does the policy permit a viatical settlement option that might be important to the insured? If the insured is, or is concerned about becoming, ill, this option could be important enough to affect the decision on keeping the policy. Is it a cash or term policy? A term policy may have no cash value and so offer no benefit upon termination. A term policy may also be so inexpensive that it is sensible to keep it in force for a few years to see what develops. Are there other methods of eliminating the possible future estate tax? How do they compare with the cost of the insurance? If a family limited partnership and the higher exclusion can solve the taxpayer's estate tax problem, perhaps maintaining insurance is not necessary.

Even after a complete analysis of the options, taxpayer's actions may still be constrained by the terms of the irrevocable insurance trust.

EXAMPLE

Taxpayer's husband died five years ago and $500,000 life insurance proceeds were paid into an irrevocable life insurance trust he established well before death. Should she keep this trust? The analysis is different because the trust cannot be effectively terminated by ceasing annual gifts. The funds are already in the trust. The analysis is also different because the trust is not really an insurance trust at this stage. It is a trust holding investment assets. Distributing assets out of the trust if the trust was structured for GST tax benefits will waste those benefits. If the insurance that is distributed to the surviving spouse and the estate eventually exceeds the new increased estate tax exclusion, an avoidable tax will have been created. The taxpayer will lose the asset protection benefits the trust affords as well as the management structure.

Should a taxpayer take action on an existing trust still owning insurance? It depends on a wide range of factors. What about an older insurance trust for which the insurance has already paid out? This is a different type of analysis, as shown in the latter example.

If, based on general dissatisfaction and the hassle of maintaining the trust, a client still wants the trust ended, then the estate planner should evaluate the discussion at the beginning of this chapter on terminating irrevocable trusts. This might be difficult to achieve for the typical insurance trust, which provides for further trusts and eventual distribution to children or other heirs. Courts may be reluctant to jeopardize the interests of these remainder or contingent beneficiaries. If they are all adults and all consent, there might be some chance for termination. An estate and probate attorney should review these issues.

Contrary to the knee-jerk reactions of some taxpayers to cancel policies, insurance planning will remain an important part of a comprehensive estate plan after the 2001 Tax Act. The only proper and intelligent way for an estate planner to complete any estate plan is to consider all of the taxpayer's assets, cash flow, and objectives, and to involve all of the family advisers (accountant, attorney, financial planner, insurance consultant, and so on). Properly planning for the new exclusion and bypass trust options discussed earlier requires evaluating the entire estate plan. If the taxpayer might still face an estate tax or have a liquidity need, the analysis of insurance will be similar to prior law.

If you begin to modify your client's planning in light of the higher estate tax exclusion, you should also evaluate the need for, amounts of, and applications of insurance under the new plan. This will involve a consideration of all the planning discussed in this book that is applicable to the taxpayer. The following example illustrates but one of myriad possibilities.

EXAMPLE

Assume that John Doe, like many taxpayers, has no confidence in the government really repealing the estate tax. While he views the increasing exclusion as a good sign, he will continue to plan as if his heirs will get nailed. So, his initial reaction, after reviewing the various planning options for a bypass trust discussed earlier is to fund a bypass trust to the maximum extent possible. Further, there is something about paying a nickel more in tax than he has to that annoys him. So, he wants a dynastic (perpetual) bypass trust with a broad sprinkle power. That way, whatever the government does next, his family will be best positioned with the most flexibility to minimize taxes. The problem with the approach just described is neither Doe nor his surviving spouse will be comfortable with what will eventually be one-half the family net worth in a trust with his children and other heirs as beneficiaries. What does any of this have to do with life insurance? Depending on Doe's age and health, he might be able to supplement the amount available to the surviving spouse with life insurance. This could take the form of a moderate policy payable outright to the spouse, an increase in coverage in an existing insurance trust, or some other option. The point is that if the taxpayer wants to secure maximum tax advantage, he can use insurance to supplement the assets or cash flow available to his surviving spouse to meet personal as well as tax goals.

Given the uncertainty of how the 2001 Tax Act estate tax rules will be handled and how complex planning has become for many, a general rule for planning new insurance trusts is to include as many options and as much flexibility as the client is comfortable with. Estate planners should consider split-dollar insurance arrangements, described later in this chapter, as well as the choices of trust protectors and other techniques discussed in the context of dynasty trusts and bypass trusts.

Planning after Estate Tax Repeal in 2010

Under the modified carryover basis rules, insurance will still have a place in planning for the wealthy after the repeal of the estate tax in 2010. The following example illustrates this kind of planning.

——————— EXAMPLE ———————

Husband dies leaving assets with $1.3 million of predeath appreciation to his son and a house worth $4 million, with $3 million of predeath appreciation, to his surviving wife. However, because Husband was concerned about his surviving wife's remarrying, he had the bequest to her limited to a life estate ending on her remarriage. She had full use of the residence for her life, but on her death or remarriage, the house would be transferred to his son. The surviving wife's ownership interest in the house will lapse on the occurrence of an event, i.e., her death or remarriage, so it will not qualify for the basis adjustment.

 Husband should analyze whether better methods exist to handle the preceding situation. He might purchase a $4 million survivorship or second-to-die life insurance policy to benefit the son after the death of the second parent. This would give the son the economic value of the house and the husband the comfort of bequeathing the house outright to his wife and qualifying for the basis step-up. The cost and likely timing of incurrence of the capital gains tax (reduced by planning options reasonably available, such as the home sale exclusion) should be weighed against the anticipated insurance premium costs.

How can you plan for insurance needs without knowing what the law will be? Taxpayers may not feel a need to acquire additional insurance for estate liquidity based on the increase in the exclusion from $675,000 to $1 million in 2002 and thereafter to $3.5 million. But then again, in 2011 the exclusion drops back to $1 million. Inflation alone can push the estate into a high estate tax position if in 2011 the tax is back. What should taxpayers do? Buy insurance coverage they will not need if the estate tax is ultimately repealed? Defer insurance purchases until the law becomes more certain? The problem with the latter approach is the risk that premiums will be substantial or health issues may preclude the person from obtaining coverage. Another approach might be to consider term insurance with conversion options or insurance with guaranteed insurability options later on.

Given the uncertainty of how long the modified carryover basis rules will last, taxpayers should endeavor to infuse as much flexibility as they are comfortable with into any new insurance trusts. Consider split-dollar insurance arrangements, discussed below.

A few final points also warrant consideration. An insurance policy can provide a substantial income tax benefit. The assets inside the insurance policy can grow and compound without triggering any income tax. Further, as noted previously, insurance provides a measure of asset protection from claimants and creditors. These benefits will remain important regardless of the status of the estate tax.

SPLIT-DOLLAR INSURANCE ARRANGEMENTS

Private split-dollar (also called "family split-dollar") arrangements are split-dollar insurance arrangements in which the split in insurance ownership is between different individuals (or entities, such as trusts controlled by those individuals), who are usually, though not necessarily, related. For example, the split could be between an insurance trust owning an interest in an insurance policy on the husband/insured and the noninsured spouse (or another trust or entity or family member), who owns the remaining interests in the policy.

The typical private split-dollar arrangement provides for an irrevocable life insurance trust (ILIT) to own the net death benefit and the spouse of the insured to own the remaining interests (cash value) in the policy as the financial party. In lieu of the spouse, any number of different types of irrevocable trusts can be substituted. This arrangement is sometimes referred to as a *two trust format*. Using an irrevocable trust as the financial party provides the insured a greater degree of control over the arrangements, particularly the cash value buildup in the policy. This is achieved because the insured will presumably dictate, within the constraints required by applicable tax law, the terms of the second trust. However, as with all private split-dollar arrangements, there can be no legally binding obligation to pay anything to the insured.

If the second trust is formed by the spouse, not the insured, and is structured in a manner that avoids its inclusion in the spouse's estate (e.g., through a dynasty trust or children trust), then the entire insurance proceeds (including the interest in cash value that is typically included in the spouse's estate if not spent down) could escape estate taxation. This trust would have to be drafted in a manner that would not grant the spouse any rights causing inclusion in her estate of the interests it holds in the policy cash value. Note that to effect this type of planning benefit, the gift tax considerations on forming and funding this second irrevocable trust have to be addressed.

For the results intended from a private split-dollar arrangement to be realized, the transactions must be characterized by the IRS as a split-dollar insurance arrangement. The IRS in recent pronouncements has been clamping down on split-dollar arrangements.

Uses for a Private Split-Dollar Insurance Arrangement Post-2001 Tax Act

A private split-dollar arrangement is worth considering to ensure that insurance proceeds are excluded from a taxable estate and the taxpayer either wants to preserve access to the policy cash values for retirement or other financial needs or, because of uncertainties about the estate tax, wants to minimize current gift tax consequences of funding insurance premiums.

 Private split-dollar insurance arrangements offer an excellent planning tool. If taxpayer is unsure about tying up large value in an insurance policy held by an irrevocable trust until the outcome of estate tax repeal becomes more certain, a private split-dollar insurance arrangement is a great technique since it can enable him to reach through to the policy's cash value buildup. Also, with the $1 million lifetime gift exclusion, the use of private split-dollar arrangements can enable taxpayer to transfer greater value during his lifetime without incurring a gift tax.

Planning after Estate Tax Repeal in 2010

The continued existence of the gift tax, even if the estate and GST taxes are eliminated in 2010, will encourage the use of split-dollar insurance as a viable method of transferring valuable assets through insurance plans after the estate tax repeal. Wealthy taxpayers will persist in their efforts to transfer wealth and to avoid using up unnecessarily their $1 million lifetime gift tax exclusion.

If the estate tax is to be repealed, or if the exclusion is increased sufficiently that life insurance is no longer required, then just as with the analysis of insurance trusts, a split-dollar arrangement may no longer be warranted. In such cases, insurance and estate advisers can investigate unwinding the arrangement.

GRANTOR RETAINED ANNUITY TRUSTS

A grantor retained annuity trust (GRAT) is a tax technique used to leverage gifts made to children or other heirs (except not to grandchildren or anyone subject to GST tax).

EXAMPLE

In 2002 and thereafter, taxpayer can gift away $1 million of assets during his lifetime without incurring any tax. Assume that he is 50 and has a family business worth $3 million. He wants to give stock to his three children who are active in the business. If he gave away all of his stock at one time, he would incur a substantial gift tax, say, approximately $1 million [($3 million gift − $1 million exclusion) × 48% tax rate]. Instead, if he used a GRAT, he could reduce the value of the gift of stock to substantially less than $3 million and in this way decrease, or even eliminate, the gift tax. Regardless of the changes in the estate tax, the gift exclusion remains set at $1 million, making GRAT planning an important technique.

A GRAT provides a discount in value for gift tax purposes because during the term of the GRAT, the grantor receives a periodic (annual or more frequent) distribution. On a present-value basis, this results in a reduction in value for current gift tax purposes. This periodic annuity can also ensure an adequate cash flow in future years during the term of the trust.

EXAMPLE

Taxpayer contributes some of his securities portfolio to a family limited partnership (FLP) and then contributes some portion of the FLP interests to one or more GRATs, each for a different number of years. During the time period of each GRAT, he will receive an annual, monthly, or quarterly annuity payment for the term of the trust. Following the term of the trust, the assets would be transferred in full to his heirs. This transaction would discount the value of the assets used for gift tax purposes. The basis of the discount is that although the gift is being made today, the heirs must wait a period of years to receive it. Thus, the current value of the FLP interests would be reduced to their present value (i.e., reflecting the discount for the annuity payment to be made back to grantor).

Factors Affecting Tax Benefits of GRATs

Five factors affect the value of the gift you make to children or other heirs through a GRAT:

1. The value of the property contributed to the GRAT. If interests in an FLP or LLC are used to fund the GRAT, an appraisal must be obtained to determine its value and appropriate discounts.
2. The annuity percentage selected. The higher the percentage annuity payment to be made periodically to the grantor during

the GRAT term, the lower the gift tax value. However, the reduced gift tax value comes at a cost, i.e., leakage of additional payments from the GRAT to the grantor and hence back into the taxable estate. Also, if the GRAT does not produce enough income to make the annual payments, principal (e.g., some of the FLP interests) used to fund the GRAT will have to be paid back to the estate.

3. The annuity term selected. The longer the period for which the annuity payments will be made by the GRAT, the lower the value of the gift to the remainder beneficiaries (e.g., the grantor's children) for gift tax purposes. Thus, the longer the term, the better the tax result. However, if the grantor does not survive the specified GRAT term, the entire principal of the GRAT is pulled back into the estate.

4. The frequency of the payments under the GRAT, whether annual, quarterly, or monthly. The more frequent the payments, the greater the value of the grantor's retained interest and the lower the value of the gift for gift tax purposes. The frequency, however, must be weighed in light of the administrative burdens it creates and the potential cash flow problems. Annual is easiest.

5. The "Applicable Federal Rate" (interest rate determined under tax law guidelines) available for the month in which the GRAT is created. When these are at low levels as a result of a decline in market interest rates, GRATs can be an especially attractive planning technique.

In combination, the preceding factors will determine the value of the gift on creation of the GRAT (and hence the amount of gift tax that may be due). The GRATs are "grantor trusts" for income tax purposes, and therefore no additional income tax returns are required. The results are simply reported on the taxpayer's personal income tax return. The use of GRATs can be contrasted with the use of the note sale to an intentionally defective irrevocable trust (IDIT), discussed later in this chapter.

Tax Relief Changes Affecting GRAT Transactions

The 2001 Tax Act did not directly affect the GRAT technique. However, three changes indirectly affect this planning technique:

1. The increase in the estate tax exclusion will enable many taxpayers to avoid the estate tax, thus diminishing the need for GRAT planning. However, in 2011 the tax is scheduled to return; planning should not be ignored pending the resolution of the uncertainty as to what will really happen with the tax.
2. Estate and gift tax rates have been reduced, but the benefits will be marginal and should not significantly affect GRAT planning.
3. The gift tax exclusion does not increase beyond $1 million, so for families seeking to pass on significant wealth while they are alive, the GRAT technique will remain useful.

The bottom line for tax planning is that many taxpayers who have large estates or who are elderly or infirm will find that planning with GRATs to reduce estate taxes is still advisable. Even if the estate tax is repealed, the $1 million gift exclusion will continue the need for GRATs for large gift transactions.

Post-2001 Tax Act Planning for Existing GRATs

Taxpayers who have existing GRATs in place can do little to change them because they are irrevocable transactions. However, depending on state law, if all the beneficiaries are adults, terminating the GRAT might be possible. This will raise issues in that a GRAT must include a provision prohibiting paying the grantor the value of the grantor's interest in advance (called a "no commutation" clause). However, if the GRAT was appropriate as to the grantor's planning needs when drafted, barring major changes in the value of the estate or financial needs, it will often remain appropriate, even if the need for it may have lessened (e.g., as a result of the increase in the exclusion to $1 million from $675,000).

Unsuitable Uses for GRATs

GRATs are not an appropriate tax planning technique for generation-skipping transfer (GST) tax planning, because of a technical trap called the estate tax inclusion period (ETIP), explained in Chapter 1. Simply stated, a taxpayer cannot allocate the GST exemption to protect a GRAT from GST tax until the GRAT ends. At that time, the assets in the GRAT will have likely appreciated, and the planning benefits will be compromised. Given the value of dynasty trust planning to the wealthy and the uncertainty of whether the estate tax will really be repealed, GST planning remains important. Although a GRAT can leverage lifetime gifts to minimize gift tax, it is not an effective tool for leveraging gifts for GST tax purposes. Another technique, the sale to an intentionally defective irrevocable trust, can be used to leverage gifts for allocation of the GST exemption.

SALES TO INTENTIONALLY DEFECTIVE GRANTOR TRUSTS

The sale to an intentionally defective irrevocable trust (IDIT) is a sale to a trust that is intentionally structured to qualify as a grantor trust for income tax purposes, while being excluded from the grantor's estate for estate tax purposes. This is an aggressive planning technique that could potentially offer substantial estate and GST tax savings.

The defective grantor trust is an irrevocable trust on which the grantor (who formed and funded the trust) pays the income tax on income earned by the trust. With nearly a 40 percent marginal income tax rate under prior law, this was the economic equivalent of a large additional transfer by the grantor to the trust, without incidence of additional gift tax. Even under the reduced income tax rates post-2001 Tax Act, this benefit can still be significant.

NOTE

After 2009, a gift transfer to a trust will be treated as a completed gift, and hence gift tax will be assessed, unless the trust is treated for income tax purposes as wholly owned by the donor or the donor's spouse (a fully grantor trust). This rule might make the use of IDITs problematic if the transfer to an IDIT under this new rule is viewed as incomplete for gift and estate tax purposes. Future regulations may help clarify the consequences.

The theoretical basis for this tax position is that the classification of a trust as a grantor trust under the tax laws makes the grantor primarily responsible for the payment of the income taxes on the trust. Thus, by paying income taxes, the grantor is meeting a legal obligation. Not surprisingly, the IRS has taken a contrary view in private letter rulings in which it has held that payment of trust income taxes is an additional gift to the trust. If the IRS successfully challenged payments of income taxes, these payments would trigger additional taxable gifts. This risk should be weighed against the benefits of the additional economic benefits conferred on trust beneficiaries and in light of whether the making of additional taxable gifts is reasonably consistent with the taxpayer's estate planning goals.

In the context of the IDIT, its defective, or grantor trust, status is even more important. In addition to the income tax benefit described in the preceding paragraph, the intent in an IDIT transaction is for the grantor to sell assets to the trust that may appreciate significantly. If the IDIT is a grantor trust, no gain for income tax purposes will be triggered on the sale or note payments made to the trust. If the IDIT were not so classified, then gain would be triggered.

The grantor sells to the IDIT assets that are expected to appreciate substantially after the sale (at a rate greater than the interest rate paid by the IDIT to the grantor). Since it would be anticipated that the IDIT would purchase interests in a family limited partnership (FLP) or family limited liability company (LLC), the discounts inherent in the valuation would leverage or boost this return.

The trust pays for the property by executing an installment promissory note to the grantor. The IDIT is a grantor trust that for income tax purposes is not treated as a separate entity. Because the trust is not recognized as a separate tax-paying entity, the grantor's sale of assets to the trust is equivalent to a sale to the grantor. Therefore, no gain or loss is recognized for income tax purposes on this transaction.

Also, the trust earnings after the sale remain taxable to the grantor for income tax purposes. Thus, when an IDIT is successfully structured as a grantor trust for income tax purposes, the income, gains, and losses of the trust are reported on the grantor's personal income tax return and not on a separate tax return filed by the trust.

For selling assets to the trust, the grantor receives back an interest-bearing note, with interest payments at a rate required by applicable tax law.[9] When rates are low, the IDIT technique can be especially favorable. This interest rate would be accompanied by a balloon payment at the end of the note term. Consideration should be given to some principal amortization during the term. The premise of the arrangement is that if the transaction is properly structured, the asset is valued at the face value of the note, and therefore there is no gift.

NOTE

If grantor dies and the estate holds the installment note, the note will not qualify for a step-up in tax basis, and the assets sold to the defective trust will retain their carryover (i.e., low) tax basis. The assets sold to the defective trust will not receive a step-up in tax basis on death because they are not taxed in the decedent's estate.

If the carryover basis rules become effective in 2010, this downside to an IDIT transaction will no longer be relevant for estates larger than those subject to the $1.3 million/$3 million basis adjustments. This is because there will no longer be a relative downside to the IDIT if there is no basis step-up on the seller/decedent's death.

At some future date, the note should be unwound, preferably before the grantor's death. If it is advantageous to eliminate the note under current law (i.e., the 2001 Tax Act prior to 2010), this can be accomplished by the IDIT selling the assets it owns and using a portion of the proceeds to pay off the note due to the grantor from the sale. Alternatively, the grantor might opt to repurchase the assets from the IDIT for their then fair market value. The payment by the grantor to the IDIT also should not trigger any taxable gain to the IDIT, again because the trust is a grantor trust. In this latter scenario, when the hopefully highly appreciated assets held by the IDIT are repurchased, they would be included in the grantor's estate. Under current law, on the grantor's death, such assets would receive a step-up in tax basis and the capital gains would be permanently avoided.

> **NOTE**
>
> Under the 2001 Tax Act, in 2010 the modified carryover basis rules come into play and there may not be a step-up in the income tax basis of these assets. In that case, a major drawback of the IDIT technique will be eliminated.

Gift and Estate Tax Considerations of IDITs

Despite the preceding income tax considerations (e.g., grantor trust status), an IDIT transaction can be structured to qualify as a completed gift transfer for gift and estate tax purposes.

The IDIT technique raises several gift, estate, generation-skipping, and income tax issues. In addition, the technique should be compared with that of a GRAT and the latter's tax consequences. The major differences are that the IDIT has greater leverage, and hence tax benefit, but is not based on firm regulatory guidelines as is a GRAT. For this reason, both techniques should be analyzed.

GST Tax Considerations of IDITs

An IDIT could arguably be the most valuable generation-skipping transfer (GST) leveraging technique available. The IDIT transaction could theoretically be structured to have a gift value of $1, against which GST exemption could be allocated. However, under prior law in determining whether the IDIT should incorporate GST planning, and if so how, consideration had to be given to whether the grantor wished to structure the IDIT transaction in filing a gift tax return or would prefer not to file a gift tax return in order to allocate GST exemption.

 The requirement to file a gift tax return to allocate GST exemption to an IDIT transaction prior to the 2001 Tax Act was a major risk many taxpayers felt uncomfortable taking. However, the automatic allocation rules can now be used as an affirmative estate tax device to avoid the need to file a gift tax return for an IDIT transaction. Simply structure the IDIT trust so that any gift to the trust will result in an automatic GST allocation under the new rules, and presto, the transaction remains invisible to the IRS. An IDIT sale to a dynasty trust post-2001 Tax Act may be an excellent estate planning technique for large estates.

Even if the planning tip above is pursued, it will not ensure that the IDIT transaction will be "invisible" for gift tax purposes. This is because many advisers structuring IDIT transactions have advocated cash gifts to the trust in the amount of, say, 10 percent of the value of the transaction. This is done to provide an economic basis for the loan—for example, there are assets other than those being sold to support the transaction. If this is done, GST exemption would have to be allocated to the cash gift or the cash gift would have to be reported as a gift.

The manner in which estate planners structure the transaction is important. If the taxpayer has, for example, an Alaska inter vivos asset protection trust or establishes a dynasty trust under his will, the IDIT could be protected by GST exemption and then pour over at some future date into the dynasty trust.

A key advantage of the IDIT over the GRAT transaction is that because of the GRAT's payments of the annuity amount to the grantor, an estate tax inclusion period (ETIP) exists, and therefore no GST exemption can be allocated until the termination of the GRAT (see the discussion of ETIP in Chapter 1). In contrast, with an IDIT transaction, there is no ETIP, so GST can be allocated at the outset. This is a valuable leveraging technique, especially when the

IDIT is purchasing assets for which substantial postpurchase appreciation may occur. The discounts on value to be achieved through a FLP or LLC will contribute to the appreciation potential over the gift tax value.

Tax Relief Changes Affecting IDIT Transactions

As noted, the automatic GST allocation may have solved the concern many taxpayers had over filing a gift tax return to allocate GST exemption to an IDIT transaction. If the defective trust to which the sale occurs in the IDIT transaction is classified as a GST trust under the new GST allocation rules, which is almost assured, then it is unnecessary to file a gift tax return notifying the IRS that an allocation of the GST exemption has been made to the trust. It will occur automatically.

For large estates, the scheduled increases in the applicable exclusion and GST exemption, particularly between 2005 and 2009, create a great opportunity for IDIT and other aggressive planning. Moreover, with the IDIT, taxpayers needn't wait, because the technique offers tremendous leverage. It might be possible to structure a transaction sooner and add to it later.

If a carryover basis regime is really allowed to happen, a major detriment of the IDIT technique for substantial estates—the risk of the transaction not being unwound before death so that heirs receive assets without a step-up in basis—may not really matter.

Post-2001 Tax Act Planning for Existing IDITs

Existing IDIT transactions are likely to be continued because this technique was generally used by substantial estates. These estates are likely to remain subject to a significant estate tax as long as the tax exists. Furthermore, because an existing IDIT transaction is not revocable, the defective trust probably cannot be unwound (but see the earlier discussion of the termination of an irrevocable trust). However, the methods used to unwind the note to evidence the sale in the past will still serve the grantor who determines that terminating the ongoing installment sale transaction is advisable.

Planning for New IDITs

If the joke is that Jack Kevorkian and Tony Soprano will be booking appointments for lots of grandmothers for December 2010 while the estate tax is still in its one-year repeal, estate planners should be well aware that IDITs will be the name of the game in December 2009. Maybe the best comment on the IDIT transaction is the Nike commercial, "Just Do It!"

Taxpayer was certain that the estate tax would be repealed and dismissed his estate planner's calls to address revising his estate plan as merely an attempt to hustle some more business. In about December 2009 taxpayer realizes that the estate tax will be back. He has one month left to take advantage of the $3.5 million estate tax exclusion and a similar $3.5 million GST tax exemption. His estate planner suggests using a sale to a defective grantor trust to fund as much as possible of the estate into a dynasty trust to obtain a grandfather protection from the reinstated estate tax. The IDIT will save the day.

DYNASTY TRUSTS

Dynasty trusts can be referred to as self-funded trusts since the grantor is the one contributing assets to, or funding, the trust. Yet the grantor remains a beneficiary. These trusts can be called perpetual trusts because they can continue forever. They are referred to as domestic asset protection trusts because they can be used to protect the grantor's assets without the need to move the trust to an offshore tax haven jurisdiction such as the Cook Islands. For simplicity, they are referred to in this book as *dynasty trusts* because the combination of all these benefits is the development of a dynasty trust for the grantor's family.

Dynasty trusts constitute a key planning tool. Given the uncertainty of what Congress might do next, many taxpayers would do well to secure tax benefits for as long as possible, instead of waiting to see what the next Congress will serve up. A dynasty trust, especially a domestic asset protection dynasty trust, which Alaska and Delaware law can provide, is potentially the most powerful tool to address this planning uncertainty.

The objective of the dynasty trust concept is that assets would be removed from the taxpayer's estate as well as the spouse's estate. These assets can be maintained in perpetuity, outside the GST, estate, and gift tax systems. Dynasty trusts must be formed in a state that has eliminated the rule against perpetuities. This is a legal concept that in general terms limited the duration for which a trust could last. If the assets of the trust are to be made available to the grantor, then a further restriction is that the state selected for the trust must be a state that permits a grantor to make a completed gift to a trust, such that the assets in that trust are protected from creditors, yet still permissible to be distributed to the grantor. Alaska and Delaware are the two most popular states for these types of trust.

Although the assets in a dynasty trust could be available to either the taxpayer or spouse, and even their children, the ideal approach is to retain those assets in the dynasty trust whenever possible so that the tax protection (afforded by the allocation of estate tax exclusion and GST exemption) will not be wasted. The assets of the trust can be reached by any family members specified, including the grantor, but the longer they remain in trust the greater the eventual tax benefits. It is unwise to remove assets unless they are really needed, because distributions that are not spent may become subject to estate and GST tax in the future. Thus, the ideal is to continue to grow dynasty trusts outside the estate and transfer tax systems for the eventual use of grandchildren and future heirs. The leverage in multigenerational tax savings can be tremendous.

These funds can also serve as a last resort or safety net in the event a malpractice or other claim somehow destroys the taxpayer's asset base.

Retaining the right to be a discretionary beneficiary of a dynasty trust could cause the IRS to challenge the position that the assets of the dynasty trust are not taxable in the taxpayer's estate. It could also be a basis for malpractice claimants or other plaintiffs to argue that they should be able to reach the assets in the dynasty trust to satisfy claims. The laws concerning dynasty trusts are relatively new, and compared with insurance trusts and other more common and established techniques, unproven. Taxpayers must evaluate these risks with advisers before proceeding.

A common technique used when funding dynasty trusts is to make gifts to the dynasty trust with leveraging techniques to maximize the tax benefits. This can be done with IDITs or more simply by transferring noncontrolling interests in FLPs or LLCs, valued with discounts for lack of control and marketability.

Structure and Operation of a Dynasty Trust

A common approach used to structure a dynasty trust is to name an Alaska or Delaware bank or trust company to serve as cotrustee. Not only does this provide objective and professional management, but from a legal perspective, having a cotrustee licensed and operating in Alaska or Delaware creates a substantial connection (nexus) to support the position that the favorable laws of that state will apply to the grantor of the trust. The following example illustrates how a dynasty trust typically might operate.

EXAMPLE

Taxpayer is an anesthesiologist and concerned about malpractice claims. He forms a dynasty trust in Alaska in 2001. He transfers $100,000 in cash and marketable securities to the trust, which are invested in the Alaska bank or trust company selected to serve as cotrustee. This further supports his nexus to Alaska and the application of Alaska law.

> He maintains a substantial $3 million brokerage account with a financial adviser he trusts and has confidence in. Taxpayer doesn't really want to lose investment control over his portfolio or the assistance of the adviser. He transfers $2.2 million of the securities portfolio to a family LLC formed on the advice of his attorney in 2001. He did not transfer the remaining $800,000 based on his attorney's advice that he must retain reasonable assets for living expenses and emergencies in his own name. He then gifts, in 2002 when the exclusion increases to $1 million, a 40 percent interest in the equity of the LLC to the dynasty trust. This 40 percent interest is valued at $650,000 [$2.2 million × 40 percent less discounts for lack of control and marketability].
>
> Taxpayer remains manager of the LLC and thus has some reasonable measure of control. Further, his trusted financial adviser continues to advise him concerning investments on most of the portfolio.

The assets transferred to the dynasty trust can include cash and marketable securities. It is often advisable to have some assets such as cash or securities deposited directly in an institution in Alaska or Delaware. The bulk of the assets transferred to a dynasty trust are more typically interests in a closely held FLP or LLC to leverage the discounts for tax purposes. An FLP or LLC also provides the grantor with greater control and asset protection.

If the taxpayer is married, the transfers in the example could be increased with proper planning to utilize the exclusion available to him and his spouse. The generation-skipping transfer tax exemption would be allocated to protect the assets so transferred. This technique could also be combined with the IDIT (note sale to defective grantor trust) technique for further leverage, as discussed previously.

Tax Relief Changes Affecting Dynasty Trusts

The 2001 Tax Act has made several changes that affect dynasty trust planning. Perhaps the most significant development is the increase in the estate tax exclusion and the eventual increase and matching of the estate tax exclusion with the GST exemption. The result is that as of January 2002 taxpayers were able to contribute up to $1 million (and if married, taxpayer and spouse could contribute up to $2 million) to a dynasty trust. These amounts are set to increase substantially if the estate tax exclusion and GST exemption increases, as enacted, are allowed to occur. In fact, by 2009 a taxpayer is able to gift $3.5 million to a dynasty trust. Together, taxpayer and spouse will be able to contribute $7 million. All these figures can be increased substantially by using the leveraging techniques described in this book.

The 2001 Tax Act has introduced substantial uncertainty into estate and related planning. It has probably heightened the mistrust many taxpayers feel about the tax system. How else is one supposed to feel about a "repeal" of the estate tax that lasts but one year, 2010? As a result, many taxpayers believe, and probably wisely so, that they should grab the tax benefits while they can. So if the exclusion increases, gift more to a dynasty trust. The dynasty trust is ideal in that the estate and GST benefits can be preserved forever. It is also ideal in that few taxpayers will be comfortable making irrevocable gifts that they can never benefit from. The dynasty trust, if it proves sustainable when attacked in future years, is the best of all planning scenarios because the grantor can secure a tax benefit, yet remain a beneficiary of the trust. This fact should entice far more taxpayers to gift greater amounts out of their estates.

The post-2001 Tax Act system retains a maximum lifetime gift tax exclusion of $1 million, as explained in Chapter 1. The maximum funding of a dynasty trust while the taxpayer is alive (e.g., up to the $1 million maximum) and again at death (perhaps with the remainder of the estate) will enable heirs to circumvent the gift tax with respect to the assets, including appreciation, in the dynasty trust. The dynasty trust assets will never be included in the estates of the taxpayer's children (or other heirs), so they cannot be subject to a gift tax. Thus, if a grantor's child wants to have a significant asset transferred to his child in a future year, the trustee of the dynasty trust can do so without imposition of a gift tax.

The possible demise of the estate tax will mean an increased emphasis on income taxation to raise revenues. The dynasty trust provides a valuable income tax planning tool as discussed in previous chapters. The states where dynasty trusts are located are unlikely to charge state-level income tax. Over many years, the compounded benefits of this tax savings can be substantial. Further, a trustee of a dynasty trust with a broad discretionary distribution power under the dynasty trust agreement can distribute funds to any beneficiary. This will draw out taxable income to the beneficiaries receiving such distributions. The result is that the trustee will have some latitude to sprinkle taxable income to the beneficiaries in the lowest income tax brackets. As the Congress seeks to raise revenues in future years, the income tax may be the way. If history is any guide, the projected budget surpluses that were the basis of the 2001 Tax Act will disappear faster than a Hershey bar on the set of *Survivor*. Having substantial assets in a dynasty trust with broad discretionary distribution powers will give trustees some planning room.

Few taxpayers believe that the estate tax has disappeared. The common perception is that it has merely been cleverly disguised for political benefit. If so, the estate planner can advise taxpayers to fund most or all of their estate into a dynasty trust (at death if a taxpayer is not comfortable with doing so now); if the tax is reinstated, or the exclusions reduced, heirs will be protected since previously formed irrevocable trusts should not be reachable.

Dynasty trusts, whether formed now to reduce estate taxes and protect assets, or funded at death to protect descendants, should become an increasingly popular planning tool.

Essential Decisions for Dynasty Trust Planning

Many decisions that must be considered in dynasty trust planning have been affected by the 2001 Tax Act.

Distribution Provisions

The preferable way to draft a dynasty trust document is probably for distributions to be solely in the discretion of the trustee. Any mandatory distributions, under any other type of standard, will distribute assets out of the protective cover of the dynasty trust. Any such mandatory distributions will remove the GST tax protection, asset protection benefits, or related protective features.

Dynasty trusts have often been drafted with all distributions being totally discretionary to the trustee. This can be done for several reasons, including, as noted above, GST planning and asset protection planning. For GST planning, it is preferable to keep assets retained in a trust unless distribution is necessary, because retained assets can be passed on, in many instances to the next generation, without incurring additional estate tax. Thus, purely discretionary trust distribution standards enable trustees to retain monies that are not needed. In contrast, a trust that requires the trustee to distribute income and specified percentages of principal at specified beneficiary ages would defeat the intended dynasty trust benefits. This latter approach would cause all mandated payments to lose their tax-favored protection. From an asset protection perspective, required distributions will then be reachable, once distributed, by the beneficiary's creditors, divorce claimants, and so forth. If such a vague standard as "in the trustee's discretion" is used, it may be wise to prepare nonbinding side letters offering more detailed discussions and recommendations as to when and how distribution should be made.

If, in light of the 2001 Tax Act changes, the taxpayer decides to gift substantial assets to a dynasty trust (e.g., to take advantage of the increased exclusion in future years) the estate planner should reevaluate the distribution provisions to make sure that the taxpayer and spouse, if any, are adequately protected.

Although consideration might be given to a mandatory distribution based on an annuity trust concept, the benefits of no mandatory distributions should be considered. An annuity-type payment can be illustrated as follows: Each January 31, calculate 4 percent of the principal balance. Pay this amount in equal monthly installments by the last day of each month of that year. Also, distributions of income with periodic principal distributions (e.g., one-third at ages 25, 30, and 35) or discretionary rights given to the trustee to invade principal, similar to those for a typical children's trust, may not be appropriate for the same reasons.

EXAMPLE

Under pre-2001 Tax Act law taxpayer planned to contribute $500,000 to a dynasty trust. Since it was only a small component of his estate, he was not concerned about using a vague and broad discretionary distribution power. Now, however, he has decided to take advantage of the increasing exclusion for himself and his spouse by transferring more assets, in fact, a significant portion of the estate. His estate planner might want to reevaluate having a distribution committee, different distribution standards, and other precautions.

What distribution standards should be used? If the taxpayer is comfortable, a vague and broad standard is best. This gives the trustee authority to minimize distributions and thus keep assets within the protective envelope of the dynasty trust. Should the trustee be given the right to purchase personal use property and make it available for any beneficiaries? In most cases, this is a good idea. For example, the trust can buy a house for the beneficiary to use. How large must the exclusion be before the taxpayer becomes concerned about contributing too much to the trust? If the trust is flexible, the income tax, management, and asset protection benefits are so substantial that all assets could be so held if the taxpayer were comfortable with such an arrangement.

 Many of these decisions are similar to those discussed earlier in the context of a bypass trust. Estate planners should review the issues covered in that section concerning a dynasty trust.

Trust Divisions and Subdivision

When the dynasty trust is started, it might be organized as one large pot trust for the benefit of the taxpayer, the spouse, if any, and all descendants. However, on the taxpayer's death (or if married, following the death of the last of the taxpayer and the spouse) should the trust be divided so that each child would have a separate trust? Or should the dynasty trust be retained as a single pot trust for everyone? Alternatively, should it be divided into separate trusts at every generational level? What about at the next generation and generations after that? Most taxpayers divide the trust at the generation of their children. Beyond that, continued divisions could become unwieldy as family lines grow. Each taxpayer should weigh the pros and cons with careful consideration to the administrative costs.

Perpetual Trust Term

A key objective of the dynasty trust concept is that the trust should last perpetually, or until funds are exhausted. The ramifications of this for trust drafting, planning, and in particular for investing are substantial. Where is the real time horizon when formulating the trust's investment strategy if there is no duration or final payout? The trust's longer time frame to take advantage of GST and asset protection benefits creates needs that are different from the more typical or shorter term trust used in other trusts.

Trust Protector

When a trust is designated as continuing for a perpetual period of time, an institutional cotrustee would be named to take advantage of the laws of a state which permits perpetual trusts. Because of the use of an institutional trustee, and the long term of the trust, an additional safeguard of appointing a person to serve in the status of trust protector may be warranted. (See the section on bypass trusts). Many of the concepts are similar. Should the trust protector be empowered to order a distribution and termination of the dynasty trust if the estate and GST taxes are totally repealed? If so, is it worth jeopardizing the many nonestate/GST benefits? For taxpayers wealthy enough to engage in this type of planning, it is likely that the control, professional management, and asset protection benefits would warrant keeping the trust intact regardless of estate tax repeal.

Who should be named trust protector? Successor? What powers should be given? This is even more complex for a dynasty trust than for a typical bypass trust, which is only intended to last until the death of the last of the grantor and spouse.

Investment Adviser

The trend is for increasing specialization with respect to trust functions. For the vast majority of trusts still existing, and certainly in almost all past trusts, a person or institution named as trustee was responsible for all trust functions. With the recognition of the importance of investment diversification and the increasing acceptance of the Prudent Investor Act, it has now become permissible to delegate or direct money management functions. Thus, it is becoming much more common for a person or institution to serve as an administrative trustee and have yet another person or institution named as investment adviser to handle money management decisions. The taxpayer should consider appointing an institutional administrative trustee located in Alaska or Delaware to obtain access to Alaska's or Delaware's favorable laws. However, where there is a long-established and successful relationship with a financial adviser or money manager, that person could be named as the investment adviser to manage the marketable securities portion of the dynasty trust's assets.

Removal of Trustee

Given the long duration of a dynasty trust (forever is a long time), estate planners should review whether the dynasty trust document should include a right of someone (beneficiaries by vote, trust protector, or another party) to remove or replace trustees. Typically, this right is limited to replacing an institutional trustee with another institutional trustee. This provision could be drafted in a somewhat restricted manner so that the beneficiaries, if given the right to remove a trustee, won't be able to simply go "trustee shopping" until they find a trustee willing to let them dissipate money in any fashion they wish.

Implementing a Common Post-2001 Tax Act
Dynasty Trust Plan

Forming and then operating a dynasty trust involves several steps, but
there is not really a set sequence. For example, it is necessary to address the types of assets to be transferred to the dynasty trust when
drafting the trust, although the assets obviously cannot be transferred
until the trust is drafted and signed. Estate planners should expect to
implement the following procedures:

- Determine which state the dynasty trust will be based in. This
  must be a state that has repealed the laws restricting the duration for which a trust can exist (the "rule against perpetuities"). If the taxpayer setting up the trust wants to be a
  beneficiary of the trust, he will have to select a state that permits self-settled trusts (e.g., Alaska or Delaware).

- Help the taxpayer make the numerous decisions necessary to
  draft a dynasty trust. This includes the selection of trustees. As
  discussed previously, choose a bank or trust company in the
  state where the trust is to be based, to create a sufficient
  connection for that state's laws to apply (nexus). Select quasi-
  fiduciaries (investment adviser, trust protector, distribution
  committee, etc.) and the detailed provisions governing these
  positions. Make sure that the powers and responsibilities of
  each fiduciary and quasi-fiduciary are coordinated to avoid
  overlap or contradiction. Determine how and when trust assets
  may be distributed.

- Have the trust drafted and signed.

- Obtain a tax identification number for the trust, if required.

- Determine what assets to transfer to the trust. This is usually
  a multistep process in that often another entity is created, such
  as an FLP or LLC, to facilitate the transfer of assets, and in
  particular to qualify the assets transferred for valuation discounts (explained elsewhere in this chapter). If the estate is
  large enough, an IDIT might be useful to leverage the transfers to the dynasty trust. With any of these approaches, the

additional entities will have to be formed, gifts made, and documents drafted. This might include, in addition to forming an LLC, drafting the operating agreement governing it; contributing assets, such as securities, to the LLC in a manner that does not trigger any adverse income tax consequences; and then having an appraisal of the LLC membership interests that are being given to the dynasty trust.

- A gift tax return will have to be filed reporting the gifts made to the dynasty trust. If, however, the dynasty trust is funded at death, the transfer will be reported on an estate tax return (or once the tax is repealed in 2010 on the replacement tax filing the IRS will require, as explained in Chapter 7).

- The estate planner and client should review and revise any wills, as needed, and if the client has parents or other persons who may bequeath assets to him, they should also review and consider revising their wills and/or trusts so that bequests are made instead to the dynasty trust when appropriate.

- Once the dynasty trust is formed and funded it will operate. This will require a review of investments to ensure maximum income and estate tax savings, often with the objective of minimizing current income taxes while investing for long-term growth. This typical scenario must be monitored as circumstances change, beneficiaries' needs for funds change, and so forth. Annual income tax returns will have to be filed in the state where the trust is based and with the IRS. Reports may have to be furnished to other fiduciaries or quasi-fiduciaries. Information may have to be solicited from beneficiaries to determine distribution decisions. Beneficiaries may have to be informed of investment or distribution decisions.

- If all proceeds as planned, assets in the dynasty trust will grow outside the transfer tax system, generate lower (or no) state-level income taxes, protect the assets from claimants and creditors, and provide flexibility to have assets or cash flow allocated to the grantor and descendants as needed. The trust should continue perpetually, or until the funds have been reduced to a level where it is no longer economically efficient to maintain.

Post-2001 Tax Act Planning for
Existing Dynasty Trusts

An existing dynasty trust is an irrevocable trust that cannot be changed. Considering the uncertainty of future tax legislation, the maximum $1 million gift lifetime exclusion, the tremendous nontax benefits, and the costs incurred in establishing the structure, it is probably unlikely that the taxpayer would want the trust terminated. Further, even if that were the case, it would probably prove difficult, if not impossible, to terminate a trust that was drafted in a comprehensive manner.

CHARITABLE REMAINDER TRUSTS

Charitable remainder trusts (CRTs) have always been a popular planning tool to reduce income taxes. They have also been a popular estate planning technique when combined with an insurance trust to replace the wealth given to the charity with a comparable amount for heirs outside the estate. CRTs should remain popular after the 2001 Tax Act.

A CRT is a split-interest trust that provides for the payment of income to the grantor (and typically a spouse if grantor is married when setting up the trust). Thereafter (e.g., on grantor's death, or if applicable on the death of the last of grantor and spouse), the remaining assets in the CRT are paid to a charitable beneficiary.

A taxpayer who decides to use a CRT would donate property (e.g., real property, stock, business interests) to a charity and receive a charitable contribution tax deduction in the year of the donation for income tax purposes.

With the scheduled decreases in income tax rates, setting up a CRT may enable taxpayers to claim deductions in a year when they are in a higher income tax bracket.

The charity will receive the full benefit of the property at only some future time. For example, taxpayers can reserve an income interest in the charitable remainder trust for life and the life of a spouse as the income beneficiaries. After the death of the last of the grantor and spouse, the charity will obtain full use and benefit of the donated property.

The savings in income taxes, federal gift or estate tax, state inheritance tax, and probate and administrative costs can enable transferring substantial benefit to a deserving charity at a very favorable cost.

A CRT used in a manner such as that illustrated in the following example can be a tremendous estate and financial planning vehicle.

EXAMPLE

Taxpayer purchased a high-tech stock long ago for a nominal price. The value per share has skyrocketed, and the aggregate value is now several million dollars. The stock pays almost no dividends. Taxpayer is about to retire and needs more cash flow to cover living expenses. He is also concerned about diversifying; he has become aware of the importance of asset allocation to the risk and return of his portfolio. Because this stock has become such a substantial portion of the estate, he is anxious to take action. However, selling the stock would trigger a substantial capital gain. He could instead donate the stock to a CRT and receive back a monthly payment for life (and even for the life of his spouse as well) The trust could sell the stock and invest in a diversified portfolio planned to generate greater cash flow. The trust will not recognize any capital gains tax on sale. As a result, taxpayer can effectively have the entire investment, undiminished by capital gains tax, working to generate a monthly distribution from the CRT. The financial benefits are potentially tremendous.

If the estate tax is in fact repealed, and the income tax remains the focus of future congressional efforts to raise revenue, CRTs could become even more popular. Further, if the modified carryover basis rules become reality, taxpayers might not benefit heirs with a stepped-up basis by holding highly appreciated stock. Thus, there will be less incentive to hold appreciated assets in contrast to simply pursuing a CRT.

CRATs and CRUTs

A charitable remainder annuity trust (CRAT) will provide a fixed annuity to the grantor or the people designated in the trust agreement. The minimum rate of return to them cannot be less than 5 percent and it must be a fixed or determinable amount. The beneficiaries' income is calculated based on the fair market value of the property transferred to the trust. Once the trust is established, no further contributions can be made to it. Where the trust income is insufficient to meet the required annual return, principal must be invaded.

A charitable remainder unitrust (CRUT) provides a variable annuity benefit to the grantor or the other beneficiaries designated in the trust agreement. The minimum rate of return to the income beneficiaries must be 5 percent. This rate of return is calculated on the fair market value of the property determined on an annual basis. This requires an annual appraisal, which for any property that is difficult to value (e.g., closely held business interests and real estate), could be prohibitively expensive. For this reason, an annuity trust approach is likely to prove more appropriate when such assets are to be contributed. The trust may provide that if the annual income earned by the trust property is insufficient to meet the required distribution to the income beneficiaries, principal may be invaded. If principal is not required to be invaded, then the trust must provide that the deficit (i.e., the amount not yet paid out) will be made up in later years. NIM-CRUT (for net income make-up charitable remainder unitrust) is the name given to a CRUT structured to accomplish this. Once a unitrust is established, additional contributions may be made in later years under certain conditions.

Requirements That CRTs Must Meet

The following list provides a brief overview of the complex and detailed technical requirements for CRTs:

- A CRT cannot have a payout greater than 50 percent of the fair market value of the assets contributed. If a CRT fails this test, the trust income beneficiaries will be taxed on all of the trust income. The value of the remainder interest to be received by the charity, determined on the date the property is contributed to the CRT, must be at least 10 percent of the value of the property.

- A CRT can only have one grantor.[10]

- The trust must be irrevocable. Once formed, it cannot be changed. The trust must not be subject to a power to alter, amend, invade, or revoke for the benefit of a person other than a charitable organization.[11] For example, if the grantor retains continuing control over the unitrust amount, this could be a prohibited retention of power. To avoid violating this requirement, the retention of power must be sufficiently limited to avoid the grantor-trust rules.[12]

- The trustee's investment opportunities are subject to permissible parameters. To qualify as a CRUT, the trust document cannot restrict the trustee from investing the trust assets in a manner that could result in the realization of a reasonable amount of income or gain annually from the sale or disposition of trust assets to pay the unitrust amount.[13] The IRS has indicated that the trustee must be free to invest assets in a manner that will permit the assets to realize a reasonable rate of return.[14]

- The trust document must contain either a CRAT or CRUT payment. Some flexibility is provided in exceptions to the general CRAT and CRUT rules.

- The unitrust payment may be paid after the close of the tax year for which the amount is due, provided the payment is made within a reasonable time of the year end.

- The required unitrust payment amount must be paid to one or more named "persons" (an individual, trust, estate, partnership, association, company, or corporation), all of whom must be living at the time the trust is created.[15]

- On expiration of the last noncharitable income beneficiary, all of the trust's assets must be either transferred irrevocably to or for the use of a charitable organization.[16]
- Additional contributions may be made to a CRUT after the initial funding. This contrasts with a CRAT, to which no additional contributions may be made.[17]
- The trust must contain a provision that addresses incorrect determinations of value concerning the trust corpus.[18]

Tax Relief Changes Affecting CRTs

Lower income tax rates will somewhat lessen the income tax benefits of CRTs. The increase in the estate tax exclusion and possible repeal of the estate tax might affect how some taxpayers structure CRT transactions. Many taxpayers combine CRTs with the purchase of life insurance to replace the value no longer passing to children or other heirs. The increase in the estate tax exclusion might motivate some of these taxpayers to own the insurance directly instead of using a trust. For the pros and cons of this issue, see the earlier discussion of insurance trusts.

Planning for New CRTs

For taxpayers who are confident that the modified carryover basis rules will come into play and who have more appreciation in their estate than these rules will address, a previous downside to CRTs is eliminated. This might increase the incentive among some to make use of this planning tool. To the extent that taxpayers can qualify for the low capital gains rate applicable to assets held over five years, the income tax benefit of CRTs will be reduced. It is important to remember, however, that the only sure way to ascertain the income tax impact of a CRT is with a projection to determine the real income tax effect in light of the increasing applicability of the alternative minimum tax (AMT).

CHARITABLE LEAD TRUSTS

The charitable lead trust (CLT) is the opposite of the CRT. In a CLT, the charity receives an income interest and a designated heir the remainder. The CLT is an estate-planning technique intended to substantially discount the value of assets to be transferred to heirs, either by gift or under the taxpayer's will. The basic structure for charitable lead trusts is to make a contribution of some amount to the trust. The assets given would remain in the CLT for a long period (the longer the period the more substantial the gift or estate tax reduction). Each year while the CLT is operative, a required distribution will be made to charity. A common technique has been to have this required distribution made to a donor-advised fund. This enables the heirs to indicate a preference for the charity that should receive the annual distributions from the trust. At the end of the specified time period, the assets would pass to the designated heirs. This is typically children, but could be anyone. If, however, the persons named as beneficiaries after the charitable interest ends are skip persons, such as grandchildren, the GST issues must be addressed (see Chapter 1).

Four possible benefits of the CLT technique:

1. A substantial reduction in gift or estate tax costs results from the intervening interest given to the charity (the payments during the CLT term come between the taxpayer's ownership of the asset and the designated heirs receiving the assets).

NOTE

If the estate will not be subject to gift or estate tax as a result of the increased exclusions of the 2001 Tax Act, then this benefit may be irrelevant. If the estate and GST taxes are actually permanently repealed, which is not how the law presently reads, then the transfer tax benefit of the CLT will disappear.

2. The use of a CLT defers the time period until the designated heir receives the assets, as illustrated in the following example.

EXAMPLE

Many parents have set the term of a CLT established for each child to coincide with the 65th birthday of that child. In the event the child dissipates inherited assets prior to retirement, the CLT can provide a safety net. Further, deferring these amounts until retirement will enable the parent to provide an incentive for the child to earn a livelihood during the interim period before the distribution of CLT assets.

NOTE

The deferred time period has and remains, even without any tax benefits, a plus provided by the CLT technique. When an heir in a wealthy family receives significant assets, deferment can protect the heir and ensure that the heir retains an incentive to be a productive member of society. This use will remain.

These personal benefits remain intact regardless of the 2001 Tax Act changes.

3. A CLT, especially when combined with a donor-advised fund at a major charity, can provide an ideal mechanism to inculcate the values of philanthropic giving to heirs, as seen in this example.

EXAMPLE

Father establishes a $1 million CLT for his 40-year-old son. Each year for 25 years, a significant amount of money will be given to a charity that will, under the terms of a donor-advised fund agreement, have to consult the son to apply the distribution. This can involve the son in planning and even implementing a significant and ongoing charitable giving program.

---

4. All appreciation of the principal of the CLT assets over and above the annual annuity or unitrust payment to the charity will enure to the beneficiary gift and estate tax free.

> **NOTE**
>
> CLTs can provide an excellent method for removing future appreciation from an estate. The need and benefit of this will depend on the size of the estate, the year the taxpayer dies, and what the exclusion will be in that year.

Tax Relief Changes Affecting CLTs

The basic changes of the 2001 Tax Act, increasing the exclusion and eventually eliminating the estate tax, have led many advisers to predict the obsolescence of CLTs. This would be unfortunate. First, until the estate tax is repealed, CLTs remain an excellent tool for reducing estate taxes for wealthy elderly taxpayers without the need to outlive some specified trust term, as with a GRAT. Further, and perhaps most importantly, CLTs provide an excellent tool for personal, non-estate tax objectives of planning.

Planning for New CLTs

Since it is impossible to know the year a taxpayer will die or the amount of exclusion applicable in that year, estate planners could use a CLT in the taxpayer's will to minimize estate tax. To accomplish this, a provision would have to be drafted to consider the increasing exclusion. The simplest way to do this would be to periodically revise the will. Another approach would be to estimate the estate and then use a formula to fund the CLT that varies based on the size of the applicable exclusion.

Planning for Existing CLTs

Existing CLTs are irrevocable trusts with charitable interests. It is unlikely that the mere changes in tax law enacted as part of the 2001 Tax Act would entice a court to permit the termination of such a trust. Further, if the CLT is already completed and funded, the taxpayer would have realized the gift tax benefit from the funding.

CHILDREN TRUSTS

Trusts for children and grandchildren are one of the most common estate-planning techniques. Although these can be motivated by a range
of tax objectives, they are primarily established for nontax motives, to
provide college or other benefits for heirs while protecting an imma-
ture heir from access to significant funds. The 2001 Tax Act won't
change these important nontax goals, but it has made changes that affect trust planning. One of the most important changes is the enhancement of the Code Section 529 college savings plan rules, which
make this a more viable option for many people (see Chapter 2).

Trusts for children are formed to provide control and protection
for assets given and/or bequeathed to them. An important goal for
many is to fund future education costs for children or grandchildren.
Funding such costs through trusts gives the taxpayer substantially
more control than using custodial accounts, is likely to result in the assets being counted less for financial aid purposes than if the assets
were held directly by the heir, and will protect the assets from
claimants, in contrast to complete exposure if simply saved in the taxpayer's own name.

Before proceeding with a child's trust, the taxpayer should consider that if all assets are transferred to the child's trust, the grantor
loses the benefit of the lower graduated income tax brackets that the
child could realize by retaining some portion of the assets. On the
other hand, retaining assets in the child's name (or more likely in a
Uniform Gift Transfer to Minors' Act account) would exposes those
assets to the child's control at a much younger age than the age at
which the child could access principal of the typical trust. It would
also further complicate the family's financial planning with additional accounts.

When planning for gifts to children, or trusts for the benefit of
a child, the kiddie tax must be considered. Any gifts to a custodial
account will be subject to the kiddie tax. If instead a trust is used for
the child, the kiddie tax will apply to distributions from the trust.
The trustee of a child's trust will have to weigh the benefits of retaining income in the trust and subjecting it to trust tax rates versus
distributing the income to the child so that the kiddie tax may apply.

To some extent, the compressed tax rates applicable to such trusts can be controlled through investment planning. Index funds, growth stocks with a buy-and-hold strategy, tax-exempt bonds, and other strategies can minimize exposure to the highest trust tax rates. The Code Section 529 plan offers an excellent option for minimizing current and future income taxes if the funds will be used for qualifying educational expenses.

Tax Relief Changes Affecting Children Trusts

The 2001 Tax Act has made changes that affect planning for existing and new trusts that taxpayers might consider establishing for a child, grandchild, or other heir:

- Income tax rates have been lowered, making the income tax costs of trusts somewhat less onerous.
- The estate tax exclusion and GST tax exemption both are increased substantially. For many taxpayers, this will remove the incentive to make the annual $10,000 gifts to reduce their estates.

 Taxpayers who could afford to make annual gifts before the 2001 Tax Act should not necessarily discontinue such gifts as a result of the increase in the exclusion. Remember that in 2011 the tax is back with only a $1 million exclusion.

- As noted previously, Code Section 529 college savings plans have been dramatically enhanced (see Chapter 2). Carefully consider these plans before making additional contributions to any trusts or forming new trusts.

Planning for New Children Trusts

As with any irrevocable trust after the 2001 Tax Act, if the taxpayer's estate is likely to be in a range where the increasing estate tax exclusion may make planning unnecessary, estate planners should consider including as many options and flexible provisions in an irrevocable child or grandchild trust as are consistent with the taxpayer's personal goals and objectives. As discussed, annual gifts might still be appropriate, and unless the new and improved Code Section 529 plans are suitable, trusts for children and grandchildren similar to those that were used in the past will remain a useful planning technique.

Planning for Existing Children Trusts

As with any irrevocable trust, terminating a child's or grandchild's trust will not be easy and, because of important personal benefits, might often be a mistake. Carefully consider the exposure to claimants, divorce, college aid, and other risks the child or grandchild will face by termination of the trust.

FAMILY LIMITED PARTNERSHIPS AND LIMITED LIABILITY COMPANIES

Family limited partnerships (FLPs) and limited liability companies (LLCs) are entities formed under the laws of a state (typically the state where the taxpayer resides, unless the entity is to own real estate, and then it may be formed in the state where the real estate is located). The FLPs, and more recently LLCs, are popular techniques to accomplish planning objectives.

They provide an important measure of control through the terms of the partnership or operating agreement and through the designation of a selected person as general partner or manager. A parent can exert substantial control, even when most of the FLP or LLC interests are given away. The provisions of the FLP agreement or the LLC operating agreement can create a structure to control assets even after death.

FLPs and LLCs can help minimize estate and gift taxes through discounts. Discounts are reductions in the value of the underlying assets as a result of their being held by an FLP or LLC, as seen in the following example.

EXAMPLE

Taxpayer owns real estate worth $1 million and contributes it to an FLP or LLC. He then gifts 10 percent interests to each of his children. Since each child will have a noncontrolling and difficult-to-market interest, it may be valued for, say, $65,000 instead of $100,000.

Partnership and operating agreements can facilitate succession management and planning, thus contributing to overall estate planning. The governing agreement can address the control and management of the enterprise following the death of the principal. Provisions that govern details of operations, working capital, and so forth can create a structure for the new generation.

FLPs and LLCs can help protect assets from claimants and creditors. A creditor who receives a judgment and seizes an interest in an FLP or LLC has no control over management or distributions and merely becomes an assignee. This entitles the creditor to whatever distributions are made. If income exceeds distributions, this can create a phantom income problem (cash flow distributed less than income reported for tax purposes). These characteristics create a substantial disincentive to a claimant.

These vitally important nontax benefits of asset protection, control, avoidance of ancillary probate, and so forth should ensure the continued popularity of FLPs and LLCs as planning tools regardless of what happens with the estate tax.

Tax Relief Changes Affecting FLPs and LLCs

No particular changes were directed at FLPs and LLCs. However, the increase in the estate and GST exclusion might lessen the need for many taxpayers to use FLPs and LLCs to obtain discounts that reduce estate and gift taxes. However, a gift tax will remain with a maximum $1 million exclusion, which will result in the continued use of FLPs and LLCs for gift transfer planning to achieve discounts.

Taxpayers who are skeptical about the eventual repeal of the estate tax should use FLPs and LLCs to fund estate leveraging techniques, dynasty trusts, and similar vehicles. To take advantage of the increases in the exclusion before Congress changes its mind or inflation erodes the benefit, it will be helpful to use FLPs and LLCs just as in the pre-2001 Tax Act environment.

Planning for New FLPs and LLCs

There is another important benefit of FLPs and LLCs. In view of the uncertainty of the estate tax repeal, FLPs and LLCs offer a mechanism to maintain control over gifts to children without the inflexibility of an irrevocable trust. For example, FLPs and LLCs can be used as substitutes for trusts. Often a parent will establish an irrevocable trust for the benefit of a minor child. The trust could own assets directly connected with the family, which the parent gives to the trust for the benefit of the child. The purpose is to control the child's use of and access to the assets, to protect the child's assets from a failed marriage or creditors, and to pass income to the child at a lower tax bracket (once the child has reached age 14 and is no longer subject to the kiddie tax). An FLP or LLC can also accomplish these goals in most instances with greater flexibility. The child's interests are protected from divorce or creditors because of the restrictions on transfer in the partnership or operating agreement. The parent as general partner, or as manager if an LLC is used, has substantial control over the assets and, subject to certain tax restrictions, significant control over distributions out of the entity. Importantly, unlike an irrevocable child's trust, changing the terms of a partnership or operating agreement simply requires having a lawyer draft a new amended and restated agreement and having the partners or members sign it.

Planning for Existing FLPs and LLCs

Advise any taxpayer who is questioning whether to unwind an existing FLP or LLC because of an assumption that the estate tax benefits will no longer be needed to think carefully. The many nontax benefits, all of which should have been addressed when planning the entity, are unaffected by any estate tax change. Why sacrifice the asset protection benefits and control rights in the event they become important at a later date? The taxpayer already has incurred the costs in setting up the structure and agreement.

CHOOSING APPROPRIATE ESTATE PLANNING TECHNIQUES

This chapter provides an analysis of many popular estate planning techniques. The objective has been to explain each technique and discuss the impact of the 2001 Tax Act on that technique. Thus, estate planners can review the status of any technique they have previously used or are presently considering for a particular taxpayer. This makes it possible for advisers and estate planners to discuss in an informed manner the steps that their clients should take next.

7 CARRYOVER BASIS CHANGES SCHEDULED FOR 2010

Basis, sometimes referred to as tax basis, is a fundamental income tax concept that must underlie any estate or related planning for the post-2001 Tax Act environment. How are gains and losses on the sale or exchange of an asset generally determined? In a simple transaction, this gain or loss is calculated by subtracting the cost or investment in the asset (its tax basis) from what is received on selling the asset (the amount realized). Basis is also necessary to determine the depreciation that can be claimed on a real estate investment property or on furniture, fixtures, or equipment used in a business or investment activity. Without a determination of basis, it is impossible to calculate income tax.

The two concepts of tax basis and amount realized can be considerably more complicated than those presented below in the example.

EXAMPLE

An investor buys a parcel of raw land on January 1, 1995, for $500,000 in cash—no loans, no mortgages, and no other fees. This is his tax basis in the land. On March 15, 2001, the investor sells his land to a buyer for $750,000 in cash. Again, there are no loans, mortgages, or fees. The investor realizes $750,000 on the sale. His gain is $250,000 (the $750,000 realized amount minus his $500,000 tax basis). The investor has to determine his tax basis in the land to determine his taxable gain, and must be able to prove the figure to the IRS in the event of an income tax audit.

The tax basis and the amount realized must be adjusted for many items. The following note provides a checklist highlighting some common adjustments made by tax advisers and illustrates the tremendous complexity involved in determining and tracking tax basis.

NOTE

TAX BASIS

+ Purchase price
+ Cost of any capital improvements (lasting improvements, e.g., a new roof or an addition)
+ Ancillary costs to acquire the property (e.g., legal fees, title insurance, recording fees)
− Any losses (e.g., from fire, theft, or condemnation)
− Depreciation claimed on the property

AMOUNT REALIZED

+ Cash received on the sale
+ Fair value of any other property received (e.g., the investor in the above example could have sold his land for $700,000 in cash and a U.S. government bond worth $50,000)
+ Amount of debt that the buyer is relieved of

The previous simple example of an investor purchasing raw land is here expanded to illustrate some of these concepts.

EXAMPLE

When the investor purchases the property, legal fees associated with the purchase have to be added to his tax basis in the land (i.e., capitalized). These legal fees also have to be distinguished from other legal fees related to ongoing business operations of the investor, which would instead be deducted currently as business expenses. The cost of title insurance, clearing title, and related fees would all be added to the investor's basis in the land. If the investor makes certain types of improvements to the land, their cost would be added to his tax basis in the land (e.g., sewers and roads or general grading costs). On the other hand, if the investor expends funds for specialized grading, berm, and other improvements that are an integral part of the design structure of a building, those costs would not be capitalized as part of the land (which would be added to his basis in the land) but rather would be capitalized as part of the basis in the building. The distinction is important because these costs, if capitalized as part of the cost of the building, would be subject to depreciation that would reduce his tax basis. Thus, the tax basis in the building and in the land would have to be tracked separately. If the investor builds a manufacturing building on the property, he would have to determine the tax basis of the permanent improvements made, which would be added to basis. He would have to track and subtract from basis the depreciation deductions claimed for income tax purposes. If repairs are made, he would have to determine whether they had to be capitalized (since they would have benefit for more than one tax year) or if instead they could be deducted in the year incurred as an ordinary and necessary trade or business repair expense. If the investor purchases fixtures to be used in the manufacturing building, it would have to be determined whether the fixtures are permanently attached to, and hence treated as part of, the realty, or if instead they are more properly characterized as movable personal property. If realty, the cost of the fixtures would be added to the basis in the property. If movable personal property, it would not.

If the investor gives the property in question to his son, his son would have to determine the investor's tax basis in the property given to him. This would require that the son complete all of the analyses previously indicated, possibly without the benefit of the father's records and assistance.

This example merely illustrates common issues related to a simple real estate investment. The actual record-keeping and decision-making process on determining and tracking basis is more complex and burdensome and requires a concerted and carefully planned effort by the taxpayer, or even the services of a qualified accountant.

RECORD-KEEPING BURDENS ASSOCIATED WITH
BASIS RULES

The complexity and difficulty of monitoring the items included in tax basis are the very reason Congress, in the 1997 Tax Act,[1] made major changes affecting income taxation of home ownership. The cornerstone of these changes was the elimination of the prior rules that had permitted clients to roll over the gain realized on selling a house into a new or replacement house or exclude up to $125,000 of gain if over age 55. Instead, a single new exclusion was provided for, without regard to age. The maximum gain that can be excluded is $250,000 for a single taxpayer, or $500,000 for a couple filing a joint tax return. The objective was to eliminate for the vast majority of taxpayers the complex record keeping required to determine a home's tax basis, improvements, and so forth. Congress recognized the burdensome, if not sometimes impossible, nature of this task. Keep this objective in mind when evaluating the new carryover basis rules.

Record Keeping for a Home

Despite the home sale exclusion rules introduced with the 1997 Tax Act, most taxpayers should still retain basis and related records for their home. The need for record keeping begins when they buy a home. After the closing (a meeting, usually at a lawyer's office or bank, where all the final calculations are made and all of the papers are signed to transfer ownership of the house to the buyer), the original deed and title insurance policy should go into a safe-deposit box, with a copy kept for home records. A copy of the closing papers (the HUD-1 RESPA form) should be retained in the taxpayer's tax files. This is the standard real estate settlement form that shows all of the payment and financial transactions, including mortgage, for a home purchase or sale. It is advisable to make a copy of the closing papers and keep them in a permanent file to track the investment (tax basis) in the home. Anytime improvements are then made to the home, copies of the receipt and canceled checks and other documents are then added to the permanent house file.

Repair versus Capital Improvement

The rules that come into play with the 2001 Tax Act make it ever more important to properly identify the distinction between a repair and an improvement. A repair is deducted currently and is not added to the cost basis in the property. On the other hand, an improvement is a capital expense, is added to the tax basis in the assets involved, and hence could affect heirs' capital gains tax if and when they sell the asset involved. It is also essential for the executor to know this information to make the necessary calculations as explained later in this chapter.

Classification as Personal Property, Not Real Property

To apply the basis rules, it is important to understand common income tax planning to maximize depreciation deductions, which will affect the adjusted basis of assets. Dollars effectively allocated to personal property will become the basis of that property and not of real property. Property classified as personal may be depreciated much more rapidly than real property. Personal property can often be depreciated over a five- or seven-year period using accelerated depreciation methods (calculations that push more of the depreciation deductions into earlier years). This contrasts favorably with commercial real property (buildings, improvements, etc.), which must be written off over thirty-nine years. Therefore, the more property that can be treated as personal property (furniture, equipment, planters, certain plumbing hookups, for example), rather than as real property (buildings and their structural components), the more rapid the depreciation deductions will be.

In general, for property to qualify as personal property, it must meet the following two tests:

1. It must be movable (e.g., a bookcase anchored with screws) rather than inherently permanent (e.g., built–in furniture that cannot be removed without destroying it).

2. It must be an accessory to the conduct of the business rather than an integral component of the building where the business is located. For example, special plumbing hookups and additional exhaust fans in a restaurant can be considered accessories to the business, whereas a roof is essential to the nature and function of the building.

The following questions offer guidance for determining whether property can be considered movable:

- Is the property permanently attached to the building, or can it readily be detached and moved? Removable hooks, adhesives, and screws will be more indicative of movability than would cement and permanent adhesives.

- How difficult and time consuming is it to move the property in question? Are special permits, personnel, or equipment necessary to move it, or can regular maintenance people move it?

- How much damage will be done to the property being moved and to the building it is being moved from (the built–in furniture mentioned earlier)?

- Has the particular property or similar property been moved in the past?

Planning for personal property should be kept in mind when building or renovating any commercial building. In some situations, it may be possible to redesign certain types of property to make it qualify. If the plans called for expensive imported tile cemented to the lobby floor of the building, perhaps a nonpermanent cement could enable the property to qualify as personal property. Expensive paneling could be fastened with removable screws instead of being glued or nailed permanently to the subwall. The additional labor costs to install with screws should be compared with the additional future tax benefits.

The following are examples of different types of property that may qualify for favorable depreciation deductions:

- *Department store.* Decorative lighting fixtures, display racks, carpeting, movable partitions, escalators, removable paneling, certain planters, curtains, and hookups for computers in the credit collection department.

- *Supermarkets and restaurants.* Counters, display racks, waste compactors, signs, certain exhaust fans, certain plumbing and electrical hookups, kitchen equipment, refrigeration equipment (including pumps, condensers, and similar equipment), and trash bins.

- *Office building.* Furniture, equipment, removable files and bookshelves, removable paneling, carpeting, decorative light fixtures, certain hookups, electrical connections, and possibly a special raised floor to accommodate computer equipment. Certain portions of security systems, special telephone and other equipment, and their support systems may qualify.

Any commercial building may have a large portion of costs that qualify for favorable tax treatment. In many cases, however, the components may be so integrated into the building that the IRS could argue that they do not qualify. In either event, the impact of this planning on the new basis rules has to be considered.

THREE BASIS RULES: STEPPED-UP, CARRYOVER, AND MODIFIED CARRYOVER

If monitoring the tax basis of a home is generally acknowledged as complex, monitoring the tax basis of every asset a taxpayer has owned has been clearly understood as being a substantial burden, if not an impossible task. The situation is exponentially worse for an heir who must determine a decedent's tax basis in a particular asset. As a result, the estate tax rules include a concept called *stepped-up basis,* which eliminates the need for heirs to determine the income tax basis of assets they inherit. This has been the law and will remain the law until 2010 when heirs will be required to determine the tax basis of inherited assets.

This rule is similar to the requirement for a donee of property received as a gift during the donor's lifetime to determine the donor's income tax basis.[2] More specifically, the basis of property received as a gift is the adjusted basis of the donor, subject to a few special rules. If the donor's tax basis is greater than the fair value of the property at the date of the gift, the basis for determining a loss is limited to the fair value of the property on the date of the gift. This is to prevent the donee from recognizing a tax loss for income tax purposes on property received as a gift. The second special rule is that if the donor giving the property had to pay gift tax on the gift, the adjusted basis of the property is increased by the amount of gift tax paid, so long as the increase is not to an amount more than the fair value of the property.

It is necessary first to understand how the stepped-up basis rules of current law (which remain law until 2010) work before it is possible to understand the *carryover basis rules* that are the basis of the new law (to become effective in 2010). Once the concept of a pure carryover basis is clear, then the even more complex rules enacted as part of the 2001 tax law, called *modified carryover basis rules,* can be analyzed.

STEPPED-UP BASIS EXPLAINED

The assets included in a taxpayer's gross estate currently receive a tax basis equal to the fair market value at the date of death (or the alternate valuation date, which is the date six months after the date of death).[3] With the basis of assets stepped up (or stepped down in the event of a decline in value), the tax consequences of unrealized gains or losses occurring before death are eliminated. There are some exceptions, such as for farm and business property that can benefit from special valuation rules to reduce estate tax. However, the general rule, that assets owned by the taxpayer at death receive a new tax basis equal to their fair value, can permit heirs to avoid any gain inherent in the assets.

EXAMPLE

Taxpayer owns a building with an adjusted tax basis (investment, less depreciation, plus improvements) of $200,000 and a fair market value on the date of his death of $1,000,000. Had he sold the building, he would have realized a taxable gain of $800,000 [$1,000,000 – $200,000] and paid an approximate federal and state income tax of about $200,000. However, since he died holding the building, his heirs will inherit it with a new tax basis of $1,000,000. The tax basis is stepped-up to the fair value at death. If the heirs sell the building the next day, they will have no taxable gain. They have saved $200,000.

The benefit of the stepped-up basis rules has been that they eliminate capital gains tax, but more important, they eliminate the need to hire Sherlock Holmes to identify the decedent's tax basis in the property.

NOTE

Another rationale for the elimination of the carryover basis rules of prior law is that it was a form of double taxation. Decedents' estates would pay estate tax on all their assets, so it would be unfair to charge their heirs a capital gains tax when they sold the same asset. It would amount to two taxes on the same assets. Now that the estate tax is being eliminated, no double taxation will occur, so there should be no reason, from a tax perspective, to *not* have a carryover basis and hence the capital gains tax. It is now only one level of taxation.

CAPITAL VERSUS NONCAPITAL (ORDINARY) GAINS AND LOSSES

The carryover basis rules enacted as part of the 2001 Tax Act also provide that the character of property in the hands of the decedent carries over to the hands of the heir. There are exceptions.

To understand the general carryover basis rules and some of the special rules enacted as part of the 2001 Tax Act that affect art, copyrights, and similar property, it is necessary to understand the characterization of an asset as capital or ordinary.

EXAMPLE

If land represented inventory, and hence ordinary income property to the decedent who subdivided land and sold building lots as a livelihood, then the land inherited by his heirs not only would have the same tax basis as it did to him, but would also be characterized as ordinary income property.

Capital gains and losses are the gains or losses realized on the sale (or certain other transfers or events that are treated like sales by the tax laws) of capital assets. An asset is simply anything of value that the taxpayer owns. Capital assets include stocks and bonds (for anyone except a stockbroker or dealer), a house, a piece of raw land held as an investment, and so forth.

According to its technical definition as provided by the tax laws, a capital asset is any property held by a taxpayer except the following:

1. Inventory (stock in the taxpayer's trade). This is generally property held for sale to customers in the ordinary course of business. Examples include the goods a retail store holds for sale such as clothing, or forty lots in a subdivision that a developer is holding for sale. For real estate, security brokerage firms, and other dealers, the key test is whether the developer held the property primarily for sale to customers in the ordinary course of his business. Tax advisers have to look at all the facts and circumstances surrounding the transaction, such as the taxpayer's intent, the amount of advertising done, other sales of similar property to customers, the portion of the income earned from such sales compared with the taxpayer's other sources of income, the time devoted to the project, and

the period for which the asset was held (investments tend to be held longer than inventory).

2. Depreciable property and land used in taxpayer's trade or business.

3. A note or accounts receivable that arose in the ordinary course of business.

4. Copyright, literary, musical, or artistic composition, letter, or memorandum if the taxpayer created it, or if the taxpayer's investment (tax basis) is determined by reference to the person who created it.

NOTE

If the taxpayer's father painted a picture and gave it to his son, the picture would not be a capital asset and the son would not realize capital gains when selling it. If the taxpayer purchased a picture at auction and sold it several years later, he would realize capital gains, assuming he was not an art dealer. Special rules apply to this type of asset after 2009 under the 2001 Tax Act.

CARRYOVER BASIS EXPLAINED

Carryover basis is simple to explain (although tough to implement). Consider the following modifications to the earlier example used to explain step-up in basis.

EXAMPLE

Taxpayer owns a building with an adjusted tax basis (investment, less depreciation, plus improvements) of $200,000 and a fair market value on the date of death of $1,000,000. Had owner sold the building, he would have realized a taxable gain of $800,000 [$1,000,000 – $200,000] and paid an approximate federal and state income tax of about $200,000. If he dies in 2010 or later owning the building, his heirs will inherit it with the same $200,000 tax basis he had, not a tax basis of the $1,000,000 fair value at death. If the heirs sell the building the day after his death, they will have a taxable gain of $800,000, the same gain the owner would have had. The real difficulty for the heirs will be to locate the owner's records of improvements to the building, depreciation deductions, closing costs, and so forth, to demonstrate tax basis.

Carryover Basis Rule Modifications

Although a pure carryover basis rule would have met the objective of replacing an estate tax with a capital gains tax, Congress sought to minimize the impact of these rules on smaller estates. Thus, Congress enacted a modified carryover basis rule that permits some amount of basis adjustment. For smaller estates (some 98 percent of decedents), this means that the net effect is similar under the 2001 law as it had been under the prior one (the rules that existed before the 2001 Tax Act and that remain effective until 2010)—no estate tax and a step-up in basis. As is explained in this chapter, every estate will be allowed to step up $1.3 million in assets. Thus, if an estate is sufficiently under $1.3 million such that it is unlikely to exceed that amount by the time of the taxpayer's death, all assets in the estate will receive a step-up in basis.

 Every executor (sometimes called personal administrator) should create records showing the basis of all assets held by the estate. These records should show a description of the asset, decedent's adjusted tax basis, the fair value at death, and then finally the tax basis to the heirs.

 Although it is easy to assume that most taxpayers will be well under the $1.3 million basis adjustment, taking a cavalier attitude to planning under the new rules can be a costly mistake:

- Congress has raised and lowered the income tax rate many times. The rules applicable to capital gains taxation have changed many times, sometimes favorably and sometimes not. There have been periods when the favorable benefits of capital gains have been entirely eliminated. If taxpayers don't plan the basis adjustment for maximum advantage and keep records to prove it, future changes when Congress decides it needs additional revenues could prove a significant and avoidable cost.

■ No one knows what his estate will be at his death. Uncertainties from an inheritance, lottery winning, or insurance payoff to the estate could easily cause an average-net-worth taxpayer's heirs to be taxed under the new system.

Although most taxpayers' heirs won't be taxed under the new carryover basis rules, it is prudent for many taxpayers (and all advisers) to consider and plan for the new rules. The following sections provide guidance in accomplishing this goal.

Basis for the New Rules

Readers who think the purpose of the new rules is to ensure that accountants will be fully employed might be right. But Congress primarily had an economic motive. It was made a political imperative that the estate tax be repealed. Repealing the estate tax system raises two issues. First, how can Congress replace the revenue loss? Second, from a technical standpoint, how are new basis rules to be provided—since the old rules are repealed with the estate tax? As for revenue loss, a portion of it is made up by, in effect, substituting a capital gains tax for the estate tax. If the taxpayer doesn't pay the estate tax, Congress will eventually catch heirs with a higher capital gains tax. So was the death tax really repealed, or did the chameleon just change colors? The technical issue is that repealing the estate tax also repeals the rules governing the step-up in basis of assets owned by a decedent. Under prior law (which remains effective until 2010), filing an estate tax return reflects the fair value of all assets owned by the decedent. These are the values that the assets in the decedent's estate would take on as their basis (i.e., the level that the basis would be stepped up to). The logic of this system was that the taxpayer paid a toll charge, in the form of the estate tax, to obtain the benefit of the basis step-up. With the 2001 legislation, the toll charge has been removed, so Congress felt that the benefit also should be eliminated. The result is that new rules, and a new tax system, must be provided involving carryover basis without regard to the estate tax. This is the objective of new Code Section 1022.

If the new system works as planned, it would be a transition from a 55 percent death tax that cannot be controlled to a 20 percent capital gains tax, the timing of which can be controlled (e.g., taxpayers can decide when to sell an asset, and which asset to sell, making it possible to control when the tax will be incurred).

THE GENERAL CARRYOVER BASIS RULES

The general concept underlying the new rules introduced in Code Section 1022 is that when the estate tax is repealed, assets will, subject to exceptions to be discussed, retain their prior tax basis once in the hands of heirs. This is the same rule that has always applied to gifts, and it will continue to apply to gifts.

Character of Property and Recapture

Property acquired from any decedents who die after December 31, 2009, is to be treated as if transferred by the decedent to the heir as a gift. Assets received as gift transfers will have the same tax basis to the donee (heir) as they did to the donor (decedent)—carryover basis (subject to several exceptions). This gift rule is the same under the post-2010 law as under prior law.[4] This means that not only will the tax basis of the decedent generally carry over to the heirs, as noted, but the character of the property, whether as ordinary income or capital gain property, will also carry over to the heirs. This is important, because the characterization of property as capital gains property can have substantial income tax benefits on sale. Similarly, if the property inherited was depreciated and hence subject to depreciation recapture on sale (some portion of the gain that would otherwise be treated as capital gains must be characterized as ordinary income and taxed at a higher rate), that taint will also carry over to the heirs.

Definition of Property "Acquired from" the Decedent

The general rule noted in the preceding paragraph applies to property *acquired from* the decedent. This term must be defined to aid in an understanding of when the new rules will apply. Property acquired by devise (real property received from a decedent), bequest (personal property received from a decedent), or inheritance, or by the decedent's estate, will be deemed *acquired* from the decedent.[5] In addition, property transferred by the decedent as a gift during his lifetime is deemed acquired from the decedent for purposes of the new rules.[6] Any other property that passes from the decedent by reason of the decedent's death is passed without consideration (i.e., not paid for by the recipient); it too is deemed acquired from the decedent. This includes property the decedent owned as a joint tenant with the right of survivorship or as a tenant by the entirety. For jointly held property between spouses, the property is generally deemed one-half owned by each spouse.[7] This means only one-half the value of jointly held property can be stepped up in value.

Joint tenants indicates possessory interest in the same property where all cotenants own a whole or unified interest in the entire property. Each joint tenant has the right, subject to the rights only of the other joint tenants, to possess the entire property interest. The traditional common-law definition of a joint tenancy requires the presence of the four unities: unity of interest (each joint tenant must have an identical interest); unity of title (the same will, deed, or other document must confer title to all joint tenants); unity of possession (each has the right to possess the entire property interest); and unity of time (the rights of each joint tenant must vest at the same time).

Property transferred by the decedent to certain trusts will similarly be subject to the new rules. Property transferred to a *qualified revocable trust* (QRT) (not to be confused with a QPRT, or house trust, discussed in Chapter 6) will be subject to the new carryover basis rules.[8] Finally, any other trust with respect to which the decedent reserved a right to change the beneficial enjoyment of the trust property by exercising a right reserved to the decedent to alter, amend, or revoke the trust, will be treated as property acquired from the decedent and subject to the new rules.[9]

Exceptions to the General Carryover Basis Rules

The first of many exceptions and special rules is that the decedent's basis will not always be the exact tax basis to the heir. The basis to the heir will actually be the lesser of the adjusted basis of the decedent in the property[10] or the fair market value of the property at the date of the decedent's death.[11] This means, in short, the lesser of basis or fair value, not a pure carryover basis.

The 2001 tax system already isn't simple. An executor will have to create records more complex than those under prior law. The executor will have to determine the decedent's adjusted tax basis in each asset and still identify current fair market value information for each asset as of the date of death (although the complexity of a second calculation at the alternate valuation date won't be necessary). But this is not the entire picture; more complexity is yet to come in the form of two modified increases to basis, explained in later sections of this chapter.

EXAMPLE

Decedent dies on March 1, 2010, owning a rental property valued at $575,000 and worth $650,000. Assume neither of the special basis adjustments (discussed later in this chapter) is allocated to the property. The adjusted tax basis in the hands of the heirs, on which they will determine their capital gain when they sell it, is $575,000.

EXAMPLE

Decedent dies on March 1, 2010, owning a rental property valued at $575,000 and worth $450,000. The adjusted tax basis in the hands of the heirs, on which they will determine their capital gain when they sell it, is the lesser of decedent's adjusted tax basis or the fair value at his death, or $450,000.

The implication of this rule is that the executor will have to determine the fair value of every asset in the estate, just as under present law. This may require an appraisal for nonmarketable assets such as real estate and closely held business interests, which can be complex and costly. The lesson is that estate planners should urge all taxpayers to keep complete records of the cost basis of assets. It will save their executors and heirs substantial headaches, time delays, costs, and IRS audit problems.

$1.3 MILLION BASIS ADJUSTMENT FOR ESTATES

One of the major exceptions the new law provides to the general carryover basis concept is that every decedent can increase the basis of assets to eliminate $1.3 million of taxable appreciation.[12]

EXAMPLE

Taxpayer's estate consists of a house worth $600,000, for which he paid only $300,000 (his tax basis), and stocks worth $2.5 million that he bought for only $1.5 million (his tax basis). He can allocate $300,000 of special basis adjustment to increase the basis in the house to its $600,000 fair value, effectively eliminating any gain. He can allocate $1 million of special basis adjustment to the securities, thus effectively eliminating any gain. When the estate utilizes this special modified carryover basis rule, heirs will not have to pay capital gains tax on the predeath appreciation when they sell the assets. Without this special tax break, the $1.3 million in appreciation could have ultimately cost the heirs $260,000 in capital gains tax.

The purpose of this rule is to prevent the majority of estates from bearing the burden of passing on capital gains tax to their heirs. Just as the applicable exclusion amount under prior law kept estates of under $675,000 from paying estate tax, the $1.3 million basis step-up modifies the carryover basis rules to enable most estates to avoid the complexity. When this is combined with the basis adjustment that a spouse can use and the $3 million special basis adjustment on transfers of assets to a spouse only a tiny percentage of estates will face the carryover basis complexity.

NOTE

It is not estates of $1.3 million and under that will be able to avoid the impact of the carryover basis rules; rather, it is estates with not more than $1.3 million in *predeath appreciation* that will receive this benefit. Thus, even an estate of $10 million or more may avoid the tax consequences of carryover basis. Thus, it is really not small estates that benefit from this rule, but any size estate. If Congress had really intended to exclude only smaller estates, the law could have been written so that only estates of less than some specified size, say $2 million, would have this benefit. But, like much of the 2001 Tax Act, tax breaks have been geared to benefit the wealthy.

The actual mechanics of this special basis adjustment are somewhat more complicated and involve a bit of jargon. The basis increase allocated to a particular asset is the *aggregate basis increase* allowed under the new allocation rules to that asset.[13] The aggregate basis increase in 2010 is calculated as follows:

- $1.3 million, as explained above.[14]
- Plus, any increase in the $1.3 million for inflation (explained later in this chapter).
- Plus, any capital loss carryovers.[15]
- Plus, any net operating loss carryovers under Code Section 172. These are taken into account to the extent that these losses would have been permitted to be carried over from the decedent's last income tax return to the next year's income tax return had the decedent lived.
- Plus, any loss deductions for built-in losses that would have been permitted as deductions under Code Section 165 as if the

property inherited from the decedent had instead been sold for its fair value prior to the decedent's death.[16]

 These new modified carryover basis rules present tremendous administrative difficulties. The rules apply to all property acquired from the decedent. Thus, joint assets, assets held in qualifying revocable trusts (QRTs), will all be subject to these new allocation rules. However, the executor of an estate has the legal right to make decisions concerning only probate assets. Nonprobate assets will thus present a particular challenge.

Married couples can substantially augment this $1.3 million basis increase with the additional basis adjustment described in the following section.

$3 MILLION SPOUSAL BASIS ADJUSTMENT

A married taxpayer may qualify for an additional $3 million basis adjustment. Similar to the $1.3 million basis step up, this is another major modification of the general carryover basis rules. This additional basis increase, unrelated to the $1.3 million basis increase, is for property acquired by a surviving spouse.

NOTE

The amount of predeath appreciation that can receive a step-up in basis if the taxpayer leaves everything to a surviving spouse is $4.3 million ($1.3 million and $3 million). This amount can be increased further by factoring in the special home sale exclusion rules discussed later in this chapter.

Note that the increase is only available if there is a surviving spouse. Thus, the estate tax laws will continue the substantial favoritism historically shown to married couples. It is not clear why Congress decided to add this special benefit.

Requirements to Qualify

For assets to qualify for the basis step-up, they must be "qualified spousal property" (QSP).[17] Congress knew instinctively that taxpayers and planners needed more estate tax acronyms to keep the rules confusing! QSP includes QTIP or outright transfer property.

Qualified Terminable Interest Property

Qualified terminable interest property (QTIP) qualifies.[18] This is a trust from which the surviving spouse will receive income for life and is property that passes from the decedent.[19] The surviving spouse has a qualifying income interest for her life.[20] This requires that the surviving spouse be entitled to receive all of the income from the assets in this trust, payable to her at least annually. Alternatively, the surviving spouse may have an interest for life in the property.[21] No person can be given a power to appoint any part of the QTIP assets to anyone other than the surviving spouse during the surviving spouse's lifetime.[22] This means giving a power to someone to appoint the QTIP property after the death of the surviving spouse will not disqualify those assets from the $3 million basis step-up.[23]

EXAMPLE

Husband wishes to bequeath $5 million of assets with a $2 million tax basis, and hence $3 million of predeath appreciation, to a QTIP trust for his third wife. On her later death, Husband wants the assets distributed to the children from his first marriage, but he is not certain in what proportions or how (in trust or not). He gives his brother a power of appointment to designate the proportions and when the class of persons consisting of his children from his first marriage may receive these assets. If this power is exercisable during his third wife's lifetime, the assets bequeathed to the QTIP will not qualify for the $3 million basis step-up. If this power is only exercisable after the third wife dies, the assets so bequeathed should qualify.

NOTE

The definitions of different types of powers of appointment will no longer appear in the tax laws once the estate tax is eliminated.

In determining whether payments to the surviving spouse will qualify as constituting all the income payable at least annually, the new law directs the IRS to issue regulations governing how an annuity will qualify as the appropriate type of income interest. This provision addresses a recent trend in trust drafting of structuring distributions to an income beneficiary as a unitrust payment rather than income. For example, after the fair value of all QTIP assets as of January 1 is determined, the trustee then pays the surviving spouse 5 percent of that value in monthly installments over the year. This distribution approach is consistent with modern investment principles such as investing for total return, which consists of dividends and interest (which would constitute income for QTIP purposes) and capital gains (which would otherwise not constitute income for QTIP purposes). A total return investment approach should maximize the distributions to both current (income) and remainder (those who receive the trust after the death of the spouse) beneficiaries.

In determining whether a transfer of property qualifies for QTIP treatment, an interest in property, such as a fractional or percentage share, will qualify.[24]

Outright Transfer Property

Outright transfer property qualifies.[25] This is basically any property acquired from the decedent that is transferred directly to the surviving spouse.[26] Property will not qualify for the $3 million basis adjustment as outright transfer property if the interests passing to the surviving spouse will lapse on the occurrence of an event or contingency, the failure of an event or contingency to occur, or the lapse of time. The example following illustrates this type of disqualification.

However, the property transfer should still qualify if the termination of the spouse's interests is because of the death of the surviving spouse as a result of the application of a simultaneous death

---
EXAMPLE

Husband dies leaving assets with $1.3 million of predeath appreciation to his son, and a house worth $4 million, with $3 million of predeath appreciation, to his surviving wife. However, because Husband was concerned about his surviving wife's remarrying, he had the bequest to her limited to a life estate. She had full use of the residence for her life, but on her death the house would be transferred to his son. The surviving wife's ownership interest in the house will lapse on the occurrence of an event, her death, so it will not qualify for the basis adjustment.

---

clause (a provision in a will or under state law that states which spouse should be presumed to have died first in the event both spouses die from a common disaster or at approximately the same time the basis adjustment will be available). Also, if the surviving spouse dies within six months of the date of the first spouse's death, and the asset is passed elsewhere, this condition will not prevent the benefit of the $3 million basis adjustment.[27]

Ownership Requirements

To qualify for the spousal basis increase, the assets involved must be owned by the deceased spouse on his death.[28] If property is owned jointly by the deceased spouse and the surviving spouse, the decedent will be presumed to own one-half of the property.[29] If the property is owned by the decedent and a joint tenant who is not the decedent's spouse, then the property will be treated as owned by the decedent based on the proportion of the value contributed to the property's acquisition by the decedent.

EXAMPLE

Husband and a friend purchased land for $500,000, with Husband contributing $300,000 and the friend contributing $200,000. Husband will be treated as owning ⅗ of the property.

What if Husband and his friend later built several buildings on the property, each contributing different amounts at different times? What if the friend contributed valuable services by assisting in physical construction of the property? The analysis becomes quite complex and would have to consider the fair market value of the property before each improvement, the cost of each improvement, and who paid how much. The value of the services rendered and the income tax consequences if the friend received a greater interest in the property for rendering services, would be relevant.

If the decedent received the property by gift, bequest, devise, or inheritance, he will be deemed to own a proportionate share of the property.[30]

EXAMPLE

Father gave each of his four children an equal interest in the family ranch. Son will be treated as a one-fourth owner since there are four joint tenants with the right of survivorship.

The decedent will be treated as owning property held in a qualified revocable trust (QRT) that the decedent funded with assets during his lifetime. In general terms, this is the popular revocable living trust.

The decedent will not be deemed the owner of assets because of possessing a general power of appointment over those assets.[31] The purpose of this rule is to prevent married couples from creating trusts giving the other spouse a general power of appointment so that basis will be increased on death.

Terminology of Spousal Basis Increase

The actual mechanics of this spousal basis adjustment are that a portion of the aggregate spousal basis increase is to be allocated under the new rules to each qualifying asset.[32] The aggregate spousal basis increase in 2010 is $3 million,[33] plus any increase in the $3 million for inflation (see later section in this chapter).

Maximum Basis Increase

The maximum basis increase, when the $1.3 million general increase and the $3 million spousal increase are both used in full, is still limited to the fair market value of the property involved.[34]

EXAMPLE

Husband dies with an $8 million estate consisting of an interest in a closely held business. His tax basis (investment) in the family limited partnership (FLP) operating the business is $4.5 million. The theoretical maximum basis increase on his bequest of the FLP interests to his surviving wife is $4.3 million [$1.3 million + $3 million], but the FLP interests cannot be increased by more than their fair value of $8 million, so the maximum basis increase permitted is only $3.5 million [$8 million − $4.5 million], not $4.3 million.

Planning for the New Spousal Basis Adjustment

Because no one can know who will be the surviving spouse, a planning objective under the new post-estate tax system, similar to the objective under the old law, will be to divide assets between spouses. This ensures the greatest likelihood of maximizing the basis increase regardless of who is the first to die.

Dividing assets is actually somewhat different, and more complex, than planning under current law (the current estate tax system, which will generally remain in place through 2009). Under current law, the planning has been based on dividing the value of assets between spouses. Under the post-2009 modified carryover basis system, taxpayers will need to divide assets based on appreciation. This is not only more complex but will require more careful monitoring.

——————————— **EXAMPLE** ———————————

Husband and Wife have a combined estate of $6.5 million consisting of a house valued at $2,000,000, purchased for $500,000, stock purchased at $1,000,000 valued at $1,000,000, and real estate worth $3,500,000, purchased for $500,000. The total estate has appreciation of $4,500,000 [$1,500,000 on the house and $3,000,000 on the real estate]. Under current law, Husband and Wife could divide assets by giving the Husband the house and stock, and Wife the real estate so each owns sufficient value of assets to take maximum advantage of the applicable exclusion and the graduated estate tax rates. Under the new system, however, this approach won't suffice. The assets will have to be divided so that the appreciation on assets is equally divided. The stock could be owned by either and would not be relevant since there is no appreciation (this could obviously change as time goes on and the stock appreciates or depreciates in value). The house and real estate would have to be divided equally, or alternatively, the house could be owned by one spouse and the real estate divided in a manner that equalizes the appreciation between spouses.

INFLATION INCREASES FOR BASIS ADJUSTMENTS

The basis increases for $1.3 million and $3 million in applicable appreciation are subject to increases for inflation. The inflation increase will be based on the increase in the cost of living adjustment for a particular calendar year, using 2009 (the last year before the modified basis adjustment rules become operative) as the base year. The adjustment is to be made using set rules[35] whereby the amounts of inflation increases will be rounded down as follows:

- $100,000 for the $1.3 million adjustment applicable to all taxpayers

- $250,000 for the $3 million spousal basis adjustment
- $5,000 for the $60,000 adjustment for nonresident aliens (as discussed later in this chapter)

COMMUNITY PROPERTY LAW AND THE NEW CARRYOVER BASIS RULES

General Features of Community Property

Generally all property acquired by a husband and wife during their marriage while they are domiciled in one of the community property states belongs to each of the marriage partners, share and share alike. They share not only in the physical property acquired but also in the income from the property and their salaries, wages, and other compensation for services. At the same time, each may have separate property. They may also hold property between them in joint tenancy and generally may adjust between themselves their community and separate property (e.g., using a transmutation agreement). Couples can state in a prenuptial agreement prior to marriage that they will not be bound by the community property laws of their state of domicile.

Generally, community property assets retain that character even after the parties have moved to a noncommunity property state, unless the parties themselves are able to adjust their rights between themselves. This is important with respect to their actions regarding the assets held. For example, the restructuring of title to any assets presently owned individually or in joint name could affect the characterization of the asset as community property. In the event of a future divorce, the present steps taken by either or both parties with reference to titles to assets could affect each person's retention of assets at such time.

Property acquired before marriage retains the form of ownership it had when acquired—separate, joint, or other. Property acquired during the marriage by gift or inheritance by one of the parties retains the character in which it was acquired. Property purchased with community property is community property, and property purchased with separate property is separate property. Property purchased with commingled community and separate property, so that the two cannot be separated, is community property.

New Basis Step-Up Rules and Community Property

For community property, a special rule applies that may provide for a full basis step-up. This is a significant benefit for community property. A surviving spouse's one-half share of community property assets will be treated as if acquired from the decedent and subject to the carryover basis rules. To obtain this benefit, at least one-half of the interests in the asset must be treated as if owned by the decedent under the decedent's state's community property law.[36]

THREE-YEAR RULE TO RESTRICT DEATHBED PLANNING TECHNIQUES

The purpose of the rule restricting taxpayers from engaging in certain so-called deathbed planning techniques within three years of death is to protect income tax revenues. Since there is no estate tax after 2009, and there will still be a $1 million gift tax exclusion, what will stop taxpayers from shifting assets between high and low income tax bracket taxpayers to obtain basis step-up?

EXAMPLE

A terminally ill patient, Tom, has an estate consisting of modest assets. The patient, however, has a close friend, Ida, who owns a particular Internet stock she purchased for $1 that is now worth $1 million. Ida sees the benefits of obtaining a basis step-up so her heirs can avoid capital gains tax. She transfers the stock to the close friend who is terminally ill, Tom. When Tom dies, he can bequeath the stock, with basis step-up, back to Ida. Ida can now sell the stock and avoid capital gains tax because the tax basis in the Internet stock received a free basis step-up from Tom. This is an obvious abuse that has to be controlled to protect the integrity of the new tax system.

Congress sought to limit such abuse by preventing basis step-up on transfers within three years of death.[37] This rule provides that the basis of assets transferred within three years of death cannot be increased under the modified carryover basis rules for the $1.3 million adjustment by any assets acquired by the decedent within the three-year period ending on the date of death. This restriction applies to property acquired by gift. A spouse can transfer property within three years of death to obtain a basis step-up under the $3 million spousal basis step-up unless the transferor spouse received the assets as a gift.

 Consider interspousal transfers prior to death. There is a three-year rule, but it provides for an exception for interspousal transfers.[38] Thus, if one spouse is on his or her deathbed, consider transfers from the healthy spouse before death to obtain a full basis step-up. Durable powers of attorney should be amended to address this opportunity.

ALLOCATING BASIS ADJUSTMENTS

The basis adjustment for the $1.3 million and $3 million are to be made by the executor appointed under the decedent's will. The executor's determination will be governed by state law unless and except as changed by the decedent's will, revocable living trust, or other governing instruments. The executor will report the allocations as made on a tax return.[39] Once made, the allocations will be binding except as the IRS may indicate in future regulations.

NOTE

Many taxpayers assume that if the estate tax is eliminated, the requirements to file an estate tax return will be eliminated. The requirements will continue, and in many respects will be more complex and difficult. Further, since the rules will be new and different, for larger estates the cost and time under the new post-estate tax repeal law may actually be greater than before. Even for smaller estates that do not need to file a return, equivalent records will have to be maintained to establish the tax basis for property.

The allocation of basis adjustments may be made on an asset-by-asset basis.

The basis allocation will be simple for most estates in that the amount of basis increase permitted will exceed the predeath appreciation in the assets.

EXAMPLE

Taxpayer dies with $2 million in assets, which have a tax basis of $1 million. The $1.3 million basis adjustment alone (without consideration of the spousal $3 million adjustment) enables executor to step up the basis of every asset so that no predeath appreciation will ever be taxed. This is relatively simple in that there is no conflict, as contrasted with the next example.

Although there are no conflicts between heirs in the preceding example, simple may still not be an appropriate description of what the executor will face. The executor will have to obtain the tax basis and fair market value of all assets, including joint assets and revocable living trust assets over which the executor may have no control.

The real issue under the new modified basis adjustment rules will arise when the aggregate basis increase is not sufficient to ensure for every heir the elimination of capital gains tax.

EXAMPLE

Taxpayer dies, unmarried, with $3 million in assets, which have a tax basis of $1 million. The $1.3 million basis adjustment cannot enable the executor to step up the basis of every asset so that no predeath appreciation will ever be taxed. Some assets will have a built-in tax cost (i.e., a tax basis less than fair value); others may not. The decisions as to how the executor should make such an allocation are complicated and could create considerable disputes between beneficiaries.

EXAMPLE

Assume the same facts as in the preceding example except that there are three children—a son and two daughters. The $3 million estate consists of the following assets:

- House—value $1 million, basis $250,000.
- Business—value $1 million, basis -0-.
- Stock—value $1 million, basis $750,000.

How should the basis increase of $1.3 million be allocated? It could be done proportionately to relative appreciation. The house has $750,000 of the total $2 million of appreciation so that $487,500 [$1,300,000 × $750,000/$2,000,000] of the basis adjustment could be allocated to the house. But what if the son plans on living in the house indefinitely so that it won't be sold? What if the son will qualify for the home sale exclusion rule on a portion of the gain? In these cases, since gain will not be triggered for a long time, it would be preferable to allocate basis to other assets more likely to be sold sooner. What if the son is the executor? Can you trust him to allocate basis fairly and not favor the assets he is inheriting? One solution would be to include detailed allocation rules in your will. Another approach is to include a different person who is independent. What if taxpayer left each child one-third of each asset versus giving the house to one daughter, the business to the son, and the stock to the other daughter? The factors to consider, and the risks and issues that can arise, are almost endless.

IRD and the Modified Carryover Basis Rules

Taxpayers cannot use basis increase on property that is income in respect of a decedent (IRD) property (sometimes called Code Section 691 property). For example, the assets in IRA accounts cannot be allocated any portion of the basis step-up under the modified carryover basis system. This is because the basis step-up is not intended to avoid unrecognized income on IRA and other assets. The basis adjustment is for non-IRD assets.

LIABILITIES AND THE MODIFIED CARRYOVER BASIS RULES

General Income Tax Rules for Encumbered Property

Under the income tax laws, if a taxpayer sells property that is subject to a liability, the liability is treated as part of the amount realized, and hence, it can contribute to the determination of the taxable gain when the liabilities exceed the tax basis in the property sold. These rules are not changed by the 2001 Tax Act. However, because of the repeal of the step-up in basis rules that gave property a tax basis equal to its fair value on death, taxpayers are more likely to unexpectedly face a tax cost.

Liabilities in excess of the adjusted tax basis will not be considered for determining whether gain is recognized on acquisition of property from a decedent by the decedent's estate or any beneficiary that is not a tax-exempt entity.[40] This rule prevents the repeal of the estate tax stepped-up basis from triggering gain on assets held with liabilities in excess of basis. The following examples indicate the impact of these new rules on highly leveraged real estate investments.

--- **EXAMPLE** ---

Taxpayer purchased real estate for $100,000 and, after it had appreciated to $2,000,000, mortgaged the property for $1,500,000. The mortgage liability exceeds the basis in the real estate by $1,400,000. On taxpayer's death, his estate will not recognize gain on the property. Further, when his estate distributes the real estate to the heirs (assuming that the $1.3 million or $3 million basis adjustments are not applied to this property), the heirs will also not recognize gain on the receipt of the property.

EXAMPLE

Assume the same facts as in the preceding example. Heirs will receive the real estate with a tax basis of $100,000, the same as taxpayer's, and subject to the mortgage. This assumes that the lender could not, or chose not to, call the mortgage as a result of borrower's death and the transfer of the real estate to the estate and from the estate to the heirs. If there is no available basis adjustment, the heirs would recognize a $1,400,000 capital gain when they sell the property (but no gain when they inherit).

EXAMPLE

Assume the same facts as in the first example, except that the executor applies the $1.3 million and a portion of the $3 million basis adjustments to the real estate. The basis of the real estate can thus be increased by $1.9 million to its $2 million fair value, which exceeds the $1.5 million mortgage. The heirs will therefore not recognize gain when they sell the property.

Charitable Gifts and Liabilities

The new carryover basis rules could have provided an opportunity for taxpayers to circumvent congressional intent for the new law. Congress wanted to prevent taxpayers from financing a property, giving the money received from the financing to their heirs, and then donating the property subject to the mortgage (or other financing arrangement). If permitted, this would enable taxpayers to circumvent the carryover basis rules. Heirs would have cash with a basis equal to its value (the cash from the financing), and the encumbered property would be donated to a charity and disappear from the taxpayer's balance sheet, including the financing. The charity could then sell the property and not report any gain because a charity, under the general rules, would not have to report gain on such a transaction. If permitted, this would enable taxpayers to avoid the income tax consequences of new Code Section 1022(g). The 2001 Tax Act has prevented this type of planning so that now the taxpayer's heir will end up inheriting the property with the liability. Gain won't be recognized as a result of receiving an asset with a liability in excess of the tax basis in the asset. However, the heir will inherit the same tax problem: To dispose of this encumbered asset, the heir will have to recognize taxable gain.

GAIN ON DISTRIBUTIONS FROM ESTATES AND TRUSTS

A common drafting technique for wills has been to state that a specific dollar amount (in tax jargon a pecuniary bequest) rather than a percentage would be given to fund (transfer the requisite assets to) a bypass trust to preserve the then $675,000 exclusion amount (which increased to $1 million in 2002, and further in later years). This has important income tax ramifications.

EXAMPLE

Taxpayer, at death, has a particular mutual fund worth $250,000. When the estate is settled eight months later and the bypass trust funded, the mutual fund is worth $600,000. Taxpayer's will bequeaths an amount up to $600,000 to a bypass trust for the benefit of the surviving spouse and children. The executor funds this bypass trust with the mutual fund. The tax basis to the estate in the mutual fund is $250,000. Gain of $350,000 [$600,000 – $250,000] must be recognized.

(This example is reevaluated later in this chapter in light of the new law after 2009.)

EXAMPLE

Grandparent transfers various assets to a trust for the benefit of several grandchildren. When each grandchild reaches age 35, he or she is to receive $35,000. When the first grandchild reaches age 35, the trustee transfers stock with a tax basis of $24,000 and a fair market value of $35,000. The trust must report a gain of $11,000 [$35,000 – $24,000].

Generally, no gain or loss results from a transfer of property from an estate to a trust or from a trust to a beneficiary under the terms of the governing instrument. There are several exceptions. Where the distribution is of appreciated property distributed in satisfaction of a right to receive a specific dollar (pecuniary) amount, gain may be recognized for income tax purposes.[41] The example on page 245 illustrates this type of situation. Similarly, as shown in the example above, a trust must recognize taxable gain or loss where a cash bequest is satisfied by distribution of other property.[42]

Special Use Valuation Rules and Income Recognition

To understand the 2001 Tax Act changes as they relate to special use valuations and income recognition, some background information is necessary. To minimize the estate tax burden on estates, including certain interests in closely held business or real estate assets, Code Section 2032A provides special valuation rules. These rules are an exception from the general rules of valuing assets at their fair market value under the standard of a willing buyer and a willing seller. For example, if a taxpayer uses land as a parking lot for a business, but a developer could build an office building on the land, the price a developer would pay for the best use of the property, not the price a purchaser would pay for parking lot land, is used. This general valuation rule can create a tremendous hardship for farm or family businesses where assets are used in the business at a lesser value than fair value. The special valuation provisions of Code Section 2032A are intended to mitigate this hardship. A major drawback of taking advantage of the special use valuation is that the basis step-up that assets receive on death is limited to the special use valuation (increased by any gain recognized, as explained later). This lower basis could trigger an unintended income tax cost, so a special income tax rule was provided for that contingency.

The special rule provides that if an estate had to recognize taxable income as a result of a distribution of special use valuation property to a qualified heir, the amount would be limited to the amount that the fair value (not the special use value) of the property on the date it was transferred exceeds the value of the property on the date of death. This rule eliminated any taxable gain to the extent that the value of the property on the date of death exceeded the special use valuation of the property.

2001 Tax Act Changes

If an executor distributes appreciated assets to satisfy a beneficiary's right to a pecuniary bequest, the estate will recognize gain only to the extent that the fair value of the property on the date of distribution exceeds the value of the property on the date of the decedent's death.[43] This new rule is necessary after 2009 when the modified carryover basis rules come into play. Prior to 2009 (prior to the changes made by the 2001 Tax Act), this special rule for determining gain only applied to distributions of special use valuation property, not any other property, because it was only in that context that the unfairness would arise.

―――――――――――――――― **EXAMPLE** ――――――――――――――――

Reconsider the example of the taxpayer who, at death, has a particular mutual fund worth $250,000. He purchased the mutual fund for $50,000 years earlier. When the estate is settled eight months after taxpayer's death, the mutual fund is worth $600,000. His will bequeaths an amount up to $600,000 to a trust (it is no longer a bypass trust since there is no longer an estate tax after

2009) for the benefit of his surviving spouse and children. The executor funds this trust with the mutual fund. The tax basis to the estate in the mutual fund is $50,000, carryover basis, not the $250,000 fair value at death, as it would have been under pre-2001 tax law. If the executor allocated some portion of the $1.3 million or $3 million spousal basis step-ups permitted under the system that becomes applicable in 2010, the $250,000 basis could be achieved under the new law.

However, for this example, assume that no such allocation is made (the basis adjustments are allocated to other assets). Gain of $550,000 [$600,000 – $50,000] must be recognized if no special rule is provided for. This new special rule states that the gain cannot exceed the amount of appreciation from the date-of-death value, or the $250,000. Thus the gain under the post-2009 law should be the same amount as under prior law of $350,000.

The result of the special rule is that even if the executor doesn't make an allocation of basis to an asset with predeath appreciation, the gain the estate will realize for income tax purposes will not be greater under the post-2001 Tax Act rules than it was under prior law. Similar rules will be provided by the IRS to address the comparable income tax problem by trusts.[44]

EXAMPLE

Based on the facts in the preceding example, the heir's (the trust's) tax basis should be the tax basis of $50,000 increased by the $350,000 gain recognized, or $400,000. The difference between the $400,000 basis and the $600,000 date of death value, or $200,000, is exactly the amount of gain not recognized by taxpayer's estate because of this special rule. The result is that if the heir (trust) sells the mutual fund, it will then realize the gain. Thus, this special rule defers the timing of recognizing gain; it does not eliminate it.

NOTE

The special rule discussed in this section is yet another instance where an estate will have to determine and document the fair market value of assets at death, the decedent tax basis in assets, and other data. Record keeping under the new rules will continue to employ estate accountants.

What happens to an estate's tax basis in the property if this special rule applies? The basis of property to an heir (what the heir will use to calculate income tax when later selling the property) is the basis before the exchange, which is the tax basis on purchase of the property during the owner's lifetime, increased by the amount of gain the estate must report.

It appears that losses will continue, as under prior law, to be deducted when an estate distributes property with postdeath depreciation to satisfy a pecuniary obligation.

EXAMPLE

Testator's will states that $50,000 should be distributed to his favorite attorney. The executor distributes stock that testator paid $80,000 to purchase. The estate should be entitled to a $30,000 loss deduction.

SPECIAL RULES FOR INHERITED ART AND CREATIVE PROPERTY AFTER 2009

The general rule under the 2001 Tax Act is that not only will a tax basis in property carry over to (become the tax basis for) heirs, but the character of property as a capital asset (the gain on which would be taxed at more favorable capital gains rates) and the holding period (the time of ownership, which can affect the capital gains tax rates applicable to assets on sale) also carry forward and apply to heirs. (The status of an asset as capital or not is discussed in a preceding section.)

Prior law provided that creative property, such as music, art, or copyrights, that the taxpayer received as a gift (more technically, art, when the tax basis was determined in part or wholly by reference to the tax basis of an earlier holder, such as the donor who created and gave the taxpayer a sculpture) would not be characterized as a capital asset.

The 2001 Tax Act provides that such property is to be characterized as constituting a capital asset. This rule is a special exception to the general modified carryover basis rules of the 2001 Act.[45]

EXAMPLE

A craftsperson buys clay for $10 and makes a sculpture worth $20,000 and bequeaths it to an heir. Under prior and current law, the heir's tax basis is $10. Under prior law, the sculpture would be an ordinary (noncapital) asset to the heir because it was not a capital asset to the craftsperson. Under this new special rule that becomes applicable in 2010, it is a capital asset to the heir (unless another exception applies).

SPECIAL RULES FOR DONATIONS OF CERTAIN CAPITAL ASSETS

General Restrictions on Contribution Deductions

The amount that can be deducted for charitable contribution purposes is limited. Specifically, the new law reduces the contribution deduction by two items. The first is the gain that would not qualify as long-term capital gain. This is determined as if the property were sold for its fair value on the date it was donated.

The second reduction applies if either a gift is made to certain private charities (called private foundations) or a donation is made of tangible personal property unrelated to the charitable purpose of the charity (e.g., art donated to a hospital). In these two situations, the amount of the gain that would have been characterized as long-term capital gain is applied to reduce the charitable contribution deduction.

2001 Tax Act Changes

The special rule characterizing certain inherited art, copyrights, and other property as capital gain property will not apply to charitable contributions of such property.[46]

> ### NOTE
>
> As noted previously, the 2001 Tax Act changes the character of inherited art and other property for purposes of determining income tax on the sale or exchange of that property. It does not change the rules for purposes of determining the deduction available if that type of property is donated to a charity .

These new rules thus affect the results under the prior law rules, which otherwise remain intact.

PERSONAL RESIDENCE INTERPLAY OF HOME SALE EXCLUSION AND CARRYOVER BASIS RULES

The 2001 Tax Act liberalizes the home sale exclusion rules for estates and heirs. To understand the changes, estate planners must know the home sale exclusion rules.

General Rules for Excluding Gain on the Sale of a Principal Residence

The house sold must have qualified as the taxpayer's principal residence for at least two of the five years prior to the sale.[47] To add some flexibility, clients who don't meet the full two-year test may qualify to benefit from a portion of the $250,000 maximum exclusion if they had to move because of a job change, health problem, or other qualifying excuse.[48]

If the residence was partially used for personal purposes as a principal residence and partially used for business purposes (e.g., for rental or as a home office), the full exclusion may not be available. To the extent that depreciation was claimed on the property after May 6, 1997, the exclusion will not be available. This means that depreciation prior to such date will not have an adverse impact; depreciation from a home office or rental use after that date will.

The maximum gain that can be excluded is $250,000 for a single client, as stated above, or $500,000 for a couple filing a joint tax return. To use the higher $500,000 exclusion, one of the spouses must have owned the house for at least two of the preceding five years. Both spouses must have used the house as a principal residence during at least two of five years preceding the sale. There has been some leniency toward taxpayers who fail some of the preceding requirements for reasons beyond their control. As noted previously, if they fail the two-of-five-years ownership and use rule, or the once-every-two-years sale rule as a result of a change in employment, health, or certain circumstances to be specified in Treasury regulations, they will qualify for a partial exclusion.[49]

Home Sale Exclusion Problem in the Post-Estate Tax Repeal Environment

The home sale exclusion rules did not provide for any leniency on the death of a taxpayer. This will be even more problematic when the step-up in basis rules are eliminated and such leniency might be necessary. Under current law (the law that will exist through 2009 when the modified carryover basis rules become effective), if a taxpayer purchases a

---

EXAMPLE

Taxpayer purchased a home for $40,000. It appreciated to $290,000, or a $250,000 increase. If he sells the home prior to his death, the gain could be excluded from taxation under the home sale exclusion rules. If however, he dies owning the home, the exclusion would not apply but his heirs would obtain a step-up in basis in the inherited home. Thus the basis would be increased from $40,000 to the fair value of the home on taxpayer's death, or $290,000. If the heirs sold the home, no capital gains tax would be due.

house that appreciates prior to the purchaser's death, the appreciation would qualify for a basis step-up at death and the capital gains would disappear. The preceding example illustrates this scenario.

After 2009, the modified carryover basis rules will not always guarantee a step-up in the tax basis of a home. Unless this issue is specifically addressed, heirs could face a capital gains tax (as the example below illustrates) they might have avoided under prior law. The new rule described below seeks to address this problem.

EXAMPLE

Taxpayer Smith purchased a home for $40,000. It appreciated to $290,000, or a $250,000 increase. If Smith died owning the home, and the $1.3 million/$3 million spousal basis adjustments were not allocated by his executor to the home, the heirs would obtain a carryover in basis in the home they inherited, or $40,000. Thus, if the heirs sold the home, a $250,000 capital gains tax would be due.

Extension of Home Sale Exclusion Rules to Estates

An estate or trust may qualify to exclude the gain realized on the sale of the decedent's personal residence. Your client's estate could qualify for this benefit, an heir who inherited the property from the client (e.g., his child) could qualify, and a special trust referred to as a qualified revocable trust (QRT) could qualify.

EXAMPLE

Taxpayer Jones purchased a home on July 1, 1997, for $100,000 and lived in it until he died June 30, 2003; at that time the home was worth $500,000, an appreciation of $400,000. Assume that his executor did not elect to allocate any of the $1.3 million/ $3 million spousal basis adjustments to the home. Jones's estate sold the home after his death for $500,000. The executor could use the $250,000 home sale exclusion to eliminate $250,000 of the $400,000 capital gain.

When an executor considers which assets should receive an allocation of the $1.3 million/$3 million spousal basis adjustments, consideration should be given to maximizing the use of the home sale exclusion available to estates. This can increase the maximum capital gains that can be avoided under the laws applicable after 2009 to $4,550,000 [$1,300,000 general basis step-up + $3,000,000 spousal basis step-up + $250,000 home sale exclusion]. Remember, this is not value of assets that can be increased, but rather, appreciation.

Definition of a Qualified Revocable Trust

NOTE

A qualified revocable trust is not the same as a qualified personal residence trust. Confusion will abound. Good for accountants, lawyers, and other estate planning professionals, but not easy for laypersons.

A qualified revocable trust (QRT) is a grantor trust that is treated as owned by the grantor. The income earned by the trust is taxable to the grantor (the person who set up the trust) during the grantor's lifetime.[50] The common QRT is the popular revocable living trust. A trust will not qualify as a QRT if it is a foreign trust.[51] If the grantor can only exercise power over the trust with the consent of another person, the trust will not qualify as a QRT.

EXAMPLE

A trust can be characterized as a grantor trust if a related nonadverse trustee can be given the right to distribute income and principal among a class of trust beneficiaries without an ascertainable standard to achieve grantor trust status.[52] Such a trust would not appear to qualify as a QRT under the new law.

Decedent's Use Available to Heirs

An heir, say a child inheriting a parent's home, can count the time periods for which the parent owned the house, or used it as a residence, in determining if the heir qualifies for the home sale exclusion. The home has to be used for two of the five years before sale as a principal residence. The decedent's use and ownership can be combined with that of the heir, as the following example illustrates.

EXAMPLE

Taxpayer purchased a home on January 1, 2003, for $100,000 and lived in it until he died December 31, 2003, when the home was worth $340,000. He only lived in and owned the home for one year and thus does not meet the requirements for the home sale exclusion. He bequeaths his home to his partner, who is in need of additional cash. If the partner sells the home immediately, he will have a capital gains tax to pay. Instead, he resides in the home as his principal residence for one year and then sells it for $360,000. The partner can add decedent's ownership and use of the home to his and thus qualify to exclude up to $250,000 of the gain when he sells the home. He need not wait to qualify for the two-year use period based solely on his own use.

NOTE

It appears that the heir can count his use of the property and the decedent's ownership toward the time period calculation. Thus, if the decedent owned the house but the heir used it, the exclusion may be available.

NOTE

Under current pre-2010 law, a surviving spouse can add the deceased spouse's use and ownership to determine if the exclusion is available. Thus, the post-2009 modified carryover basis law extends this benefit.

SPECIAL RULES APPLICABLE TO
FOREIGN TAXPAYERS AND TRANSACTIONS

Modified Basis Adjustment for
Nonresident Aliens Severely Limited

The basis adjustment available to most estates, which permits the basis of assets to be increased by up to $1.3 million under the system to become applicable in 2010, is reduced to a nominal $60,000 for nonresident aliens.[53] Further, the adjustment for capital loss carryovers,[54] net operating loss carryovers under Code Section 172, and any loss deductions for built-in losses that would have been permitted as deductions under Code Section 165 to a resident taxpayer, will not be permitted to a nonresident alien.

 Evaluate any estate tax treaty between the United States and the country in which the particular nonresident taxpayer is a citizen. There may be benefits to offset this harsh limitation.

Basis Adjustments Not Permitted for
Certain Stock Holdings

No basis increase is permitted on stock in a foreign personal holding company (FPHC),[55] a domestic international sales corporation (DISC),[56] a foreign sales corporation (FSC),[57] or a passive foreign investment company.[58]

Gain on Transfers to Certain Foreign Trusts and Estates

Under pre-2001 Tax Act law, if appreciated property were transferred to a foreign trust or estate, gain had to be recognized. The 2001 Tax Act extends this rule.

Testamentary transfers starting from 2010 by a U.S. estate to a nonresident alien will be treated as a sale or exchange of those assets at their fair value.[59] The concept behind this rule is that once assets are transferred to a nonresident alien, they will be outside the reach of the U.S. taxing authorities. Therefore, the capital gains tax is executed on transfer.

Basis Reduction for Foreign Investment Company Stock

Gain from the sale or exchange of a foreign mutual fund or investment company stock is treated as ordinary income, and not capital gain, under special rules. The basis of such stock becomes its fair market value on death. This special rule is repealed after 2009 when the estate tax is repealed and the new modified carryover basis regimen begins.[60]

REPORTING REQUIREMENTS UNDER THE NEW MODIFIED CARRYOVER BASIS RULES

The new modified carryover basis rules require lots of IRS reporting—good news for accountants, more hassles for everyone else.[61] The new reporting requirements, just like the 2001 tax law generally, are even more complex than prior law. Is this why they called it tax "relief"? The new reporting requirements must address the complexity of advising heirs of their tax basis in inherited assets.

Complex Tax Return Required

The executor must file a tax return with the IRS reporting specified information, although the new reporting requirements will only apply to estates over $1.3 million.[62] This is the amount below which no appreciation will be taxed under the modified carryover basis rules.[63] (As discussed in the section that follows, for estates of $1.3 million or less, the tax basis of all assets will be stepped up so the IRS need not worry about reporting.)

> **NOTE**
>
> The preceding rule is limited to the $1.3 million figure, as inflation indexed. It is not increased by the amounts for losses and loss carryovers (explained earlier).

For estates with less than $1.3 million in assets (not appreciation), executors should compile the same information even if an IRS tax filing is not necessary. This information will be necessary for heirs to determine the tax basis of assets they sell. Further, if an heir, say a son, has a large estate, it is possible that the heir's executor will have to file a tax return on his death. The information from the father's estate will be necessary for the son's executor to file a tax return.

NOTE

These rules are confusing in that the modified carryover basis rules refer to $1.3 million of appreciation, not $1.3 million of assets. However, the reporting requirements are based on $1.3 million of assets. The rationale for the difference is simple. The IRS will assume that for assets of estates under $1.3 million in total value all assets will have a tax basis equal to their value at the date of the decedent's death (similar to the step-up in basis rules under current law). The issue of whether the $1.3 million in basis step-up protects all assets cannot apply for estates with less than $1.3 million, even if all assets have a zero tax basis. Over this amount, taxpayers will have to prove tax basis.

If the $1.3 million and the $3 million basis adjustments don't apply to the property, reporting will be necessary. This means that any property received by gift by the decedent within three years before the decedent's death must be reported, because no basis adjustment will be permitted.

Planning Perspective for Smaller Estates

Estates under $1.3 million will presumably not be required to file any type of tax return. As noted, executors of such estates should still collect and organize similar information, because each heir will have to have documentation of the tax basis in assets inherited. What this also means (which is the same as under current law) is that for estates not

---
EXAMPLE

Father died and his entire estate is valued at $850,000. His estate is left to his only heir, his son. The estate consists of a house that the son, as executor, believes to be worth about $350,000, and $500,000 of mutual funds. The value of the mutual funds is fixed and clear, but what about the house? Under current law, in 2001, for example, with a $675,000 exclusion, the son would have made every effort to have the house appraised at the lowest value possible to minimize the value of the estate and hence minimize estate taxes on the value in excess of $675,000. After 2009, under the new modified carryover basis rules, son would endeavor to do just the opposite, up to a point. The higher the son could have the house appraised—but not in excess of $800,000 (the amount that when combined with the $500,000 of mutual funds would trigger the requirement for the estate to file with the IRS)—the better. Why? As long as the estate is under $1.3 million in value, there is no reporting requirement. Under this threshold, the incentive will be to value any asset with an uncertain value (real estate, closely held business, art, etc.) as high as possible since that value will be the value to the heir and will determine the income tax the heir will have to pay on selling the property.

---

required to file, the incentive will be to justify the highest value possible for any assets in the estate since these assets will become the tax basis of the assets to the heirs.

Special Rule for Nonresident Aliens

E.T. may not be able to afford to phone home after this one. For non-resident aliens (noncitizens), estates over $60,000 will be subject to the reporting requirements. The only assets considered are those potentially subject to U.S. taxation, generally tangible property located in the United States. Tax treaties may affect this consideration. These treaties are bilateral conventions (agreements) between the United

States and the nonresident alien's country of citizenship. For example, a treaty may provide that only the home country, not the United States, may tax a nonresident alien's estate.

Tax Return Requiring Participation of Executor and Others

In many instances, the executor may not have complete information to file the required tax return with the IRS. For example, a trust may own assets included in the decedent's estate or the decedent may have owned assets jointly with someone so that the assets pass by operation of law outside the probate estate. In such cases, the new reporting rules direct the executor to describe the property and list anyone who has a beneficial interest in the property, such as a joint owner. These rules could be extremely burdensome and difficult to implement. For many estates, several different people will have to collaborate to complete the return. For example, if before death the taxpayer transferred some, but not all, of his assets to a revocable living trust, the trustee and executor would each have information necessary for the completion of this return. Generally, this should not be an issue because the trustee and executor are often the same person. Where they are not, coordination will be necessary. For some taxpayers, this can be problematic.

EXAMPLE

Taxpayer is married for the third time and wants to leave certain assets to children from a prior marriage and a former spouse but does not want his current spouse to be aware of these bequests. He establishes a revocable living trust to hold these assets. He does not use a pourover will (a will that transfers assets to the trust for distribution after death) because he does not want to bring the trust to anyone's attention. Both the trustee and executor must cooperate. In addition, co-owners of any joint assets will presumably have information and be required to cooperate as well.

Information That Must Be Reported

The required information is similar but more comprehensive than the information required for an estate tax return under current law (which remains through 2009 in this regard). This reporting will have to disclose "sufficient information" so that the new carryover basis rule will work properly.

> **NOTE**
>
> Undoubtedly, the IRS will define the phrase *sufficient information* that executors must provide in a broad, complex, and difficult to comply with manner. But Congress came up with this messy new system—the IRS will only be trying to implement it.

The reason for the detailed reporting requirements is that heirs must know the tax basis they have in assets they inherit so that they can determine their income tax consequences when they sell property. It is necessary to provide the IRS with specific information in the following seven areas:

1. The name and tax identification number (e.g., Social Security number for an individual) of each beneficiary (recipient).[64]

2. An accurate description of the property involved.[65] For publicly traded stock, this will be simple. Likely, more complex requirements and details will be required of a closely held business or other harder-to-value assets.

3. The adjusted income tax basis of the property to the decedent.[66] This requirement was not relevant under prior law when most assets (except IRD, such as an IRA account) received a step-up in tax basis to the fair value at death (or at the alternate valuation date six months following death).

4. The fair market value of each asset to the decedent.[67] This is similar to the current law. Although the new law after 2009 is based on a carryover basis concept, the modified carryover basis approach actually adopted (which permits adjusting basis

for the $1.3 million general and the $3 million spousal amounts) requires both tax basis and fair market value data. When this is compounded by the issue of how to allocate these adjustments, the complexity is truly remarkable.

5. The decedent's holding period for the property.[68] As explained earlier, the time the decedent held the property, which is necessary for determining the capital gains consequences on the sale of property, carries from the decedent to the heirs.

6. Information necessary to determine whether any of the gain an heir would realize on the sale of the property would be taxed as ordinary income (at the maximum individual income tax rates) rather than as capital gain income (potentially taxed at the lower capital gains tax rates).[69] This could include information as to dealer status. For example, if the decedent purchased land, subdivided, and sold many lots as inventory, any remaining lots could generate ordinary income and not capital gains to the heirs. Similarly, depreciation deductions claimed on a property could cause the recharacterization of some portion of the gain as ordinary income instead of more favorable capital gains.

7. Any other information that the IRS may require in regulations.[70]

Reports an Executor Must Give Heirs

After making the preceding determinations, the executor then has to report to heirs the information necessary for them to determine their tax basis and holding period in the property.

The new law will require that for decedents dying after 2009, executors will have to provide the following information to heirs:

- Name, address, telephone number of the person filing the return. This will generally, but not always, be the executor.

- All of the information required to be furnished to the IRS, as explained in the preceding section, for the assets bequeathed to the particular heir.[71]

The executor must provide this information to each heir within thirty days of filing with the IRS.

> **NOTE**
>
> Executors will probably send this information using certified mail or have heirs sign an acknowledgment that they received this information to prove compliance. Perhaps the typical receipt and release used for probate and estate administration will include an acknowledgment of the data attached as an exhibit.

If the estate is subject to an IRS audit, the executor will undoubtedly be required to provide additional revised information to each heir. If the heir has already sold the property, then the heir will have to file an amended income tax return.

The information that the executor furnishes to the heirs will be binding on them and will inform them of their tax basis in each asset. This will create a need in large estates for heirs to carefully review the estate tax return information.

Penalties to Encourage Compliance

To ensure that the executor complies with these rules, substantial penalties are imposed for failure to meet the reporting requirements of the IRS. The penalty is generally $10,000 for failing to furnish the required information.[72] However, failure to provide the IRS the information required concerning appreciated assets that the decedent received as a gift within three years of death is only $500.[73]

If an executor fails to provide beneficiaries with the information required under the code,[74] then the penalty is $50 for each failure.[75] The new rules give executors a break. They won't be penalized if there was "reasonable cause" for not filing. Annoyance and confusion, however, are unlikely to constitute reasonable cause. If the failure is intentional, the penalty becomes more severe, 5 percent of the value of the property involved.[76]

New Gift Tax Filing Requirements

Gift tax returns still must be filed if the estate tax repeal era in 2010 is reached without another major tax bill. This is because a $1 million lifetime gift tax exemption will remain (see Chapter 6). To enforce this filing, requirements are necessary. A gift tax return will have to be filed any time the taxpayer makes a transfer that is not protected by one of the following five exclusions:

1. A gift valued at $10,000 or less during the year to one donee that is a gift of a *present interest.* This is a technical requirement that in simple terms means the beneficiary or donee must be able to realize the enjoyment of the money or have access to it when the gift is made. This requirement presents the biggest problem when gifts are made to trusts. This amount is to be indexed for inflation.

2. Medical or tuition payments that are not subject to the gift tax.

3. A transfer that qualifies for the gift tax marital deduction for gifts to a spouse, unless it is a gift to a trust for which a special spousal trust election (QTIP) is made.

4. A transfer to a noncitizen spouse that exceeds the $100,000 permissible annual gifts (indexed for inflation, $106,000 in 2001) to a noncitizen spouse.

5. A gift that qualifies for the gift tax charitable contribution deduction.

When a gift tax return is filed, an information report will have to be provided to each donee stating the name, address, and telephone number of the person required to make the report and the information in the gift tax return concerning the property that the particular donee receives.[77] This is necessary so that the donee can determine his tax basis in the property. This report to the donees will have to be furnished within 30 days of the date the gift tax return is filed. There are penalties for failing to comply.

PLANNING WITH THE NEW MODIFIED CARRYOVER BASIS RULES

Need for Immediate Record Keeping

Don't wait for the new basis rules to take effect in 2010. It is helpful from a general income tax perspective, and essential under the modified carryover basis rules, to have adequate documentation. The taxpayer's broker or financial planner should endeavor to track tax basis on financial statements. Computer tracking of tax basis using a program like Quicken can be helpful (see Shenkman, *The Beneficiary Workbook* for sample forms).

When to Sell, When to Hold

Under current law, which will continue until 2010, there is an incentive to hold on to assets for which the executor cannot determine a tax basis, such as stock received as a gift decades ago from an elderly aunt who owned it for many decades before giving it to the taxpayer. The reason to hold on to such an asset is that it would receive a step-up in tax basis on the taxpayer's death and thus eliminate the taxable gain. Another reason is that the step-up in basis would eliminate the record-keeping nightmare of trying to determine the tax basis in the property. Under the modified carryover basis system scheduled to become effective in 2010, every taxpayer will be able to eliminate $1.3 million of gain. For the vast majority of Americans, this means that they will continue to have the equivalent of a complete step-up in tax basis at death. In such instances, planning will not change. If the estate is so large and has so much appreciation that beyond the $1.3 million basis step-up and the $3 million special spousal basis step-up the taxpayer will still have gain, then the analysis about holding a particular asset until death will change.

If the taxpayer has assets that have declined in value, there may not be a benefit to selling them before death.

 If a taxpayer is on his deathbed, his accountant can determine whether from an income tax standpoint it will be advantageous to sell loss property (property with a fair market value less than its adjusted tax basis) and recognize a tax loss for income tax purposes on the final income tax return of the taxpayer.

Transferring Assets to Taxpayers in Low Tax Brackets

An affirmative income tax planning strategy will be to transfer appreciated assets to taxpayers (relatives or friends) who are in relatively low tax brackets. This tactic will enable the financial planner to obtain a step-up in basis and avoid capital gains tax. However, it is necessary to monitor the three-year rule, which, except for transfers between spouses, will effectively eliminate this type of planning.

 When transferring assets to an elderly or infirm friend or relative to obtain a basis step-up, carefully evaluate whether it is worth the following risks:

- The maximum capital gains savings might be at a 25% state and federal level, perhaps less. Compare the maximum anticipated savings, on a present value (time value of money) basis, to the risks involved, and be certain the transfer is really worthwhile.

- The taxpayer cannot legally control where the transferee bequeaths his assets. What if he changes his mind and gives the assets to someone other than the taxpayer (or a desired recipient)? No one should sign an agreement since it would memorialize a tax fraud scheme.

- If the transferee is sued or requires substantial medical care, the assets could be jeopardized.

- It is often difficult to predict how long a terminally ill patient will survive. A several-year survival period could affect a taxpayer's willingness to engage in such planning. Also, the longer the survival period, the greater the likelihood that the transferee will use the assets transferred.

- The transferee may have a surviving spouse who elects under state law to take some portion of the assets given.

- If the assets are in excess of $1 million, a gift tax might be triggered on the transfer. If the assets are difficult to value, such as a family limited partnership, an audit might be triggered.

- Consider the costs of the transfer. While stock might be relatively inexpensive to gift, transferring real estate might require a deed, mortgage recording fee, the need to obtain a lender's approval, changes in title and casualty insurance, and lease assignments.

A related issue to consider is whether a particular beneficiary is a dealer with respect to property being bequeathed. If a beneficiary is a real estate developer, bequeathing property to him might result in income eventually taxed as ordinary income, not capital gains. Given the higher tax rate, there may be a greater incentive to allocate basis adjustment to such an asset.

Negative Effect on Inter Vivos QTIP Technique

The QTIP marital trust was discussed at length in Chapter 6. This technique can be used in the form of an inter vivos QTIP while the taxpayer is alive. The inter vivos QTIP has been a useful technique to equalize estates while retaining control over assets.

─────────────── **EXAMPLE** ───────────────

Husband has a $5 million estate with a tax basis of zero. Wife has no assets. He is uncomfortable placing one half of the assets in her name, but doing so will enable her estate to take advantage of the basis step-up provisions. If Husband gave one half of the assets

> outright to Wife, she would have control over them. If instead, he gave one half the assets to a QTIP trust, they would be included, under current law, in Wife's estate, yet Husband would have control over where they would ultimately be distributed.

This inter vivos QTIP technique has been popular, and will become more popular, as taxpayers seek to divide their estates to take maximum advantage of the increasing estate tax exclusion. However, it is not certain that this technique will be successful in qualifying the assets that taxpayers give to the inter vivos QTIP for the modified carryover basis step-up under the system to become applicable in 2010. Under the new modified carryover basis rules, certain types of property interest passed on to a surviving spouse will qualify for a basis increase of up to $3 million (in addition to the $1.3 million general basis increase). However, the rules for what qualifies for the $3 million basis step-up may not include property interests that revert to a taxpayer on the death of a spouse.

Step-Ups with Living Trust Assets

Revocable living trusts might also present an issue under the new basis step-up rules. The issue is whether the property owned by a trust will be deemed owned by the decedent to qualify for the basis step-up. The decedent will be treated as owning property transferred during his lifetime to a qualified revocable trust (QRT).[78] The definition does not appear to include a revocable trust that can only be amended by the grantor with the consent of another person. This is a constraint commonly used in a revocable trust when the grantor needs some protection from himself, or when the grantor wants to ensure a greater ease of continuity in the event of disability by naming a current cotrustee. This type of revocable trust would have significant adverse consequences under the basis step-up rules.

Joint revocable trusts will not provide the step-up because the powers of appointment used in such plans will not qualify as ownership.

If the carryover basis rules actually come into being, taxpayers who have a cotrustee on a revocable living trust will have to review and possibly modify the trust agreement.

Determining the Tax Basis of an Asset

The reason the carryover basis rules were repealed in the past was that they were too complex and difficult to administer. Key differences under the new system to become applicable in 2010 are the $1.3 million general basis step-up, the $3 million spousal basis step-up, and the $250,000 home sale exclusion rules. As a result, all but the very wealthiest families will not be subject to carryover basis. For those who are, determining, and then proving basis on an IRS audit, will be a difficult task.

Taxpayers who can accept a zero basis because the $1.3 million/$3 million amounts exceed the value of the estate can use a zero basis and simply step-up.

If the facts necessary to determine the basis of property in the hands of the donor or the last preceding owner by whom it was not acquired by gift are unknown to the donee, the IRS will, if possible, obtain the pertinent information from the donor or from the last preceding owner or from any other person who possesses the relevant information. If the IRS finds it impossible to obtain the necessary information, the basis in the hands of such donor or last preceding owner will be presumed to be the fair market value of the property as determined by the IRS as of the date the property was acquired by the donor or last preceding owner.[79] How much help this will be in situations where basis cannot be determined is questionable.

Increased Liability of Executors and Trustees

Fiduciaries have an obligation to behave in a fair and impartial manner under state law. How will this obligation affect a fiduciary's allocation of basis adjustment to various estate assets under the new rules? If the will is silent on what should be done, then state law will have to be consulted. State law cannot be particularly detailed on this issue because it is so new.

 Executors who must implement the new rules with so little guidance will have to exercise caution. Professional advice on how to allocate the basis adjustments should be obtained. Further, the release issued to beneficiaries before property is distributed should expressly acknowledge the basis adjustments allocated and agree to them.

Drafting of Wills and Trusts under the New Law

Language should be added to wills and trusts that gives the executor protection from beneficiaries for any basis allocation made in good faith. Also, the document should give the fiduciary reasonable discretion concerning the allocation of the various basis adjustments to each estate asset.

Property cannot be valued at an amount greater than the date-of-death value. This is not simple for nonmarketable assets, such as stock in a closely held business. Caution would be in order and protective language should be included to protect fiduciaries.

NEW REGULATIONS FROM THE IRS

The IRS has been directed by the new law, and given the authority, to develop regulations to address the myriad issues created by the new carryover basis rules.[80] Thus there is more complexity to come. The modified carryover basis rules are exceedingly complex and raise many new questions. While many practitioners believe that the rules will never be allowed to take effect, the reality is that they are law and unless and until Congress acts to change them, taxpayers must begin planning for their impact.

8
ISSUES IN REVISING WILLS AND OTHER ESTATE PLANNING DOCUMENTS

The many changes, tremendous uncertainty, and potential for further change and modification of the estate and related tax laws make planning complex. The preceding chapters have reviewed the new rules and their impact on various trusts and other estate planning techniques. This chapter reviews the changes from the perspective of constructing an overall estate plan.

WILL DRAFTING CONSIDERATIONS

The following issues must be addressed in structuring a will or revocable living trust after the 2001 Tax Act:

- How should a bypass trust be structured in light of the changes? Should a cap be placed on the amount used to fund the bypass trust? If so, how should it be structured? Alternatively, should the selection of trustees, beneficiaries, and distribution standards be modified? As an alternative to a cap, should a disclaimer approach be used outright to the surviving spouse, who by disclaiming it, allows it to go to the bypass trust? Will this approach be practical for the taxpayer? (See Chapter 6.)

- Title (ownership) of assets must be monitored, and may have to be restructured to fund the larger bypass amount. The restructuring will have to change and be reevaluated when the modified carryover basis rules come into play in 2010.

 As noted, while the estate tax exists, a married taxpayer should divide assets between himself and his spouse approximately equally in value. Once the estate tax is repealed and the modified carryover basis is enacted, the taxpayer will still divide assets equally, but by appreciation, not value.

- The carryover basis rules are scheduled to become effective in 2010. There is little guidance on how to deal with these extremely complex rules. Should a taxpayer's will attempt to deal with this considerable uncertainty now? Should it include a directive to the executor for allocating the basis adjustment? The wait-and-see approach is dangerous for will and trust drafting. There can be no assurance that a taxpayer will be mentally and physically capable of executing a new will when the state of the law becomes better defined. On the other hand, how many contingent scenarios can a taxpayer comfortably plan for?
- Based on current law, in 2011 the estate tax will be in force with a $1 million exclusion and all the current rules. There is no certainty that a future Congress will make the repeal real and permanent. As such, wills need to reflect the possibility of the current estate tax laws remaining in force, with the $1 million exclusion.

Basic Dispositive Scheme

What changes will there be in the post-estate-tax repeal world? What type of disposition to a spouse or another beneficiary will make sense with no estate tax? Trusts should continue to be used. Consider the impact of the gift tax, which will remain. This might be the ideal opportunity for the distribution of assets to a discretionary dynasty trust by a nonmarried taxpayer (see Chapter 6).

Taxpayers with a spouse can leave property assets outright to the surviving spouse, but this will not enable them to take advantage of the GST exemption or dynasty planning. The preferable approach from a tax perspective until the estate tax is repealed is to maximize GST planning through a bypass and, to the extent necessary, QTIP trust, to eventually fund a dynasty sprinkle trust. After the estate and GST taxes are repealed in 2010, the estate can distribute directly to the dynasty trust (don't forget that for gift tax purposes there is still only a $1 million exclusion). This dispositive structure will enable a surviving spouse to make gifts to children and future descendants free of the newly constituted gift tax. Flexible discretionary family pot trusts that may be split by children after death of the surviving spouse would appear to be the ideal approach to planning without an estate tax.

Another planning issue is that the estate tax may be reimposed. What type of asset or disposition has the best chance of escaping a new tax? It would seem that if the new estate tax is similar to the current estate tax system, a sprinkle perpetual trust may be best.

There are limits on this type of planning under the new modified carryover basis rules. Estate planners must be certain that wills address the $1.3 million general basis step-up and the $3 million spousal basis step-up. This is not available with a sprinkle trust. A QTIP is eligible, however. So the objective is to have enough assets in a trust for the $3 million spousal basis step-up. This is complex to achieve since assets are not allocated to the trusts based on market values, but on the difference between the adjusted tax basis and fair market value of those assets (i.e., by appreciation) to absorb the maximum basis step-up.

When selecting which assets to distribute to the QTIP or sprinkle trust to maximize tax benefits, tax planners want sufficient assets to absorb the $3 million basis step-up (which may be much more than $3 million in fair value) allocated to the QTIP and the remainder to a sprinkle trust. There could be a formal bequest to the marital trust QTIP to obtain the basis step-up. These issues are further complicated by when an asset may be sold. Other than Code Section 1022 considerations and personal issues, the preferable estate distribution could be all to a family pot sprinkle trust.

Handling the Bypass Trust with Smaller Estates

What if the entire estate will be covered by the bypass? If the bypass is a pecuniary trust, the taxpayer may trigger taxable gain on funding the trust (see Chapters 1 and 6). This could be problematic; a pecuniary marital or fractional share disposition may make more sense to avoid this gain. Another problem is that the formula to fund the bypass may not achieve the desired result because as the exclusion increases, the amount involved may be too large relative to the size of the estate (see Chapter 1).

Revising Language to Fund Trusts

The language used under an existing will (prepared prior to the 2001 Tax Act) to fund a bypass trust may produce uncertain results. If the funding clause indicates the maximum exclusion, what if there is no exclusion? The pertinent language in every will should be revised to address this issue.

 The only practical and safe approach is to review and revise every plan and will. Being penny-wise and pound-foolish is dangerous here.

State taxes create another issue if the state of the taxpayer's residence has an estate tax that is not properly coordinated with the 2001 Tax Act rules. It may be prudent to revise the formula in the taxpayer's will to address any potential discontinuity. This complex issue will evolve as states react to the 2001 Tax Act.

EXAMPLE

Husband's estate is $6 million. His will says that the amount necessary to reduce the estate taxes on his estate to zero shall be distributed to a QTIP trust for his surviving spouse. The estate remaining after this distribution is to be distributed to a nephew. The idea was to distribute $675,000 to the nephew, and the remaining $5,325,000 in a QTIP for his wife. However, if the estate tax is repealed, the amount necessary to reduce the estate tax on the estate to zero is zero. Would that result in a distribution of the entire estate to the nephew? Even apart from the marital deduction, the increasing exclusion will result in an inappropriately large amount distributed to the nephew.

If the marital clause in a will is drafted in a manner stating that the marital bequest shall be the amount necessary to reduce the estate tax to zero, then no distribution may be made to a trust for a surviving spouse. Instead, all assets might be distributed to children or other heirs.

Addressing Modified Carryover Basis, the $1.3 Million/ $3 Million Step-Ups, and Other Post-2009 Issues

At least six issues arise in analyzing how to revise a will to address the many changes wrought by the 2001 Tax Act if and when the post-2009 modifications come into play and the estate tax is repealed:

1. Should the approach used be discretionary, nondiscretionary, nondiscretionary with guidance, or mandatory? As reviewed in this chapter, the answer will depend on the type of assets, expectations for distribution or sale, the independence of the executor, and other factors. The following sample language offers but one of many approaches that could be used.

SAMPLE PROVISION

I give, devise, and bequeath to the Trustee of the Marital Basis Increase Trust property qualifying for the spousal basis increase under Code Section 1022(c) sufficient property to take maximum advantage of the basis increase available under such provision.

If the value of such assets on the dates distributed to said Trust is less than the value of such assets on the date of my death, the

> Executor shall distribute such additional assets to said Trust necessary to increase the value at the dates of distribution to equal the value at the date of my death if such distribution is required to qualify for the basis step-up under IRC § 1022.
>
> My Executor shall fund said Trust with assets with the most predeath appreciation unless in my Executor's discretion such property should not be transferred to said Trust. The Executor, by way of example and not limitation, may choose not to allocate a specific asset to said Trust on the Executor's belief that such property will be more readily managed if distributed to a different trust or beneficiary, the expected timing of the sale of such property is remote, the difficulty in demonstrating basis is considerable, or any other factor.

2. What about assets for which tax basis is uncertain? Should these receive a full allocation as if their tax basis were in fact zero, or instead receive a partial allocation? If there is sufficient basis adjustment, the question would be moot because full basis adjustment can be allocated. If there is insufficient basis, then a decision will have to be made based on expected sale date, with basis data estimated, and so forth.

3. How should the executor address assets for which capital gains can be deferred? Which are likely to be deferred? This will require an analysis to which beneficiaries will need to contribute information. Any of the following techniques could be used to defer capital gains:

   - Real estate can be exchanged under a tax-deferred Code Section 1031 like kind exchange and avoid any current gain. If the property is suitable for such a transaction, should the executor not allocate basis adjustment to it? What criteria should be used for determining suitability?

   - A highly concentrated stock position, and in some instances appreciated real estate, could be contributed to a charitable remainder trust (CRT) and sold by the charity without any immediate tax cost, the proceeds diversified and invested, and a periodic annuity generated and paid to the donor. How, if at all, should the executor address this planning opportunity in allocating basis?

- A large position in a particular stock could be contributed to an exchange fund and diversified without incurring any capital gains cost. This type of fund is an investment partnership typically organized by a major money management firm specifically for such a purpose. They identify a large number of investors with concentrated and appreciated stock positions in different stocks so that the assembled portfolio is well diversified. They add sufficient nonmarketable assets to the mix, such as real estate, to avoid triggering the investment company rules that would result in gain being triggered on the contribution to the partnership. Should the executor be charged with obtaining an opinion as to whether certain stock should or could be handled in this manner? If so, what if Congress changes the laws affecting investment companies so that such funds are more difficult to use?

4. How should the taxpayer's home be handled? Should it be bequeathed to a specific heir who may be best situated to take advantage of the home sale exclusion? If the heir decides to sell immediately and not qualify for the home sale exclusion, should any basis adjustment be allocated to the house? Should the will expressly state that the executor, in making the allocation of basis, is to assume that the home will qualify for the maximum exclusion and not make any allocation to that extent? If so, then the burden to qualify will be on the heir receiving the devise of the home.

5. What happens to assets sold after death? Will they qualify for a basis step-up if sold prior to going to the QTIP or pot trust established under the will? Although it would seem appropriate to allocate basis adjustment based on the sale value, it is not clear what criteria the will should contain. On a present value analysis, there can be no more costly income tax than that on the assets sold during administration of an estate (i.e., because

income tax will be due more quickly than a tax a beneficiary of property may seek to defer). Should the will therefore mandate that basis adjustment be first allocated to assets sold during administration? The answers are not simple.

6. In light of the tremendous amount of discretion given to the executor, who should be named executor? The example below illustrates options for consideration depending on the circumstances.

EXAMPLE

Taxpayer has three children. Under prior law, the children may simply have been named in descending age to serve individually as executor. However, if the executor is to be given wide latitude to allocate the new basis adjustment after 2009, would it still be advisable to name the eldest son as sole initial executor? Perhaps taxpayer could name all three children as co-executors so that they could all agree on the allocation. However, three co-executors is unwieldy. Perhaps it would be better to name a professional trustee, such as a bank or trust company, that would also be impartial in making the allocation.

REVOCABLE LIVING TRUSTS

Revocable living trusts will have to be revised to conform with the many issues and changes noted for wills.

Need for Coordination

Some coordination provision to address the need for allocation of the $1.3 million/$3 million basis adjustments should be considered. The assets adjusted under the trust and those adjusted under the will all need to be considered.

Home Sale Exclusion Rules

Care will have to be taken to ensure that a revocable trust will qualify as a qualified revocable trust (QRT) under the new home sale exclusion rules. Perhaps savings language (language authorizing the trustee to correct the trust to obtain the desired tax result) should be included to help ensure that the estate will qualify for this income tax benefit. The sample language provided here offers one such approach.

SAMPLE LANGUAGE

It is the Grantor's intent that this Trust qualify as a Qualified Revocable Trust (QRT) as defined under IRC § 645(b)(1) for purposes of qualifying for the home sale income tax exclusion under IRC § 121. Grantor authorizes and directs the Trustee [or grantor might prefer the Trust Protector, instead] to make any such modifications necessary to enable this trust to so qualify if, at the time of Grantor's death, this Trust owns a personal residence of Grantor that would otherwise qualify for the exclusion under IRC § 121.

POWERS OF ATTORNEY

Gift provisions will have to be revised. For smaller estates unlikely to be subject to gift tax, those provisions might be deleted. But if so, provisions should be added to enable agents to help loved ones if the grantor is disabled. Either a provision authorizing distributions to specified persons in need or some other modified gift provision should generally be retained.

For larger estates, express language may be added to incorporate the specific right and directive to make gift transfers up to the $1 million lifetime gift exclusion. Larger estates may also wish to incorporate language authorizing or even encouraging agents to make late or even deathbed transfers to take advantage of the $3 million spousal basis step-up and the $1.3 million general basis step-up. These provisions could be added now with a proviso that they only become applicable if the modified carryover basis rules become operative. If not, the power of attorney will have to be revised at a future date, assuming the taxpayer has the mental capacity to do so.

If a taxpayer is on his deathbed, the estate planner should consult the taxpayer's accountant to determine whether, from an income tax standpoint, it will be advantageous to sell loss property (property with a fair market value less than its adjusted tax basis) and recognize a tax loss for income tax purposes on the final income tax return of the taxpayer. To facilitate this type of planning, a durable power of attorney may specifically authorize the agent to sell loss property to trigger taxable losses for income tax purposes after 2009.

NOTES

Chapter 1

1. IRC § 2210, amended by Act § 501(a).
2. IRC § 2664, amended by Act § 501(b).
3. IRC § 2001(c), amended by Act § 511.
4. IRC § 2057.
5. The trust must be subject to the laws of a state which permits dynastic trust planning.
6. IRC § 2505(a)(1), amended by Act § 521(b).
7. IRC § 2505(a)(1), amended by Act § 521(b)(1).
8. IRC § 2502(a)(2).
9. IRC § 704(e).
10. IRC § 2057(a)(1).
11. IRC § 2057(a)(2).
12. IRC § 2057(a)(3).
13. IRC § 2057(a)(3)(A).
14. IRC § 2057(a)(3)(B).
15. IRC § 2010.
16. IRC § 2057, amended by Act § 521(d).
17. IRC § 2033A(f)(1)(A)-(D).
18. IRC § 2057(f)(1)(A).
19. IRC § 170(h); IRC § 2057(f)(1)(B).
20. IRC § 2057(f)(1)(C).
21. IRC § 2057(f)(1)(D).

22. IRC § 2057(f)(2); see former IRC § 2033A(f)(2).
23. IRC § 2033A(f)(2)(A)(i), referring to IRC § 2032A(c)(2)(B).
24. IRC § 2033A(f)(2)(A)(ii), referring to IRC § 6621.
25. IRC § 2601.
26. IRC § 2612(c).
27. IRC § 2603(a)(3).
28. IRC § 2603(a)(2).
29. IRC § 2654(a)(1).
30. IRC § 2612(c)(2).
31. IRC § 2612(b).
32. IRC § 2624; 2621(a)(2).
33. IRC § 2621(b).
34. IRC § 2603(b).
35. IRC § 2603(a)(1).
36. IRC § 67(b)(2). It is analogous to the deduction under IRC § 691(c) for IRD.
37. IRC § 2613(a).
38. IRC § 2612(a).
39. IRC § 2612(a)(1).
40. IRC § 2603(a)(2).
41. IRC § 2624(c). The estate tax alternate valuation rules are available if the requirements are met.
42. IRC § 2622. Expenses are those deductible under IRC § 2053 for estate tax purposes as if the transfer were included in the gross estate.
43. IRC § 2631(a).
44. IRC § 2631(a).
45. IRC § 2631(b).
46. IRC § 2642.
47. IRC § 2642(a)(2)(A).
48. IRC § 2642(a)(2)(B).
49. IRC § 2632(c).
50. IRC § 2632(c)(2)(A).

51. IRC § 2632(b).

52. IRC § 2632(c)(2)(C); Act § 561(b).

53. IRC § 2632(c)(1), amended by Act § 561(a).

54. IRC § 2632(c)(3)(B)(i).

55. IRC § 2632(c)(3)(B)(ii).

56. IRC § 2632(c)(3)(B)(ii).

57. IRC § 2632(e)(3)(B)(ii).

58. IRC § 2632(c)(3)(B)(ii).

59. IRC § 2632(c)(3)(B)(iii).

60. IRC § 2632(c)(3)(B)(iv).

61. IRC § 2632(c)(3)(B)(v).

62. IRC § 2632(c)(3)(B)(vi).

63. This is the amount referred to in IRC § 2503(b).

64. IRC § 2642(g)(1)(A)(ii).

65. IRC § 301.9100–1.

66. Act § 564(b)(1).

67. IRC § 2632(d), Act § 561(a).

68. IRC § 2362(a)(3), Act § 562(a).

69. IRC § 2642(g)(2), Act § 564(a).

70. IRC § 2011(b), amended by Act § 531.

71. IRC § 2058, added by Act § 532(b).

72. IRC § 2106(a)(4), Act § 532(c)(8).

73. IRC § 6166(a)(1).

74. IRC § 6166.

75. IRC § 6166(a)(2).

76. IRC § 6166(a)(3).

77. IRC § 6601(j).

78. IRC § 6166(a)(1).

79. IRC § 6166(a)(1).

80. IRC § 6166(b)(1)(B)(ii), amended by Act § 571(a).

81. IRC § 6166(b)(1)(B)(ii), amended by Act § 571(a).

82. IRC § 6166(b)(1).

83. IRC § 6166(b)(1)(B)(ii), amended by Act § 571(a).

84. IRC § 6166(b)(2)(B); LTR 8428088.

85. IRC § 6166(b)(2)(C).

86. IRC § 6166(b)(2)(D).

87. IRC § 267(c)(4).

88. LTR 8136022.

89. Rev. Rul. 75–367, 1975–2 C.B. 474.

90. IRC § 6166(b)(10), amended by Act § 572(a).

91. IRC § 6166(b)(10)(A)(iii).

92. IRC § 6166(b)(6). These are items deductible under IRC § 2053 or § 2054.

93. IRC § 6166(b)(4).

94. IRC § 6166(b)(8)(C).

95. IRC § 6166(a)(1); IRC § 6166(b)(9)(B)(ii) and (iii).

96. IRC § 6166(c).

97. IRC § 6166(b)(8)(B), amended by Act § 572(a).

98. IRC § 6166(g).

99. IRC § 4947(a)(2), amended by Act § 542(e).

100. Act § 581.

101. IRC § 2032A(a)(2).

102. IRC § 2032A(b)(2).

103. IRC § 2032A(b)(1)(C).

104. IRC § 2032A(a)(1)(A).

105. IRC § 2032A(b)(1).

106. IRC § 2032A(a)(1)(B).

107. IRC § 2032A(d)(1).

108. IRC § 2023A(d)(2); § 2032A(c).

109. IRC § 2032A(b)(1)(A).

110. Rev. Rul. 82–140, 1982–2 C.B. 208.

111. IRC § 2032A(e)(2).

112. IRC § 2032A(c).

113. Act § 504(b).

114. IRC § 2032A(c)(7)(E).
115. IRC § 170(h); Reg. § 1.170A-14.
116. Reg. § 1.170A-14(c)(1).
117. Act § 508.
118. Meeting the requirements of IRC § 170(h).
119. IRC § 170(h)(1).
120. IRC § 170(h)(4)(A).
121. See, generally, IRS Publication 526.
122. IRC § 170(f)(3)(B).
123. IRC § 170(f)(3)(B).
124. IRC § 2031(c), amended by Act § 551.
125. IRC § 2210(b)(2).
126. IRC § 2056A(b)(3)(B).

Chapter 2

1. IRC § 530; Act § 213(a).
2. IRC § 911, 931.
3. IRC § 4973(a)(4).
4. IRC § 219.
5. Treasury Regulation § 1.408–2(a).
6. IRC § 408A(d)(1)(A).
7. IRC § 70(t)(2)(F).
8. IRC § 408A(c)(5); 401(a).

Chapter 3

1. Reg. § 1.641(a)-2; CCH ¶¶24,763; 24,767.01.
2. IRC § 641(a); Reg. § 1.641(a)-2; CCH ¶¶24,760; 24,763.
3. IRC § 643(a).
4. IRC § 642; Reg. § 1.641(b)-1.
5. IRC § 151.
6. IRC § 67, § 642(c); Temp. Reg. 1.67–2T. The limits on itemized deductions under IRC § 68(e) do not apply to trusts.

7. IRC §§ 162, 212.

8. *duPont Testamentary Trust Co. v. Commissioner*, 514 F.2d 917 (5th Cir. 1975).

9. *Morel v. U.S.*, 221 F.Supp. 864 (W.D. Pa. 1963).

10. IRC § 265.

11. IRC §§ 167(d); 611(b); 642(e).

12. Reg. § 1.642(d)-1.

13. IRC § 165(h)(4)(D); Reg. §§ 1.165–7(c), 1.165–8(b).

14. IRC § 642(c); Reg. § 1.642(c)-1(b).

15. IRC §§ 170(c), 642(c)(1).

16. Rev. Rul. 68–667, 1968-2, C.B. 289; Rev. Rul. 71–285, 1971-2 C.B. 249.

17. IRC § 469(a)(2); Temp. Reg. § 1.469–8T.

18. Reg. § 1.651(a)-1.

19. IRC § 651; Reg. § 1.651(a)-1.

20. IRC § 642(b).

21. IRC §§ 652, 662.

22. IRC § 651 for trusts that distribute income currently and IRC § 661 for trusts that accumulate income or distribute corpus.

23. IRC §§ 652, 662.

24. IRC § 651 for trusts that must distribute income currently, and IRC § 661 for trusts that accumulate income or distribute principal.

25. IRC §§ 652, 662.

26. IRC §§ 652, 662.

27. The deductions claimed under IRC §§ 651 and 652 are added back.

28. IRC § 642(b).

29. IRC § 643(a)(6).

30. IRC § 651(b).

31. IRC § 643(a).

32. IRC § 661(a).

33. IRC § 661(b); Reg. § 1.661(b)-1.

34. Reg. § 1.652(b)-3.
35. IRC § 663(b); Reg. § 1.663(b)-1.

Chapter 6

1. IRC § 2652(a)(1).
2. IRC § 2652(a)(3).
3. IRC § 2503(b)(1).
4. Treas. Reg. § 25.2503–3(b).
5. *Fondren v. Commissioner*, 324 U.S. 18 (1945).
6. *Helvering v. Hutchings*, 312 U.S. 393 (1941).
7. *W.D. Disston*, 325 U.S. 422 (1945).
8. IRC § 2702(a)(3)(A)(ii).
9. IRC § 1274.
10. LTR 9547004.
11. IRC § 170(c); Treas. Reg. § 1.664–3(a)(3)(ii).
12. IRC § 671–678.
13. Treas. Reg. § 1.664–1(a)(3).
14. Rev. Rul. 73–610.
15. IRC § 664(d)(2)(A); § 7701(a)(1).
16. IRC § 170(c).
17. Treas. Reg. § 1.664 3(b).
18. Treas. Reg. § 1.664–3(a)(1)(iii).

Chapter 7

1. The Taxpayer Relief Act of 1997, Public Law 105–34.
2. IRC § 1015.
3. IRC § 1014.
4. IRC § 1022(a); Act § 542(a).
5. IRC § 1022(e)(1).
6. IRC § 1022(e)(2).
7. IRC § 1022(d)(1)(B)(i).
8. IRC § 645(b)(1); IRC § 1022(e)(2)(A).

9. IRC § 1022(e)(2)(B).

10. IRC § 1022(a)(2)(A).

11. IRC § 1022(a)(2)(B).

12. IRC § 1022(b)(1); IRC § 1022(d)(1).

13. IRC § 1022(b)(2)(A).

14. IRC § 1022(b)(2)(B).

15. IRC § 1212(b).

16. IRC § 1022(b)(C)(ii).

17. IRC § 1022(c)(1); § 1022(d)(1).

18. IRC § 1022(c)(3)(B).

19. IRC § 1022(c)(5)(A)(i).

20. IRC § 1022(c)(5)(A)(ii).

21. IRC § 1022(c)(5)(B)(i).

22. IRC § 1022(c)(5)(B)(ii).

23. IRC § 1022(c)(5)(B).

24. IRC § 1022(c)(5)(D).

25. IRC § 1022(c)(3)(A).

26. IRC § 1022(c)(4)(A).

27. IRC § 1022(c)(4)(C)(i).

28. IRC § 1022(d)(1)(A).

29. IRC § 1022(d)(1)(B)(i)(I).

30. IRC § 1022(d)(1)(B)(i)(III).

31. IRC § 1022(d)(1)(B)(iii). See PLR 9308002.

32. IRC § 1022(c)(2)(A).

33. IRC § 1022(c)(2)(B).

34. IRC § 1022(d)(2).

35. IRC § 1(f)(3); IRC § 1022(d)(4)(A)(i).

36. IRC § 1022(d)(1)(B)(iv).

37. IRC § 1022(d)(1)(C).

38. IRC § 1022(d)(1)(C)(ii).

39. IRC § 6018.

40. IRC § 1022(g)(1)(A). See Treasury Reg. § 1.1001–2 for general rules.
41. Treasury Reg. § 1.661(a)—(2).
42. Reg. § 1.661(a)-2(f)(1); CCH ¶24,820.015; ¶24,902.
43. IRC § 1040(a); Act § 542(d)(1).
44. IRC § 1040(b).
45. IRC § 1221(a)(3)(C), Act § 542(e)(2)(A).
46. IRC § 170(e)(1); Act § 542(e)(2)(B).
47. IRC § 121(a); 121(b)(3)(A).
48. IRC § 121(c).
49. IRC § 121(c)(1).
50. IRC § 676.
51. IRC § 7701(a)(30)(E).
52. See PLR 8103074 and *Carson v. Commissioner*, 92TC1134 (1989).
53. IRC § 1022(b)(3).
54. IRC § 1212(b).
55. IRC § 1022(d)(1)(D).
56. IRC § 1022(d)(1)(D)(ii).
57. IRC § 1022(d)(1)(D)(iii).
58. IRC § 1022(d)(1)(D)(iv).
59. IRC § 648(a), amended by Act § 542(e)(1)(A).
60. IRC § 1246(e), amended by Act § 542(e)(5)(A).
61. IRC § 6018, Act § 542(b)(1); IRC § 6075(a), Act § 542(b)(3)(A); IRC § 6716, Act § 542(b)(4).
62. IRC § 6018.
63. IRC § 1022(b)(2)(B).
64. IRC § 6018(c)(1).
65. IRC § 6018(c)(2).
66. IRC § 6018(c)(3).
67. IRC § 6018(c)(3).
68. IRC § 6018(c)(4).

69. IRC § 6018(c)(5).

70. IRC § 6018(c)(7).

71. IRC § 6018(c).

72. IRC § 6018(b)(2); Act § 542(b).

73. IRC § 6716(a); Act § 542(b)(4).

74. IRC § 6018(e).

75. IRC § 6716(b).

76. IRC § 6716(d).

77. IRC § 6019(b).

78. IRC §§ 645(b)(1), 1022(d)(1)(B)(ii).

79. Treas. Reg. § 1.1015–1(a)(3).

80. IRC § 1022(h).

INDEX

ABOUT BLOOMBERG

Bloomberg, L.P., founded in 1981, is a global information services, news, and media company. Headquartered in New York, the company has nine sales offices, two data centers, and 85 news bureaus worldwide.

Bloomberg, serving customers in 126 countries around the world, holds a unique position within the financial services industry by providing an unparalleled range of features in a single package known as the BLOOMBERG PROFESSIONAL™ service. By addressing the demand for investment performance and efficiency through an exceptional combination of information, analytic, electronic trading, and Straight Through Processing tools, Bloomberg has built a worldwide customer base of corporations, issuers, financial intermediaries, and institutional investors.

BLOOMBERG NEWS®, founded in 1990, provides stories and columns on business, general news, politics, and sports to leading newspapers and magazines throughout the world. BLOOMBERG TELEVISION®, a 24-hour business and financial news network, is produced and distributed globally in seven different languages. BLOOMBERG RADIO℠ is an international radio network anchored by flagship station BLOOMBERG® WBBR 1130 in New York.

In addition to the BLOOMBERG PRESS® line of books, Bloomberg publishes *BLOOMBERG MARKETS*™, *BLOOMBERG PERSONAL FINANCE®*, and *BLOOMBERG WEALTH MANAGER®*. To learn more about Bloomberg, call a sales representative at:

Frankfurt:	49-69-92041-200	São Paulo:	5511-3048-4500
Hong Kong:	85-2-2977-6600	Singapore:	65-212-1000
London:	44-20-7330-7500	Sydney:	61-2-9777-8601
New York:	1-212-318-2200	Tokyo:	81-3-3201-8950
San Francisco:	1-415-912-2980		

ABOUT THE AUTHOR

Martin M. Shenkman, CPA, M.B.A., J.D., is an attorney in private practice in New York City, specializing in tax planning, estate planning and administration, and corporate work. A frequent seminar speaker on estate planning, asset protection, and related topics, he is a regular source for financial and business publications, including the *Wall Street Journal, Fortune, Money,* and the *New York Times.* Mr. Shenkman has appeared as a tax expert on television and radio talk shows nationwide. He has written numerous professional articles and some thirty books. The author received a Bachelor of Science degree in accounting and economics from The Wharton School, University of Pennsylvania, a Master's in Business Administration with a concentration in tax and finance from the University of Michigan, and the degree of Juris Doctor from Fordham University School of Law.